How History Made the Mind

How History Made the Mind

The Cultural Origins of Objective Thinking

DAVID MARTEL JOHNSON

OPEN COURT
Chicago and La Salle, Illinois

To order books from Open Court, call toll-free 1-800-815-2280, or visit our website at www.opencourtbooks.com.

Open Court Publishing Company is a division of Carus Publishing Company.

Library of Congress Cataloging-in-Publication Data

Johnson, David Martel.
    How history made the mind : the cultural origins of objective thinking /
David Martel Johnson.
        p. cm.
Includes bibliographical references and index.
    ISBN 0-8126-9536-4 (pbk. : alk. paper)
    1. Knowledge, Theory of. 2. Objectivity. 3. Philosophical anthropology.   I. Title.
        BD161 .J652 2003
        128'.2—dc22

                                                                    2003016161

Brief Contents

Detailed Contents   vii

Preface   ix

1 Introduction: Humans Are Cultural as well
   as Physical Animals   1

2 Two Forms of Naturalism: Ancient and Modern   41

3 Mind As a Product of the Greek Revolution   87

4 Reintroducing the Mind into Nature   131

5 A Short, Speculative History of Reason   173

Bibliography   211

Index   221

Detailed Contents

Preface   ix

1   **Introduction: Humans Are Cultural as well
    as Physical Animals**   1
    1.1   Is There a "Preferred Explanatory Direction"
          between Mind and Brain?   2
    1.2   The Nature of Mind, and Why the Upper
          Paleolithic Revolution Occurred So Late in Time   18
    1.3   What This Book Is About   34

2   **Two Forms of Naturalism: Ancient and Modern**   41
    2.1   Early Conceptions of Mind—An Affirmation of
          Disembodiment?   42
    2.2   The Path that Led to Modern Eliminativism:
          From Many, to One, to None   51
    2.3   Eliminativism Revisited, then Reversed   64
    2.4   Although the Mind Is Natural and Physical in
          Terms of Its Ontology, from the Viewpoint of
          Society and Culture, It Is *Not* Part of Nature   68
    2.5   The Place of Reason in History   75

3   **Mind As a Product of the Greek Revolution**   87
    3.1   Did the Hebrews Prefigure What the
          Pre-Classical Greeks Introduced Later?   88
    3.2   The Greeks' Intellectual Version of

Anti-Naturalism, Expressed in Their New
Interpretation of "Childishness" 96

3.3 Mind, Belief, and Desire Presuppose
Our Conception of Truth, and Thus, Strictly
Speaking, Are Limited to the Western
Tradition Alone 106

3.4 Frankfort, Jaynes, and the Concept of Infinity 114

4 Reintroducing the Mind into Nature 131

4.1 Finishing the Job: Mind in the Wide as well as
Narrow Sense 132

4.2 A Platonic Conception of the Universe, and
Species' "Adaptive Tricks" 139

4.3 (Wide) Mind As a Lately Discovered Ecological
Niche 156

4.4 Reason As a Still More Recently Discovered
Way of Filling the Mind-Niche 163

5 A Short, Speculative History of Reason 173

5.1 Barbarian Simplicity 174

5.2 *Lingua Franca*: Reason's Connection with
Commercialism and Cosmopolitanism 185

5.3 Reason's Connection with Indirect Practicality 190

5.4 The Goal of Science Is to Discover Truth, and
"Chauvinism" Sometimes Is True 198

5.5 How Reason Made the World a Dangerous Place 208

Bibliography 211

Index 221

Preface

J.L. Austin claimed (at the beginning of his book, 1964) that one great weakness of philosophy and philosophers was a tendency to confine attention—generation after generation—to a very few repeated examples, topics, questions, and answers. In the area of philosophy of mind and cognitive science, the cases philosophers harp on today tend to be determined by a desire to make the concerns and methods of their discipline as similar as possible to those of the physical sciences. That ideal is not objectionable in itself. But many of the people in question think of "science" in an overly narrow fashion. Accordingly, my different project here is to throw new light on the puzzle of how it is appropriate for us to think of ourselves in general, and of our minds more particularly, by setting this question against the background of certain concrete events that happened long ago in both history and prehistory. To be specific, I argue that the least misleading way of making sense of the mind is not to interpret it as an outcome of physical and physiological developments alone. Instead, we should see is as a product of at least two *cultural* revolutions that archeologists, anthropologists, and historians have discovered and described in considerable detail.

I am neither a professional historian nor a scientist. I am a philosopher who has observed certain developments taking place in fields outside his own, and then tried to appeal to, and employ, some of those developments for wider, philosophical purposes. Thus, this book is not a record of empirical research; and readers should not expect to find new evidence in it about what did and did not happen in the past. Instead, I am proposing new, philosophical interpretations of research done by other people, in order to break down artificial barriers between specific areas of science, history, and philosophy. If I am successful, then each of those fields will have become stronger, more focused, and better able to fulfill its purposes, than otherwise would have been the case. More especially, I do not believe casual, "a priori" historical speculation can provide a foundation for a scientifically adequate account of the human mind. For this purpose, rather, it is necessary to appeal to empirical facts and insights that recently have become common property through the work of historical researchers.

I dedicate the book to the memory of my parents, James and Nila. And I also propose to dedicate it to all of my teachers, or "extended parents." Among this last group, I acknowledge a special debt to John Yolton, at the undergraduate level, and to Wilfrid Sellars, at the graduate level. The first of these people convinced me that the past could act as a good source of insights for making sense of the present. The second reaffirmed that same lesson, and also brought me to see how close the relation was between philosophy and empirical science. Reformulating a Kantian saying, Sellars led me to see that "philosophy without a foundation in science is empty, and science without philosophy is blind."

Another former student of Sellars (Thomas Vinci) makes something like the same point in the preface to a recent book (1998), in a more authentically Sellarsian style. For instance, he says (vii): "Sellars regarded science and metaphysics as separate threads in a single web of philosophical inquiry." I have no quarrel with this person, whose work I respect. But even though I am fond of the elegantly poetic mode of expression this sentence illustrates, I confess that I always have found such talk more inspiring than illuminating. Therefore, I do not propose to emulate it here, and shall content myself instead with thanking Sellars for having provided a good—albeit negative—inspiration for always attempting to write as simply and clearly as possible. I have taken Charles Darwin as a stylistic model, who was a first-rate, ground-breaking scientist, but nevertheless was able to express himself in terms that any intelligent and attentive reader (with a bit of practical experience) could understand.

Let me add one further comment: I express some of the book's ideas differently, in different parts of it. This may lead some readers to ask, for example, "Is this author really talking about the human mind, or just the notion or idea of mind?" "Is the mind as he understands it an object, a function, or a certain way of thinking and talking?" I do not apologize for this tendency towards variation in expression, since (I claim) it is not a result of sloppiness or inattention. Rather, like Plato, I have resisted adopting any single, "official" expression for my ideas, because—as Aristotle warned—doing otherwise would involve the fraud of trying to achieve more precision in the subject at hand, than it rightfully allows. More especially, I believe the historical facts on which this account of the human mind is based are genuine and genuinely important ones. But that does not imply that those facts necessarily will be good guides for choosing between familiar types of philosophical theories—for example, Cartesian dualism, epiphenomenalism, behaviorism, the identity theory, and computational functionalism. Instead (as the following pages will show) they point in quite different directions.

I have benefited from comments and suggestions, on earlier versions of the book, from anonymous editorial readers of various presses. I am particularly grateful to David Ramsay Steele and his editorial associates at Open Court, for seeing what I was trying to accomplish—and why it might be significant—in a draft of the book where those matters were not yet clearly and concisely expressed. A remarkable, second-year undergraduate student, Pavel Davydov, read a still later draft of the manuscript, and offered many helpful observations. I thank him as well.

As in the case of my second co-edited book for Oxford University Press, *The Mind As a Scientific Object: Between Brain and Culture*, my daughters Kirsten and Sigrid also made a significant contribution to this volume. I commissioned Kirsten (a professional artist) to plan and paint another portrait, to be used on the cover; and Sigrid again agreed to serve as the painting's model. Readers who love art are bound to be almost as pleased with the gothic-humorous result of Kirsten's labors as I am.

Finally, I acknowledge the help of my wife Barbara. Without her patience, love, and support, this book would not have been written.

Chapter 1

Introduction: Humans Are Cultural as well as Physical Animals

The mastery of nature is vainly believed to be an adequate substitute for self-mastery.

—Reinhold Niebuhr

1.1 Is There a "Preferred Explanatory Direction" between Mind and Brain?[1]

Shortly after Steven Pinker published his book, *How the Mind Works* (1997), I saw this author being interviewed on television. As I remember the occasion, the host introduced him using something like the following words: "Here is a person who has just written a book called, *How the Brain Works*." This was an obvious mistake, since it was *not* the correct title. But even so, Pinker said nothing about the error. Instead, he continued on as if no mistake had been made at all, or as if, even though he was aware that the host had made a misstatement, he considered it such a small, trivial, and forgivable oversight that it would be pedantic to mention it.

Later—after having looked again at the first few pages of this book—it occurred to me that I should not have been surprised at Pinker's attitude towards the verbal *faux pas* just mentioned, since it fitted in well with his general view about the relation between the brain and the mind. The basic statement he makes on that topic occurs on page 21 of his book, where he says, "The mind is what the brain does." He then goes on to elaborate this same idea, and put it into a wider context, as follows:

> The mind is a system of organs of computation, designed by natural selection to solve the kinds of problems our ancestors faced in their foraging way of life, in particular, understanding and outmaneuvering objects, animals, plants, and other people.

Pinker admits (p. 24) that the mind is not *everything* the brain does. For example, the brain metabolizes fat and gives off heat; but neither of those processes has anything to do with mind. Rather, according to him, the mind is identical with all and only the brain's *informational* functions. For instance, seeing is a function of that type; understanding and using language is another; and forming and manipulating so-called mental images is a third. Pinker assumes throughout the book that there are two, roughly complementary means or techniques for understanding the mind,

---

1. An earlier version of some of the material in this first section also appears in D.M. Johnson forthcoming.

which are available to scientifically sophisticated investigators. One is to think about mind in terms of artificial intelligence and information theory, in something like the way proposed by Alan Turing. The other is to conceive of mind from the standpoint of modern biology, and more especially, in terms of Darwinian natural selection. Why does Pinker choose to emphasize just these two approaches, as opposed to other possible alternatives he might have mentioned instead? One main reason may be that both these ways of knowing are clearly connected with the detection, creation, manipulation, and transfer of information.

Jerry Fodor, in a more recent book called *The Mind Doesn't Work that Way* (2000), attacks Pinker's theory, along with other versions of the so-called "New Synthesis" (Turing combined with Darwin) on the grounds that no view of that sort is able to account for the aspects of mind that allow subjects to judge the relevance to a problem of certain data and facts, and thus to engage in abductive reasoning ("inference to the best explanation") with respect to that problem. Another way to express the same point is to say that, in Fodor's opinion, Pinker-like theories of mind are wrong, because they cannot explain how humans manage to solve the "frame problem." I think Fodor probably is right to say this. And therefore his criticism strikes me as a telling one. Nevertheless, the main point I want to make in this book is not the same as Fodor's, nor even remotely similar to it. Instead, it is a simpler and more basic criticism that applies to Fodor just as much as it also does to Pinker. It is that many present-day theorists (including the two just mentioned) overlook the important contributions to the nature of mind that have been made (a) by culture[2] considered in a general way, and, more specifically, (b) by certain definite past historical events.

What, in my view, is the fundamental error made by all the theorists I propose to criticize? The answer is that: (i) these people

---

2. The usual criterion social scientists use for distinguishing "culture" and "nature" is this: Whenever there are reasons for believing that certain characteristics belong to all the normal members of some given species (whether the human species or another), then they count those characteristics as natural ones. On the other hand, whenever they believe certain characteristics only belong to one or more particular groups of organisms within a species and not to other, physically separated groups, and when furthermore it seems clear that those characteristics are typically acquired by a process of learning from conspecifics, and thus are not directly dependent on any features of the environment, then social scientists take those characteristics to be cultural. See for instance de Waal 2001, p. 6.

have a keen desire to think, reason, and speculate in a manner typical of *natural* scientists. Furthermore, (ii) they assume that the exclusive concern of such scientists is (or ought to be) basic items (such as particles) that exist in space and time. By parity of reasoning, then, they conclude that (iii) mind must be both identical with, and completely explainable in terms of, certain parts and aspects of the brain—but not the other way around.

I do not deny that the mind is ontologically identical with the brain. But it seems to me that granting that point does not carry the further implication that the mind is also completely explainable in terms of the brain. To say the same thing another way, I do not subscribe to a metaphysics of substance or property dualism.[3] Instead, I am inclined to accept John Searle's claim that "most of our metaphysics is derived from physics (including the other natural sciences)" (1995, p. 6). Accordingly, I am willing to admit that physical categories like "quark," "molecule," and "neuron" are ontologically simpler than mental categories like "thought," "desire," "belief," and so forth; and therefore we are entitled to think of the second set of categories as extensions and elaborations of the first. Nevertheless (as I shall explain in more detail later—for example in section 2.4), existence and explanation are not the same thing; and in view of that fact, it is wrong to confuse one with the other. Still more particularly, the brain's being ontologically less complicated and more basic than the mind does not imply that, in principle, it would be possible to explain (or explain away) every conceivable problem about the second, if only one had a sufficient amount of precise, scientific information about the first.

Now let us shift our focus somewhat. Linguist George Lakoff and philosopher Mark Johnson propose and defend a particular conception of mind in their book, *Philosophy in the Flesh: The Embodied Mind and Its Challenge to Western Thought* (1999). I find what they say there interesting, if only because there are some respects in which their views are closer to mine than

---

3. This does not imply that I therefore accept the metaphysical view of materialism or physicalism instead. Rather, like J.L. Austin (Austin 1964) and John Searle (Searle 1992), I am inclined to accept the view that all such "isms" are mistaken, since the project of trying to count up all the different types of phenomena in the world puts one on a wrong and misleading track.

Pinker's. More especially, I noted before that Pinker proposes to equate the mind with the brain's informational functions (such as seeing, using language, forming mental images, and so on), and denies that we are entitled to consider any one of those functions more central or important than the others. But George Lakoff and Mark Johnson take a different view. According to them, it is both appropriate and illuminating to define mind in terms of just one characteristic function—namely, that of generating, monitoring, and employing reasonable thinking. And at least as far as that particular point is concerned, I think they are right, and Pinker is wrong. However, my position diverges from theirs when they then go on to say that mind (or "reason"—a word they take to be equivalent) is always physically embodied, "in such a way that our conceptual systems draw largely upon the commonalities of our bodies and of the environments we live in." Still more particularly, I disagree with them when they claim that "much of a person's conceptual system is either universal or widespread across languages and cultures" (p. 6). In other words, even though I already have made it clear that I do not accept dualism, I think the idea of its following from the fact that the mind is identical with the brain, that all human beings everywhere, and at all times, must have essentially the same minds, is false.

The following passage (pp. 3–4) provides a still more complete statement of Lakoff's and Mark Johnson's position:

> Reason has been taken for over two millennia as the defining characteristic of human beings. Reason includes not only our capacity for logical inference, but also our ability to conduct inquiry, to solve problems, to evaluate, to criticize, to deliberate about how we should act, and to reach an understanding of ourselves, other people, and the world. . . . Reason is not disembodied, as the tradition has largely held, but arises from the nature of our brains, bodies, and bodily experience. . . . [T]he very structure of reason itself comes from the details of our embodiment. . . . Reason is evolutionary, in that abstract reason builds on and makes use of forms of perceptual and motor inference present in "lower" animals. . . . Reason is not "universal" in the transcendent sense; that is, it is not part of the structure of the universe. It is universal, however, in that it is a capacity shared universally by all human beings. What allows it to be shared are the commonalities that exist in the way our minds are embodied.

To summarize, then, all the authors I have mentioned so far in this chapter apparently suppose that, at least in the ideal case, it would be possible for scientists to produce an exhaustive account of every "meaningful" and "purposeful" characteristic associated with the human mind, in terms of natural (for example physiological) properties of (i) the brain, and (ii) the physical environment in which the brain happened to be set. On the other hand, they do not suppose the same applies in the reverse direction. In other words, according to them, it is not also the case that—ideally—a fully informed person could give a scientifically significant account of relevant parts of the brain, in terms of the mind. To see more clearly what this claimed "asymmetry" involves, consider the following statement by Noam Chomsky, in which he sets forth some methodological principles of what he calls "naturalistic inquiry":

> In formulating a constructive research program we depart in various ways from ordinary usage with its teleological and normative conditions, which have no place in a naturalistic inquiry and merely lead to confusion if adopted uncritically. . . . The approach to language . . . mentioned earlier—and . . . other work on specific topics within the cognitive sciences—adheres more strictly to the naturalistic pattern. We want to discover how actual systems work. Simulation is of value insofar as it contributes to this end, and, that apart, there is no interest in criteria for commonsense notions like intelligence, language, understanding, knowledge, aboutness, etc. There is no reason to expect them to find a place, unchanged, in a principled theory of the mind. (1997, pp. 24, 31. See also Chomsky's paper, 1987/1990, pp. 627–28.)

Still another expression of essentially the same program is that which Patricia Churchland calls "neurophilosophy" in her book of the same title, 1986. Accordingly, all the previously mentioned authors probably would be willing to accept her notion of "mind/brain," or the idea that the two words conjoined in this phrase are trivially different—but explanatorily asymmetrical—means of referring to the same entity or set of entities.

This particular conception of the "explanatory relation" between brain and mind is very popular at the present time. Nevertheless, I am suspicious of it for at least four reasons. First, (A) empirical investigation shows that the human brain, especially when immature, is a pliable organ that is capable of adjusting itself, in both its structure and functioning, to a very wide range of internal and external influences. (A classical expression of this point appears in Penfield, 1975; a more recent statement of it occurs in Donald's book, 1991, especially p. 13.) For example, let us ask the following question: Must all such determining influences on the brain be narrowly physical ones—factors like temperature; atmospheric pressure; the amount of oxygen, alcohol, adrenaline, and testosterone in the blood, and so forth? Or have observations proved that there sometimes can be scientifically significant explanations of the brain's structure and functions that go in the opposite direction? To be still more precise, can the brain be affected by "meaningful" factors like thoughts, purposes, plans, normative standards, and patterns of thinking, as well as by factors of a more narrowly physical sort? As far as I can see, the answer is that nothing in either our everyday experience, or in the results of organized and objective scientific investigations, forces us to believe that only influences of the first kind are—or can be—genuine and effective.

Consider a pair of simple examples. A linguist says:

> science has begun to provide hard data demonstrating that children's developing neural nets are affected by the [particular] language they learn. (Conlogue 2001, p. D9)

Again, paleoanthropologist Ian Tattersall remarks:

> recent research suggests that early exposure to music (playing more so than listening, though both are effective) enhances the development of mathematical reasoning, apparently stimulating the development of neuronal circuits devoted to higher reasoning. (1998, p. 213)

On the assumption that these and similar observations are not misleading, we are entitled to wonder whether methodological principles like the ones promulgated by Chomsky in the preceding quotation really are based on objective, scientific considerations, or whether—at least in part—they are ideologically motivated. In other words, do such principles boil down to wishful claims about what, for various reasons, some people think the world *ought to* be like, as opposed to what careful observation and experiments have shown that it actually is?

My second reason for thinking Pinker, Chomsky, P.S. Churchland, Lakoff, and Mark Johnson may have taken a wrong turn is this: (B) Even though all these authors "tip their hats" in the direction of Darwinian biology, it is not clear to me that they have managed to grasp the full significance of the intellectual revolution Darwin inaugurated. For instance, recent biologists tell us that natural selection always operates in an exploratory and opportunistic fashion. To be more specific, they claim on the basis of many observations that (contrary to some views once held by Darwin himself) the development of organisms does not occur through a series of small and gradual changes, all aimed in a single direction. Instead, creatures characteristically change in a jerky, uneven way, which often involves their "moving into" ecological niches that happen to be open at the time they are "needed." (See, e.g., Deacon 1997, pp. 29–30.) This implies that the functions of any evolved bodily organ never remain entirely static and settled, but always are subject to further modifications and revision.

In fact, some biologists have introduced a technical term to clarify this point. According to them, to describe a certain property of an organism, or a function performed by a bodily organ, as an "exaptation," is a means of reminding readers that the creature or organ in question did not always have that property, and *a fortiori* was not "designed"—to use Pinker's word—to possess or perform it. Instead, it only acquired that property or function later, as a result of changed circumstances. A classic example of this point is the case of feathers. That is, some evolutionary investigators maintain that feathers originally developed as a means of insulating certain reptiles against cold, and only later acquired the additional, "accidental" function of helping some descendents of those first creatures to fly (see Gould and Vrba 1982; Tattersall 2002, p. 52, and 1998, p. 108).

Furthermore, such "delayed changes" have been especially numerous, frequent, and drastic in the case of nervous systems in general, and of the human brain in particular. Presumably, the reason for this is that organs of that type perform an enormous number of subtle monitoring and controlling tasks; and therefore they are bound to be very sensitive and responsive to changes in environmental conditions. As Tattersall summarizes the point:

there is no better example than the history of the vertebrate brain to demonstrate that evolutionary change has not consisted merely of gradual improvements over the ages. Brain evolution has not proceeded by the simple addition of a few more connections here and there, finally adding up, over the aeons, to a large and magnificently burnished machine. Opportunistic evolution has conscripted old parts of the brain to new functions in a rather untidy fashion, and new structures have been added and old ones enlarged in a rather haphazard way. (1998, p. 194)

In my view, unless we take all of the preceding observations seriously, we put ourselves in danger of turning back the clock from our own, post-Darwinian era, to the earlier time of Aristotle. In Aristotle's opinion, there could not be any genuine, proper, or "scientific" knowledge of anything whose existence stemmed from merely chance events or conditions, and which therefore fell under categories that were artificial, arbitrary, and impermanent. (See *Physics*, 2, 4–6.) On the other hand, Darwin and his successors discovered a way of extending one type of obviously legitimate and rigorous scientific thinking to objects and categories that were neither necessary nor "timeless" (in the Aristotelian sense of eternally present in the world), but were nothing more than temporarily effective results of incidental and accidental causes. At the present time, for example, biologists conceive of all existing species as temporally relative, historical entities, each of which had a beginning at some past time, and all of which eventually will become extinct at another time in the future. Again to quote Tattersall (1998, p. 26):

Species . . . turned out to be bounded entities in time as well as in space, with origins, life spans, and extinctions.

Thus, a good means of summarizing my second point is to say that if the currently popular scenario accepted by people like Pinker, Chomsky, and Lakoff were correct, then the recent scientific followers of Darwin would only be able to exorcise the ghost of Aristotle in a partial, superficial, and merely conditional way. But they could not do this either thoroughly or completely.

In the view of people like Pinker, Lakoff, Mark Johnson, Churchland, and Chomsky, the best means of making scientific sense of mind is to identify it with informational functions performed by the normal human brain. That presumably implies that the same evolutionary processes that brought brains into existence also resulted in the appearance of minds. In other words, as soon as there were human brains, then—necessarily and automatically—minds were present in, expressed by, or supervenient on them as well.[4] But now let us ask two questions. First, can the way people think and speak in ordinary life provide non-misleading clues about the nature of mind in general? If so, then rather than following Pinker in equating the mind with *all* of the brain's informational functions, it is better to suppose, in the manner of Lakoff and Mark Johnson, that the mind is only connected with those functions that are associated with reasoned thought, because we find it natural to speak and think about mind that way. Second, can cultural factors influence the mind, as well as physical ones? If the answer to this last question is Yes, then Lakoff and Mark Johnson are wrong to suppose that reason depends in a direct way on various bodily characteristics and dispositions that belong to all humans everywhere and at all times.

Thus, we ask: Could it be true that—for cultural reasons—minds did not come into existence until long after evolution already had produced the first human brain? Still more particularly, did minds only appear at a particular point in history, because of the fact that there was some important change in humans' cultural environment at the same time?

(C) Another, third reason for doubting that, in principle, it is always possible to account for mind in terms of brain, but not brain in terms of mind, is that theorists who hold this view often try to defend it by exaggerating the importance of the notions of individuality and "presentness." For example, because of the desire of such people (in Chomsky's words) "to discover how actual systems work," they tend to ignore the fact (repeatedly confirmed by observation) that successful adaptations are typically results of (i) what creatures are and do together, in a group, and (ii) what they do over extended temporal periods. By contrast, good adaptations are much less often results of what individual creatures are and do, by themselves, and during continuous—short—amounts of time. Of course, this is not to dispute the

---

4. On the notion of "supervenience," see Kim 1998, especially p. 10.

commonly accepted metaphysical principle that every organism—like every other particular occupant of our universe—only has literal existence in or at the present moment. But even so, accepting that principle does not justify one's ignoring the most basic lesson Darwin ever taught—namely, that it is not possible to understand living beings accurately and correctly, unless one thinks of them in terms of their history.

Many people subscribe to the view nowadays that the basic thing that distinguishes modern humans on one side, from all other known living things on the other, is the fact that the great majority of the activities that contribute to humans' adaptive success depend, directly or indirectly, on the fact that they are members of one or another symbolically-based culture. To say the same thing another way, that which sets us apart from all other creatures is the fact that the environments in which we live are saturated with meaning.[5] Nevertheless, the "neurophilosophical" views promoted by Pinker, Fodor, Churchland, and other people tends to obscure that point, because those theorists implicitly assume that one can explain everything knowable about humans (including their different from all other animals), just in terms of their anatomy and physiology. But this, I suggest, is to interpret a distinction in kind as if it were merely one of degree.[6]

(D) Finally, my fourth reason for doubting the correctness of the above view is not a conceptual point, but an empirical one. Some commentators say that cognitive scientists in general, and philosophers of mind in particular, have been slow to recognize the importance of the science of biology for their field. One thing

---

5. Terrence Deacon expresses this same point at the beginning of his book (1997, pp. 21–22), when he says: "Though we share the same earth with millions of kinds of living creatures, we also live in a world that no other species has access to. We inhabit a world full of abstractions, impossibilities, and paradoxes. We alone brood about what didn't happen, and spend a large part of each day musing about the way things could have been if events had transpired differently. And we alone ponder what it will be like not to be. In what other species could individuals ever be troubled by the fact that they do not recall the way things were before they were born and will not know what will occur after they die? We tell stories about our real experiences and invent stories about imagined ones, and we even make use of these stories to organize our lives. In a real sense, we live our lives in this shared virtual world. And slowly, over the millennia, we have come to realize that no other species on earth seems able to follow us into this miraculous place.

6. Again, Deacon says (*ibid.*, p. 23): "Biologically, we are just another ape. Mentally, we are a new phylum of organisms. In these two seemingly incommensurate facts lies a conundrum that must be resolved before we have an adequate explanation of what it means to be human.

I shall try to accomplish in this book is to make a similar point about still another pair of scientific disciplines. To be specific, I claim that we also should think of paleontology (especially pale-oanthropology) and archeology as unjustly neglected cognitive sciences. One measure of the theoretical importance of those disciplines is the fact that their practitioners have uncovered quite a few significant facts about our species, which neither armchair thinkers (those who appeal to common experience, memory, reasoning, introspection, and so forth), nor neurophysiologists (who study the brain) could have brought to our attention. For example, paleontological research has shown that, through the long evolutionary process that led to modern humans, there was a constant "mismatch" between physiology on one side and behavior on the other. What this means, more especially, is that there virtually always was a delay between (i) the development of larger or more complex hominid brains, and (ii) subsequent cultural advances, for which, presumably, those larger brains were in part responsible.

Let me mention two examples of this last point. At the beginning of Chapter 5 of *Becoming Human* (1998, pp. 137–38), Ian Tattersall describes the appearance in eastern Africa, about 1.9 million years ago, of a species "distinctively different from anything previously known." He is talking here about the advent of

> *Homo ergaster* (also sometimes known as 'African *Homo erectus*') . . . a creature who "sported a cranium that much more closely resembled that of later humans, boasting a braincase of about 850 ml in volume (above half the modern average), housed in a relatively high and rounded vault.

Nevertheless, in spite of the physiological advances this hominid had made over its predecessors, so far as *Homo ergaster's* behavior and culture were concerned—for instance the prey it hunted and the stone tools it made—this species remained at essentially the same level as its immediate ancestors, for a very long time. Tattersall continues:

> Culturally . . . little appears to have changed by the time Turkana boy came on the scene [an especially complete, well preserved specimen dated at about 1.6 million years ago]—although studies of

tooth wear in *Homo ergaster* suggest a greater amount of meat eating compared to *Homo habilis*, which shows the more vegetarian pattern of wear typical of *Australopithicus*. The stone tool kit and animal remains found at Turkana in the time of the earliest *Homo ergaster* do not, for example, differ significantly from those associated with *Homo habilis*.

Tattersall then adds the following reflective comment:

At first, this appears a little counter-intuitive; but a moment's thought will contradict intuition. Why should a new species—which inevitably emerged out of an old one—necessarily bring with it a new technology? Whether physical or cultural, innovations can appear in only one place, and that's *within* a species. Any individual who bears a new genetic trait or invents a new technology (which is a very different thing) cannot, after all, differ too much from his or her parents.

Four hundred thousand years after the first appearance of *Homo ergaster*, some members of this species—now developed into fully-fledged *Homo erectus*—finally made an intellectual advance that was worthy of their larger and more complex brains. Tattersall explains as follows:

A couple of hundred thousand years after fossils of *Homo ergaster* first show up . . . we do see a remarkable cultural innovation in the archeological record. Up to that time (about 1.5 million years ago), stone tools had been of the simple kind that had been made for the previous million years or so, in which the main aim had probably been to achieve a particular attribute (a sharp cutting edge) rather than a specific shape. Suddenly, however, a new kind of tool was on the scene: the Acheulean hand ax and associated tool types, which were obviously made to a standardized pattern that existed in the toolmaker's mind before the toolmaking process began. [In particular, h]and axes are large, flattish, teardrop-shaped implements that were carefully fashioned on both sides to achieve a symmetrical shape . . . . (*Ibid.*, p. 138)

The second example brings our present discussion closer to the main concerns of this book. That example is the remarkably rapid transition through which our own species passed (in Europe), when its members left behind the behavior and technologies characteristic of the so-called Middle Paleolithic period, and instead adopted those associated with the Upper Paleolithic (or "Later Old Stone Age"). Archeologists tell us that, during more than half the time *Homo sapiens* has existed, our ancestral conspecifics behaved in ways that were nearly indistinguishable from the behavior of our closest primate relatives—i.e. members of the "cousin" species, *Homo neanderthalensis.* For instance, Alan Thorne and Milford Wolpoff (1992, p. 78) say that, in the Levant (the eastern shore of the Mediterranean) where both species lived in close proximity for a long while,

> "modern" people had a culture that was identical to that of their local Neanderthal contemporaries: they made the same types of stone tools with the same technologies and at the same frequencies; they had the same stylized burial customs, hunted the same game and even used the same butchering procedures. (Also see Tattersall 1998, pp. 150–180, and 1999, Chapter 8.)

This situation only changed at the end of the Middle, and beginning of the Later or "Upper Paleolithic," approximately 40,000 years ago (again, in the case of Europe),[7] when a revolutionary event took place. Paul Mellars (1998, pp. 91–92) says that he, along with many other archeologists, consider that event

> the most radical episode of cultural, technological and general behavioral change in the entire history of the European continent.

Is this statement an exaggeration? Should Mellars have claimed instead that the most profound change in the life of European humans happened at the start of the Neolithic or New Stone Age, roughly 10,000 years ago? After all, this was the time of the

---

7. Consider the following point expressed by Steven Mithen (1996, p. 152): "Yet if we look a little more closely at the boundary . . . we see that there is not so much a single big bang as a whole series of cultural sparks that occur at slightly different times in different parts of the world between 60,000 and 30,000 years ago. The colonization of Australia, for instance, seems to reflect a cultural spark which happened between 60,000 and 50,000 years ago, yet at this time all remained relatively quiet elsewhere in the world. In the Near East a cultural spark happened between 50,000 and 45,000 years ago when the Levallois technology was replaced by that of blade cores. The cultural spark in Europe seems not to have been until 40,000 years ago with the appearance of the first objects of art. Indeed, it is perhaps only after 30,000 years ago that we can be confident that the hectic pace of cultural change had begun in earnest throughout the globe.

invention of agriculture, irrigation, domestication of animals, settled city life, and the institutions of government, military organization, and law. (For example, one informed person who takes this last view is University of Frankfort prehistorian, Jens Lüning. See the report in Lemonick 1992, p. 53.)

It seems to me that, at least from the perspective of the interdisciplinary study of mind and brain we now call "cognitive science," the answer is No. In other words, the Neolithic transition could not have been basic in a cognitive sense of the word, since it is clear from hindsight that it was a "working out" of intellectual capacities that humans had acquired much earlier. Apparently, in fact, all the elements that eventually produced the Neolithic revolution already were in place roughly 30,000 years before that time, at the start of the Upper Paleolithic era.

What exactly did entry into the Upper Paleolithic imply for the nature, properties, and conduct of human thought? Consider Mellars's following list of seven changes that occurred at that time (all extensively documented from archeological materials). These are:

(1) "The appearance of much more widespread 'blade' and 'bladelet' as opposed to 'flake'-based technologies . . . ."
(2) "The appearance of a wide range of entirely new *forms* of stone tools, some of which . . . reflect an entirely new component of conceptual or visual form and standardization in the production of stone tools . . ."
(3) "The effective explosion of bone, antler and ivory technology, involving . . . a remarkably wide range of new and tightly standardized tool forms . . ."
(4) "The appearance of the first reliably documented beads, pendants and other items of personal decoration . . ."
(5) "The transportation of sea shells and other materials over remarkable distances . . . ."
(6) "The appearance of the first unmistakable sound-producing instruments . . ."
(7) "Most dramatic of all, the sudden appearance of explicitly 'artistic' activity, in a remarkable variety of forms . . ."

Mellars fails to mention at least two other relevant points. One is that human numbers dramatically increased at the time of the Upper Paleolithic revolution (see, for example, Stringer and

McKie 1996, pp. 196–97). And a second, even more significant consideration is that—in the view of some investigators; see for instance Tattersall 2000, p. 62 and 1998, p. 232—this probably was when humans first began to think and communicate in terms of a sophisticated (for example, syntactical) language. Of course, the point just mentioned is controversial. Some (such as Deacon 1997, pp. 370ff and Mithen 1991, Chapter 10) deny its truth altogether, although still agreeing that the Upper Paleolithic Revolution was an extremely important event. Still others simply deny that language or any other fundamental human trait came into existence at the start of the Upper Paleolithic. For example, Pinker says (1994, p. 254) that human language "evolved only once." Furthermore, he also apparently assumes, consistent with his general view explained before, that it began at exactly the same time—between 250,000 and 150,000 years ago—as the first *Homo sapiens* brains appeared.

What is my own view about these matters? I think that unless we assign a central place to the Upper Paleolithic Revolution in the history of human development, we make the mistake of ignoring a significant set of empirical data about our past. Furthermore, there are good reasons for believing that this event was not primarily a physical (for example, physiological) change, but instead something cultural. For one thing, the Upper Paleolithic Revolution happened far too quickly to have been a product of evolved bodily changes. For example, there is no evidence for believing it resulted from the swift replacement of one population of humans by another—for example, by conquest followed by massacre. And we also have no reason to suppose that any important environmental change took place at roughly the same time, which somehow might have triggered this event (see Tattersall 1998, pp. 231–32).

For all these reasons, then, it seems to me that the Upper Paleolithic Revolution deserves to be thought of as an especially clear instance of "mind-brain (as contrasted with brain-mind) causality." And thus in turn, it is also presumably something that demands to be accounted for in terms of mind-brain, rather than brain-mind, patterns of explanation.

To conclude, I accept the anti-Cartesian notion that the human brain and mind are and must be the same thing—as long as one interprets "are," "same," and "thing," as they appear in that statement, in an ontological sense. Thus, what the preceding statement means, as I understand it, is that, considered at any given moment, the entities that constitute (certain parts of) a person's brain are the same as those that constitute his or her mind, and vice versa. Nevertheless, for the different purposes of understanding and explaining, brain and mind do *not* amount to the same thing. For example, one thing it means to consider matters from an explanatory rather than an ontological viewpoint is that it is not appropriate for theorists just to take account of events, properties, etc. that exist at the present time. Rather, they also should concern themselves with questions about how those items got to be what they are, and of what one reasonably can expect them to become in the future. Let me now propose a simple, concrete case. Thinking of a particular, two-fist sized bit of protoplasm—"X"—as a brain, is to consider that lump of matter as having been formed by blind physical and evolutionary forces alone, without help from any "meaningful" projects, intentions, plans, or other cultural factors. On the other hand, to conceive of that same X as a mind is to think of it in (at least) a two-fold manner: (i) as presupposing the existence and operation of a certain number of natural and physical—for example, evolutionary—events and processes, but also (ii) as being a product of various meaningful thoughts, desires, decisions, and values. The theorists with whom I disagree tend to discount or ignore the second, "mind" part of the preceding formula, because of their obsession with the "scientific" project of replacing all talk about meaning and mind with corresponding statements about the physical brain. But it seems to me that this last idea is neither helpful nor plausible, because human beings like us are not—even in the Peircean "long run"—omniscient beings who can obtain an exhaustively detailed comprehension of the workings of any part of matter in general, or of living matter in particular. Rather, we are nothing more than finite, fallible inquirers who must content ourselves with gleaning whatever information happens to be available to our limited senses, and equally limited powers of inference, from the observable surfaces of things.[8]

---

8. This remark is parallel to another made many years ago by J.L. Austin. See his 1964, Chapter 10, especially pp. 117–123.

1.2   The Nature of Mind, and Why the Upper
Paleolithic Revolution Occurred So Late in Time

> This is our natural state and yet the state most contrary to our incli-
> nations. (Blaise Pascal)
>
> The fear of the uncanny controls much of the thinking of a child
> before it becomes conversant with the order of the universe about it.
> It looms equally large in the mentality of primitive peoples. (Snell
> 1953/1960, p. 23)

Jaegwon Kim begins his book, *Philosophy of Mind* (1998, p. 1), by
reminding us of the fact that, in our daily lives, we are constantly
aware of an intuitive, largely unreflective distinction between
things that are *living* and others that are *dead*. Similarly, he says
that another fundamental classificatory distinction available to us
is this: Whenever we meet an adult human being, we are rarely in
doubt as to whether that person is *male* or *female*. He then says:

> The same is true of the distinction between things or creatures with a
> "mind" or "mentality," and those without a mind. This is probably
> one of the most basic contrasts we use in our thoughts about things
> in the world. Our attitudes toward things that are conscious and
> capable of sensations like pain and pleasure, however lowly they may
> be in the biological hierarchy, are importantly different from our atti-
> tudes toward things lacking such capacities, mere chunks of matter
> or insensate plants, as witness the controversy about vegetarianism
> and medical experiments performed on live animals.

Is Kim right about the intellectual status that belongs to this
third distinction? Or do we have grounds for doubting that the
notion of *mind* is similar, in the manner he proposes, to those of
living and *female*? To be even more explicit: Is it really true that
an organism's having a mind is something that is just as obvious,
objective, and observable to us, as those other two states, facts, or
properties? If one supposes (as Kim apparently does) that the
most essential and characteristic property of mind is the fact that
it acts as a source of all a person's consciousness and sensations,
then it seems to follow that having a mind also must be some sort
of physical (for example, physiological) condition. This is true for
all the same reasons we have for believing that being conscious

and having sensations are, themselves, physical and physiological states. Nevertheless, despite the fact that many theorists (including Kim) continue to talk this way, a shift gradually has occurred in people's theoretical conception of mentality. (For example, Paul Churchland describes this intellectual change, at the beginning of his paper, 1981.) In the 1960s, theorists widely assumed that the most important, typical, and revealing properties of mind had to do with qualia, emotions, and "raw feels." One reason they thought this was that they believed that those particular entities and properties were the ones it was most difficult to conceive of as being reduced to some underlying material substrate. Today, however, according to Churchland, we have made a certain amount of progress in proposing plausible ways in which such a reduction might be accomplished—for example, ways that qualia might turn out to be identical with activities of neurons. (Again, see the references concerning this point in Churchland's 1981.) As a result of that theoretical development, quite a few authors now have changed their views about what count as the most important and characteristic properties of mind. Instead of locating the mind's "center" in its ability to generate and maintain conscious states like qualia, quite a few of them now believe the crucial point lies in the fact that minds are able to create and employ intentional, referring phenomena like beliefs, desires, hopes, and other "propositional attitudes." Let me propose an example (parallel to, but disagreeing with, a "thought experiment" that John Searle explores in his book, 1992, pp. 70–71). Even if there were good grounds for believing that some computer-driven machine located in a car assembly plant had achieved a low level of consciousness, it still would not be natural for us to attribute a mind to that machine, unless and until it also came to be able to engage in acts of intending, choosing, believing, and desiring.

Contrary to Kim's view, the intellectual sea-change that Churchland documents constitutes a reason for supposing that the concept of *mind* is fundamentally different from those of *living* and *female*. The reason is that, unlike these others, the notion of mind is a non-physiological one that depends on certain aspects of human culture. (As mentioned before—in note 2—the usual criterion investigators employ to divide natural and physiological properties on one side from cultural ones on the other is that organisms acquire characteristics of the first sort by means of inheritance rather than learning, so that those characteristics are bound to belong to all the normal members of a given species; but on the other hand, since properties of the second kind *are* acquired by learning, it is *not* reasonable to expect them to belong to all a species' normal members.)

We know from ordinary experience that people often confuse cultural traits on one side, with physical (for example, physiological) properties on the other. Let me mention one personal, silly, and embarrassing instance of such a thing—for which I apologize in advance. Towards the end of the years I spent in Junior High School, and continuing on into the beginning of High School, I distinctly remember having believed that there was an obvious, observable, and physically based distinction between those human beings who were "cool," (as revealed by certain attitudes they had, certain clothes they wore, certain ways they combed their hair, certain kinds of music to which they listened, etc.) and all the other members of the human race, who were not cool. Of course, I no longer believe any such thing. It now seems to me—especially when recalling how often, dramatically, and arbitrarily the standards for adolescent sophistication and fashion have changed since that time—that this was nothing more than an arrogant and childish mistake. In other words, there in fact was not an objective, seeable, or even a real distinction of the sort I had in mind at all. Instead, this "objective distinction" was nothing more than a subjective, temporarily interesting, idiosyncratic product of preferences, assumptions, and choices associated with—to express the point vaguely—one special group of individuals who lived at a particular place and time, under very specific circumstances.

Kim's account of minds may have arisen from a similar confusion between nature and culture. One indication of this point is the following. Contrary to what Kim says and implies, we are *not* aware of any precise dividing line between "unminded" animals on which it is morally acceptable to perform live experiments, and "minded" ones on which such experiments are not permitted. A proof of this claim is the fact that, during the course of human history, what people have taken to be the dividing line between the two sides of this supposedly objective distinction has changed many times. (Compare Tattersall 1998, pp. 30–31.)

What are the sources of the misunderstanding I propose to attribute to Kim? The main thing operating here, it seems to me, is that he and like-minded theorists consistently underestimate the strength and depth of the influence that culturally based (or learned) patterns, institutions, and traditions can have on human thought and behavior. To express the same point another way, the thinkers in question fail to appreciate what I have called "the causal power of ideas." Of course, that is not usually true in practical contexts of everyday life. In those settings, the vast majority of people unthinkingly assume that culture plays a central role in shaping nearly everything that modern human beings are, think, and do. Nevertheless, many sophisticated thinkers—supposedly in the interest of achieving scientific rigor—feel compelled to "correct," or at least, radically downplay, any such common-sense impressions about how human beings work. For instance, I believe this is true, not only in Kim's case; but also in that of cognitivists like Chomsky, Pinker, and the Churchlands; of behaviorists like the psychologists John Watson and B.F. Skinner, and of the philosopher Gilbert Ryle. However, despite the popularity of this general intellectual program, I think it is quixotic and mistaken, for the following reason. We all are bound to agree that the basic aim of science is simply to discover truth, or—to use an equivalent expression—to find out what the facts are that actually constitute our world. And in view of that point, neither scientists, nor philosophical thinkers (like me) who try to base their opinions on the methods and results of science, can afford to turn their backs on any part of the truth—not even those parts of it that typically reveal themselves in contexts of practical experience.

Consider a few illustrations. First, a systematic undervaluing of the influence of culture, supposedly in the interests of preserving scientific clarity and objectivity, creates important problems for behavioristic theories of mind. Behaviorists are theorists who claim that science is a systematic study of observable entities, and therefore argue that there cannot be any room in science for consideration of mysterious, hidden entities that are supposedly only knowable by inference and surmise. Consistent with that methodological program, behaviorists then insist that scientists also should conceive of mind, not as an inner cause of outer, observable behavior (so that patterns of behavior are merely effects and symptoms of its presence), but as being exhaustively constituted by behavior.

In other words, behaviorists say "talk is cheap"; and therefore any scientifically legitimate account of humans must focus on what they do—for example, how they react to stimulation in well defined situations—and leave out of account all subjective considerations of personality, history, and societal and cultural background. However, one important problem with this methodology is that it often leads to results different from what behaviorists expected and intended, because conclusions drawn from observations of behavior often fail to be cross-culturally valid.

Here is a fictional but typical instance of what I am talking about: In one scene of the Hollywood film, *True Grit*, Rooster Cogburn, a cantankerous, slightly depraved, but basically honest federal Marshall (played by John Wayne) complains that, although he often plays cards with the Chinese restaurant owner, in whose house he lives, he never yet has managed to beat him. Furthermore, according to Cogburn (Wayne), the fundamental reason for this consistent string of losses is the fact that he finds it impossible to know—to conclude from observations of face, hands, posture, or the like—what any Chinese is thinking. (It is never explained in the film why the Chinese landlord does not find Cogburn's card-playing just as incomprehensible as *vice versa*; but I propose to ignore this last complication.)

A fortiori, it is reasonable to expect this same phenomenon of mutual inscrutability to occur in an even deeper and more virulent form, in situations where humans attempt to discover and describe the thought processes that occur in animals of other species. Some authors (such as Jerry Fodor—see his 1987, pp. ix–xii) argue in quasi-behaviorist style that we are justified in drawing essentially the same observational conclusions about non-human animals, as we also do about our human friends and neighbors, for the following two reasons. First, we know from experience that we are able to "read the minds" of certain domesticated animals, especially our pets. And second, we have good reasons for supposing that those creatures are fairly accurate and faithful representatives of all other, non-human animals as well.

But this Fodorean argument is fallacious. The real explanation of the fact that we usually can predict what our pets will and will not do, is not that we are able to gain insights into the workings of their minds by means of observing their behavior. Instead, the principal source of this predictive power is the artificially structured, human-dominated environments in which we force domesticated animals to live. A humorous illustration of this point occurs in a famous cartoon where "Marvello the Mind Reader" (or some such name, identified from a poster hanging on a background wall) looks down at his cat sitting in front of the kitchen refrigerator, and asks (in the caption), "Would you like something to eat?" The point of the joke, of course, is that (i) the only food available to the cat is located in this refrigerator; (ii) only humans, and not cats, are able to open the refrigerator's door; (iii) the cat has been trained to expect to eat at approximately the same time every day; and therefore, in view of all these considerations, (iv) it does not require a mind reader to figure out that the cat now wants to eat. Thus, to summarize the point, the only reason this conclusion is obvious is that, in all such cases, it is "built into" the situation itself.[9]

A related observation is this: Changes in a pet's environment sometimes will undermine one's usual expectations about how that animal will behave. Here is another imaginary situation (based on an incident in my own past). A man—call him Jones—cherishes the idea that his dog, Fluffy, is his best, oldest, and most faithful friend. Jones then receives a visit from someone of great authority and importance—"Mr. Big." And during the visit, Jones goes out of his way to treat his guest with consideration, respect, and deference. After taking note of this situation, Fluffy suddenly "switches allegiance." In other words, the dog now begins to respond to the visitor in ways that, before then, it had reserved for its master alone. Still later, when Jones has time to reflect on this change in the dog's behavior, he is forced to conclude that his earlier view of his pet as a "faithful friend" was based on illusion. Instead, he now believes the dog somehow conceives of itself as a low-ranking member of a very small pack. And therefore, the dog finds it appropriate (and safe) to behave in an appeasing, subservient way towards any creature—canine or

---

9. See the analogous arguments that Edward Reed mustered in his 1997, in favor of the idea that the traditional psychological notion of "stimulus" is both unrealistic and illegitimate.

human—that currently happens to occupy the position of pack leader or "Alpha wolf."

It is now a familiar story to say that behaviorism—with its emphasis on observable behavior—eventually fell into decline, and was largely replaced by "cognitivism." What are the main characteristics of this last-named view? The most important thing to say is that it identified the mind with certain parts, aspects, and powers of the brain. Furthermore, it claimed the best way for researchers to study and know the particular brain-parts in question was for them to make inferences from "clues" provided by subjects' observable behavior. In other words, rather than thinking of patterns of outer behavior as identical with mind, as behaviorists had done, they conceived of behavior as a source of clues—an inferential basis—from which scientists could reconstruct what the mind was like, indirectly.

With respect to cross-cultural and cross-species problems of the sort just discussed, did this transition have the effect of changing things for the better? The answer is No. For example, when cognitivist, Noam Chomsky, wrote his now famous review (1959) of B.F. Skinner's book, *Verbal Behavior*, he did not attack the views of Skinner and other behaviorists on the grounds that they failed to take account of cultural influences on the mind. Rather, his two main objections to the behaviorist program were as follows: First, he rejected the idea that scientists could discover the important properties of mind, just by paying attention to patterns of behavior—such as stimulus-response connections, schedules of conditioning, or the "law of effect"—because this ignored the crucial role played by the evolved, physical brain in determining the properties of thinking, perceiving, and speaking. Second, Chomsky objected to the notion of a "general mind"—something behaviorists believed followed from their assumption that simple conditioning (reward and punishment) led creatures to do everything they did, and to become everything they became. To be more particular, behaviorists claimed it was plausible to expect any given species of animals to form essentially the same mental principles, properties, and powers, as every other species, because experience—and conditioning on the basis of that experience—would teach all of them virtually the same lessons. According to Chomsky, however, that last idea was nothing more than a non-empirical and unscientific prejudice. In fact, he thought certain empirical findings already available were sufficient to show that, in fact, some species learned, thought, and reacted to their environment, in importantly different ways. For instance, Chomsky referred to one experimental study whose authors had concluded that "there are important qualitative differences in solution of comparable elementary problems by rats and fish" (Chomsky 1959, p. 30, note 4).

The upshot, as I see it, then, is that Chomsky rejected the extreme position Skinner had affirmed, only to adopt the opposite extreme himself. What this means is the following: Skinner believed, as just mentioned, that learning from experience, and more specifically, learning by means of reward and punishment, determined everything important about the mind. And he thought this implied in turn that, since the experience of creatures of all types was more or less similar, so that they would learn more or less the same things, they thereby would develop (to one or another degree of completeness and sophistication) essentially the same minds. By contrast, Chomsky said the mind's most important features were genetic rather than acquired by learning, and therefore researchers were only entitled to suppose that minds belonging to members of the same species (animals with approximately the same genotype) were similar. For example, he believed that minds capable of employing syntactic language were the exclusive possession of human beings.

In my way of thinking, however, Chomsky's attack on Skinner did not go far enough. Why do I say this? The reason is that, within the bounds of a given species, separate groups of individuals often learn to behave—to deal with each other and with their environment—in significantly different ways than other groups. This means in turn that all the differences just mentioned are cultural rather than genetic ones. For instance, consider the following passage (Walker 1992, pp. 31–32):

> To him [wolf-researcher Dr. Paul Paquet], interpreting animal behaviour is as much an art as a science. "I think there is more subtle cultural information passed on that we are not aware of," Paquet explains. He believes the dominant wolves transmit their culture and traditions to other pack members through their leadership. Their hunting traditions are one example. "I know some packs seem to be quite adept at tracking and killing certain animals and not others, so one pack may hunt moose not elk. That becomes a tradition."

Still another example is the different socially transmitted customs, passed from one generation to another, which researchers have noted among separate groups of our closest living genetic relations—the wild chimpanzees of Africa (see Whiten and Boesch 2001).

Are we justified in supposing, as Chomsky does, that cultural differences analogous to those just mentioned cannot have played any important role in creating what we now think of as the human mind? If the answer is No, then we have reasons for thinking that Chomsky and others like him, each in his or her own way, are in just as much danger, as Skinner was, of constructing their general accounts of mind on illegitimate, non-empirical foundations. In particular, the issue of exactly what cultural factors can and cannot do in this respect deserves a serious answer—an answer that reflects, and grows naturally out of, careful, empirical research. Furthermore, it seems to me that the sort of research in question here should not be focused exclusively on narrowly physical matters of fact (e.g. the physiological organization of the brain), but also should concern itself with human life, considered in a more general way.

It now is time to pass on to another, related topic. Why did I spend so many words in the preceding section describing the Upper Paleolithic Revolution (henceforth, the "UPR")? The reason is that this event provides a good means of exposing a weakness in the approach to mind shared by people like Chomsky, Pinker, Lakoff, Mark Johnson, and the Churchlands. To be specific, the UPR provides a concrete, clear, and important proof that cultural as opposed to physiological events sometimes have deep and lasting effects on humans' basic intellectual properties and powers.

Some theorists would deny what I just said, on the grounds that every species that manages not to become extinct soon after having evolved (including our own) does and must remain essentially unchanged throughout the rest of its history. Thus, these same individuals will say, the only criterion of evolutionary success that applies to every species is that of the species' being able to maintain or reconstruct essentially the same environmental conditions that were in place at the time its genes originally were assembled. For instance, Steven Pinker seems to agree with such a view. To focus on just one case, he says (1997, p. 525) that, as far as humans are concerned, religion and philosophy are in part the application of mental tools to problems they were not designed to solve.

What does Pinker mean by this? Repeating a theme already mentioned once before, he also says (p. 524):

> The mind is a neural computer, fitted by natural selection with combinatorial algorithms for causal and probabilistic reasoning about plants, animals, objects, and people. It is driven by goal states that served biological fitness in ancestral environments, such as food, sex, safety, parenthood, friendship, status, and knowledge. That toolbox, however, can be used to assemble Sunday afternoon projects of dubious adaptive value.

Still more concretely (*ibid.*):

> Some parts of the mind register the attainment of increments of fitness by giving us a sensation of pleasure. Other parts use a knowledge of cause and effect to bring about goals. Put them together and you get a mind that rises to a biologically pointless challenge: figuring out how to get at the pleasure circuits of the brain and deliver little jolts of enjoyment without the inconvenience of wringing bona fide fitness increments from the harsh world.

For example (p. 525):

> We enjoy strawberry cheesecake, but not because we evolved a taste for it. We evolved circuits that gave us trickles of enjoyment from the sweet taste of ripe fruit, the creamy mouth feel of fats and oils from nuts and meat, and the coolness of fresh water. Cheesecake packs a sensual wallop unlike anything in the natural world because it is a brew of megadoses of agreeable stimuli which we concocted for the express purpose of pressing our pleasure buttons.

In a similar fashion, according to Pinker, writers, critics, theologians, and others habitually assume that art, music, humor, philosophy, and religion are not just activities and methods of thinking that we happen to find interesting and pleasant. Rather, these people claim that they are deep, significant, and obviously useful parts of the mental equipment with which all normal human beings have been lucky enough to be born. But according to Pinker, this assumption is mistaken. The fact of the matter, he says, is that (like cheesecake) all the supposed mental faculties just mentioned are merely distractions that are not adaptive, and that even may be positively harmful.

However, I reject all the preceding claims Pinker makes, for several reasons. First, I admit that there are at least some cases that are like the situation Pinker discusses. Biologists say that the genera or families of cats, sharks, and crocodiles have remained essentially unchanged over a very long period. In the case of cats, for example, the length of time through which animals of that sort have continued to look, act, and make their living, in virtually the same ways, has been about thirty-four million years (see Newman 1997, p. 58). Nevertheless, creatures like these are not common in the history of life, but are rare. In fact, they only typically occur in special situations where, by chance, it is appropriate to say that "Nature has hit a bulls eye." In other words, the type of situations I am talking about are ones where a group of organisms, very early in its career, happens to stumble upon an available and unoccupied style of life that proves to have great effectiveness and durability. But in the contrasting, much more usual sort of case, the life-history of a successful group of animals shows that it was necessary for those creatures to "wander" through a large repertoire of different forms and styles of living, before they finally found a relatively permanent place or home in what Darwin called the "economy" or "polity" of nature (see for example Darwin 1859/2000, p. 81). To quote an example from p. 199 of Gould 2001), "horses began as small, four-toed woodland scamperers and ended as big, one-toed grassland gallopers." Similarly, camels are another familiar instance, where what the animals in question were like when they first evolved was quite different from what they became later (*ibid.*, p. 194). Thus, the reason they continue to survive today is that the manner of life at which they eventually arrived proved able to provide them with a stable and defensible means of support.

Does it make sense to maintain, in defense of theorists like Pinker, that even if large-scale taxa, like families and genera, are capable of changing over time, it still is true to say that every individual species included within a taxon always remains relatively fixed and unchanged? How one answers this question will depend on the particular species he or she has in mind. On the one hand, it is necessary to admit—as Darwin also did—that there are quite a number of extremely conservative species (for example clams and some types of worms) that have remained nearly unchanged since very ancient times, because nothing ever compelled them to abandon the specialized mode of life that they adopted at the very beginning of their existence. (See Attenborough 1979, pp. 39–40.) For example, a case partly similar to this is the family of sea birds we now call puffins (for example the Atlantic Puffin). These count as a relatively specialized group of organisms because of the fact that, generation after generation, they characteristically stick to more or less the same diet, reproduce in essentially the same way, live in essentially the same habitats, and so on. And because of this, even a small change in their circumstances can be enough to put them in danger of falling into extinction. But on the other hand, this is not also true of more opportunistic, "generalizing" species like rats, coyotes, crows, and herring gulls. Recent reports tell us herring gulls are now threatening the viability of some species of puffins because, in many parts of the world, they have taken over the puffins' ranges, food sources, and nesting places. In other words, generalizing animals of the sorts just mentioned seem able to change how, where, and by what means they live, in fairly drastic and dramatic ways, without thereby setting themselves on a road that leads to extinction.

Against the background of this discussion, how is it appropriate to classify human beings like ourselves? To be specific, to which of the two broad groups of creatures just distinguished are we more similar? It certainly is true to say that humans have some backward-looking, "conservative" characteristics that show them to be fairly typical members of the primate family. For instance, over time, primates considered as a group have demonstrated a tendency towards "encephalization"—the development of increasingly larger brains, and increasingly more complex nervous systems. And our species, *Homo sapiens*, is no exception, since it fits in consistently with that same tendency. (See Tattersall 1998, Chapter 2.) In spite of that, however, as far as concerns a great many of what we usually think of as mental properties, humans— and more especially modern humans, those who came after the UPR—have shown themselves to be quite different from their predecessors. In particular, they now are much more flexible and able to change than other primates. At least in this last respect, then, it seems reasonable to say that we *Homo sapiens* are more like the second, generalizing, "wandering" group of animals, than like creatures of the first, conservative sort.

In fact, at least in one way, our biological situation appears to be even more extreme than that of other opportunistic creatures like crows or coyotes, because modern humans like ourselves have gone beyond the lifestyle typical of our ancestors, by what E.O. Wilson has described as a "quantum leap."[10] In other words, instead of a progressive development through a series of small stages—the sort of picture Darwin favored—human history has passed through several, and perhaps many, radically transforming "twists." Thus, alongside the "conservative" model of cats, sharks, and crocodiles, and the "wandering" model of horses and camels, there might be a need for another, third category capable of throwing light on the fundamental nature of our own species. In addition to humans, it might be appropriate to think of this third category as also including creatures like echo-locating bats, electric eels, skunks, and flying fish. To be more concrete, what I am talking about is the fact that our species (or at least, modern humans like us) have been able to devise—or, to employ another metaphor, have been able to discover—a radically new "adaptive trick," which has had the effect of setting the course of our existence on a decisively different path from the one that was typical of our ancestors.

For the reasons just mentioned, then, Pinker is wrong to say that modern humans have extended themselves into areas of thought and action where—in view of their fixed and innately given natures—they do not belong, and where they have no realistic hope of ever finding success. Rather, a better description of the situation is to say that humans like us have managed to locate and occupy a new adaptive niche that was unknown to our predecessors. And therefore, in contrast with our ancestors (even including many earlier members of our own species), it is now the case that our long-term survival might well depend, not just on the shape, size, and capabilities of our bodies, but instead on whether we manage to solve a series of more or less abstract problems, of an artistic, philosophical, or religious nature.

---

10. See his 1975/1980, p. 272: "The growth in intelligence that accompanied this [brain] enlargement was so great that it cannot yet be measured in any meaningful way. . . . [N]o scale has been invented that can objectively compare man with chimpanzees and other living primates."

We are now in a position to return to the issue—announced in the title of this section—of why it took so long for the UPR to happen. As mentioned before, humans' entry into the Upper Paleolithic was obviously connected with the biological, evolutionary, and physiological fact that *Homo sapiens* happened to possess a special type of large and complex brain. One proof of this is implicit in the discovery of paleoanthropological historians that this revolution occurred at more or less the same time all around the world, among populations of humans that were physically isolated from one another. Nevertheless, why did this event not appear in human history at a much earlier time? Why did something like ninety thousand to 140 thousand years have to pass, since the beginning of our species (and our species' brains) before this development took place?

The philosopher, David Hume, formulated the following principle about the workings of causality (1775/1978, p. 174):

> an object, which exists for any time in its full perfection without any effect, is not the sole cause of that effect, but requires to be assisted by some other principle, which may forward its influence and operation.

What is my proposed solution to the paradoxical problem this Humean principle sets for the early history of human beings? It is this: Since physical and physiological considerations, by themselves, cannot provide an adequate explanation of the long delay in the appearance of the UPR, it is reasonable to try to account for that phenomenon another way. The most obvious means of doing this is to appeal to psychological, cultural, and historical considerations in place of physical ones. For example, one thing that might be relevant to this matter is the familiar observation that children born into cultural environments where intellectual curiosity is neither valued nor rewarded—such as in isolated, backward, "mill-town" societies, or impoverished inner-city ghettos—often develop profound mental limitations as a result of this beginning in life. In other words, no matter how potentially intelligent and talented these children were at birth, they become more likely, on average, to grow up to lead narrow, unimaginative, conservative lives, and to pass on to their own children, a proclivity to live and think in the same way. My suggestion is that something like this—but even cruder, more extreme, and more serious in its consequences—also may have happened in the lives of the earliest members of our species.

Second, we can speculate that the special brains our early ancestors possessed might have allowed them to have unusual, non-primate-like experiences. More especially, the human owners of those brains might have got occasional, vague glimpses of a previously unknown intellectual power of considering objects, properties, and events from a relatively removed, selfless, and dis-interested standpoint. And this would have been obviously different from the style of thinking other primate had employed—considering things only from an engaged, practical, and exclusively personal point of view. (This novel way of thinking I am talking about is similar to, and perhaps identical with, what Thomas Nagel calls "the view from nowhere" or "objective thought." See his 1986.)

In spite of those flickers of awareness, however, I speculate that, for many thousands of years, people like the ones just described made something like an explicit decision never to employ, participate in, or further explore that new mental capacity. What motivated this? I suggest they followed this course because they had not yet had enough time to organize their lives in a way capable of supporting the new set of problems, and the new type of society, to which such thinking inevitably would lead. In particular, they probably considered their new-found ability to be alien, strange, disturbing, and threatening. In other words, my paradoxical, semi-Freudian thesis is that our early *Homo sapiens* ancestors avoided (relative) objective thinking for a long time, because they saw it as carrying a threat of separating them from the safety, order, and familiar comfort of the world in which they always had lived. (Again, similar factors often lead present-day children in ghettos or isolated, "redneck" communities to con-clude that the life of the mind—such as school—is "not for them.")

Someone might object that none of the preceding remarks can claim to have any legitimate scientific significance, because there is no way of proving it right or wrong. Furthermore, the objector might add, all those statements add up to nothing more than an imagined projection from certain aspects of present experience into the remote past. This "likely story" is not based on any empirical considerations relevant to the historical period in question itself. In this last respect, the objector will continue, my explanatory account turns out to be similar to—and of no more value than—Thomas Hobbes's uninformed and fanciful claim that early human life was "nasty, brutish, and short."[11]

I cheerfully admit that this objection contains a certain amount of truth. But my reply to it is that my only project here is to provide a "possibility proof." Everyone agrees that we have massive factual ignorance about the period to which I am referring. And in the face of that ignorance, scientific investigators are only able to appeal to something like defense lawyers' strategy for establishing reasonable doubt about their clients' guilt. That is, a lawyer tells the jury a story that fits all the facts presented in the trial—but one in which his client is innocent. He does not claim that this is a literal account of what actually occurred. Rather, the only function the story has is to show (indirectly) that the defendant *might* be guiltless. In roughly similar fashion, then, I am trying to show that a psychological and cultural rather than narrowly physical explanation of the lateness of the UPR is conceivably correct, by proposing a consistent and, in this sense, possible account of the matter. But instead of claiming that this account is true, I only insist that it has a right to be taken seriously, because something more or less like it may be correct.

What about the comparison with Hobbes? It is important to note that neither Thomas Hobbes nor any other thinker who lived before the twentieth century had any means of knowing about the Upper Paleolithic Revolution. Furthermore, no such person was in a position to appreciate the profound intellectual changes this event introduced into human history, or to contemplate the puzzling fact that the UPR happened many thousands of years after our species already had come into existence. These two points are recent, hard-won empirical discoveries. Furthermore, (relative to previously accepted ways of thinking) they are such strange and unexpected facts, that anyone who wants to propose a scientifically based account of the basic nature that belongs to human beings needs to find some plausible way of taking account of them.

---

11. The above objector is not just a creature of my imagination, but a real person—an anonymous editorial reader for MIT Press. I am grateful to him or her for having proposed these penetrating criticisms.

1.3   What This Book Is About

Despite the fact that I had a great deal to say in the first two sections of this chapter about the Upper Paleolithic Revolution—the event that inaugurated the Late Stone Age—my main concern in the rest of the book will not be with it, but with something that happened later, in historical rather than pre-historical time. I shall try to show that it is illuminating to think of that later event as similar to the UPR. More specifically, my project is to extend something like the same points that recent archeological writers have made about the UPR, to the so-called "Greek Revolution in Thought" that occurred somewhere on the mainland of Greece around the time of Homer (between 1100 and 750 B.C.E.).

This last-mentioned revolution, as I interpret it, was a culturally grounded, intellectual invention made by one or more unusually gifted, but now unknown individuals. Its principal effect was to allow people to begin employing a new set of rules, goals, and standards for thinking. At the present time, the great majority of the inhabitants of the earth have come to adopt those same rules. In fact, many scientific and philosophical theorists now claim that those rules embody the natural, correct, and proper forms for all possible human thought. But that is a mistake, since, as a matter of historical fact, humans did not begin to think in that way (not, at least, in a strictly consistent and relatively permanent fashion), until the time of the Greek Revolution.

Much of what I shall say will focus on the notion of "reason." Some people suppose that reason is the most essential feature of human mentality. For example, the summarizing passage from Lakoff and Mark Johnson (1999, pp. 3–4) quoted before shows that those authors take this view. But Lakoff and Mark Johnson also assume that reason is a genetic endowment that belongs to every human without exception. By contrast, I shall defend the view that there was no such thing as reason, strictly understood, or the special sort of mind that reason makes possible, until after approximately 1000 B.C.E.

In some respects, Lakoff and Mark Johnson implicitly agree with this. Why, for instance, did they choose to begin the passage just mentioned with the following sentence?

Reason has been taken for over two millennia as the defining characteristic of human beings.

To state the same puzzle in still more precise terms, what led those authors to pick that particular number of years, as opposed to some other number? After all, the period of two millennia is not a majority of the time since the beginning of civilized, settled, agricultural life—which happened about 10,000 years ago. And it is merely a drop in the bucket, compared to the whole period (between 200,000 and 150,000 years) during which the species *Homo sapiens* has existed. It is even a smaller drop, if one compares it instead with the time since the common ancestor of hominids and chimpanzees was alive (roughly six million years ago), or with the whole duration since the development of primates generally (about 65 million years, or in other words, since the asteroid strike that probably caused the so-called K-T—Cretaceous-Triassic—geological boundary). (See Tattersall, Delson, Van Couvering 1988, pp. xxvi–iii.)

Lakoff and M. Johnson might have chosen this number because they thought any humans who lived earlier than three to two thousand years ago were "primitive" beings, who lacked the intelligence, sophistication, or presence of mind to speculate realistically about their nature and place in the world. But this is not a plausible or defensible idea. For example, the remains of many past cultural achievements show that at least some ancient Egyptians, Babylonians, and Chinese were intelligent and educated individuals, who were fully capable of thinking in a careful, precise way about any number of issues. Of course, none of these people had access to modern science. But the same is also true of the vast majority of humans who lived after the period of three to two thousand years ago, since modern science did not appear until much later. For example, some authors say science of that sort started during the Italian Renaissance in the 1400s. And—as we shall see—the historian, G.E.R. Lloyd, claims it did not begin, in a strict sense, until the twentieth century.

I think the real reason Lakoff and M. Johnson settled on the number of years they did, is that they were vaguely aware that some historical transition had taken place around that time, which had a profound and lasting effect on human patterns of thought. What event am I talking about? Again, the answer is the intellectual transition that occurred in Greece during the "Middle Age" that separated the Mycenaean from the later Classical period.[12]

Let me mention a further problem. Some people may feel that my main thesis is too inward-looking, restricted, and exclusive, because it only focuses on the history of Western civilization, and does not take account of any other world-cultures. For example, someone might grant that the Greek Revolution obviously was important, if only because certain themes it introduced were destined to blossom later into what we now think of as modern science. But even so, the objector will say, various other ancient civilizations (such as those of India and China) also had intellectual traditions that encouraged the gathering, assessment, and justification of knowledge. And therefore those other traditions also have a right to be called scientific. Thus again, it seems to be an obvious mistake to ignore those cultures, and concentrate on early Greece alone.

In his book, *Adversaries and Authorities: Investigations into Ancient Greek and Chinese Science* (1996), G.E.R. Lloyd follows a different procedure from the one I am recommending here. In the middle of his career as a scholar specializing in early Greek thought, Lloyd concluded that his viewpoint in earlier works had been too narrow. For example, on the first page of the book just mentioned, he says that

> it is obvious that in antiquity we are not dealing with science as we know it today, that is, with the highly institutionalized practice that is carried on in modern universities and research laboratories. On the strictest interpretation of science, we have to concede that the term is not applicable to anything before the present [twentieth] century. But that is, no doubt, to be unduly restrictive, and I shall use the term conventionally as a place-holder for a variety of specific inquiries we can identify in both Greece and China. Three of the most promi-

---

12. Again, one respect in which I think the Greek Revolution was similar to the UPR is that both were primarily cultural occurrences rather than just physical ones. Nevertheless, it also seems to me that *no* historical event (including the Greek Revolution) has been nearly as important to humans' intellectual development as that which happened at the beginning of the Late Stone Age.

nent, which will occupy much of our attention throughout, are astronomy, mathematics and medicine: a fourth is cosmology and whatever passes as natural philosophy or physics: others that could be added are geography, optics, harmonics, mechanics and so on.

I consider comparative studies like this one of Lloyd's legitimate, interesting, informative, and admirable. But in spite of that, I have not chosen to follow a path similar to his in this book, for at least two reasons—one superficial, the other deeper. The more superficial reason is that it is never a good idea to try to talk about everything; and—other things being equal—authors ought to stick to the topics they know best. My past interests have not led me to inform myself about the history of ancient China, India, or other ancient cultures, in a way that would now allow me to write an interesting and worthwhile comparative book on those subjects.

The deeper and more important reason is that Lloyd's talk about "place-holders" is disturbing to me, since it may be a sign that he subscribes to what I think of as a false and dangerous view of history. Consider the following. It is often hard to draw a clear line between (subjective) inventions on one side, and (objective) discoveries on the other, because inventions sometimes appear to be outcomes of inevitable and determinate courses of events. For instance, if Alexander Graham Bell had not invented the telephone at the particular time and place he did, there are good reasons to suppose that, at a slightly later time, someone else would have done so instead. Those reasons stem from the fact that other members of Bell's relevant cultural group were then working on roughly the same problem in roughly the same ways; and all the elements of Bell's general solution were "in the air."

Again, separate groups of people sometimes can be led to accomplish roughly equivalent things, or to develop parallel cultural institutions, simply by virtue of shared similarities in their physical situations (for example in their bodies). Why does each generation "discover" the social institution of sexual intercourse between male and female? Why do virtually all societies recognize some form of marriage? Why have historians and anthropologists never discovered any (post-UPR) human society totally devoid of religion? (For the last of these points, see the first page of Burkert 1996.) The answer seems to be that analogies in the physical, emotional, and instinctual properties of humans are enough to bring about all the things just mentioned.

As suggested before, this also may shed light on certain puzzles about the Upper Paleolithic Revolution. Even though present-day researchers know much more about the European "edition" of this historical change than any of its other versions, evidence points to the fact that similar transitions happened around the same time (60,000 to 30,000 years ago) in other parts of the Old World (Africa, the Far East, Australia). This was not likely to be a coincidence. Thus, the explanation of this rough agreement in time—i.e. the similar number of years each group needed to "mature" into the UPR—seems to lie in the simple fact that all humans possess approximately the same brains.

All this having been said, however, the case discussed in this book (as I interpret it) is different from the others just mentioned, in the following respect. As compared with them, the Greek Revolution was unique, individual, and radically contingent, because it arose out of, and was an expression of, a special cultural situation. To explain this further, let me propose a parallel from another field. Steven Jay Gould, once famously claimed that if it were possible for the tape of life to be rewound to the early Cambrian period, the chances are very small that human beings would appear again in the replay (Gould 1989, especially the first part of Chapter III; and 1996, p. 214). Similarly, I suggest that something like Gould's neo-Darwinian conception of biological evolution also applies to certain cases of human cultural and historical traditions. More precisely, we have good reason to believe that the sort of rational, objective, scientifically useful thinking employed by the overwhelming majority of people today would have been different, if history had followed another course than the one it actually did. For example, it is easy to conceive of a contrary-to-fact situation in which the ancient Chinese science Lloyd describes acted as the source of our present-day, worldwide, scientific thinking. For better or worse, however, that scenario just envisioned did not actually happen. To mention a trivial point, if the possible world we now are imagining were the real one, then it would be reasonable to expect that modern scientific thinking would attach a great deal of importance to the distinction between Yin and Yang. But the science we now possess does not do that; and that is one indication that the world just imagined is not our world.[13]

Accordingly, I claim that the Greek Revolution *created* what we now think of as reason—and thereby also, that which most people now conceive of as the mind. Furthermore (paradoxically), those who would reject this idea on the grounds of its being narrow-minded and prejudiced are themselves in danger of stumbling into the grip of an ethnocentric fallacy. What I am talking about is the mistake of assuming that anyone who fails to think in exactly the same way *as we* do *now*, thereby shows that he or she is not, and could not be, a normal, sane, cultured, or intelligent human being.

I also propose to argue (mainly in Chapter 4) that this conception of things puts us in a position to solve certain other, indirectly related problems. In particular, I shall try to show that my account of mentality points the way towards more adequate solutions to ancient puzzles about (i) what it means to say that generals or universals exist, and (ii) how it is possible for such entities to be related to concrete individuals.

---

13. Aristotle says somewhere (perhaps in Book VII of the *Politics*) that if a universal conflagration were to destroy the whole of civilization, then eventually, once order was restored, precisely the same list of the human arts and sciences would re-emerge to be affirmed once again by all people. Does Lloyd (who is a well known Aristotelian scholar) implicitly accept this same idea?

Two Forms of Naturalism: Ancient and Modern

Everything the philosopher has declared about man is . . . at bottom, no more than a testimony as to the man of a very limited period of time. Lack of historical sense is the family failing of all philosophers. . . . They will not learn that man has become, that the faculty of cognition has become; while some of them would have it that the whole world is spun out of this faculty of cognition.

—FRIEDRICH NIETZSCHE (1878/1986, PP. 12–13)

The man who has no idea of what happened before he was born always remains a child.

—CICERO

2.1 Early Conceptions of Mind—An Affirmation of Disembodiment?

In the first of the two above quotations, Nietzsche reminds us that, in the absence of a clear and objective knowledge of history, theorists are bound to make the mistake of projecting their own local, idiosyncratic concerns into the past and the future of the human race as a whole. One example of this point is the following: During the last few centuries, many Western philosophers have been obsessed with the denunciation of dualism. As mentioned before, this is the doctrine that the universe is irreducibly divided between two (or more) separate realms, substances, or states—for example the natural versus the supernatural realms, or the state or condition of being a human being on one side as opposed to that of being non-human on the other. Accordingly, it was natural for those philosophers to suppose that humans *always* have had a tendency to adopt dualistic forms of thinking. More narrowly, they supposed it was natural for all the members of our species to think of our minds as different and separated from the physical world, by virtue of being "disembodied" (to use Lakoff's and Mark Johnson's word). Furthermore, those same philosophers were also inclined to assume that the best available means of overcoming this tendency was to correct it by appealing to the monistic, naturalistic conception of the world apparently affirmed by the findings of modern empirical science.

Let me give a few concrete illustrations. In the first half of the twentieth century, John Dewey argued that philosophy was what one did with a problem, until the concepts and presuppositions associated with it became sufficiently clear to allow it to be solved by the methods of science. (I owe this way of summarizing Dewey's position to Jerry Fodor. See Dewey 1920/1960, and Fodor 1983, p. 177.) Dewey also claimed that the reason scientific facts could provide a powerful antidote to dualism was that science—simply by virtue of its inner nature—was fundamentally opposed to all forms of that view. Thus, in a course I took long ago with Sidney Hook, who had been a close associate of Dewey's for many years, Hook cynically observed that the Dewey he had known had been "infuriated by anything connected in any way with the number two."

Later, in the second half of the twentieth century, Willard Quine affirmed still another version of essentially the same idea. According to him (1969a, p. 27), a naturalistic conception of the universe—one based on the notion that it is possible to explain the existence and properties of human beings in roughly the same terms that also apply to all other existing things—was something so opposed to our usual ways of thinking, that it never even occurred to people, until very recently. In fact, Quine said that humans had only become able to contemplate the world in this special, monistic and anti-dualist way, after the methods and results of modern empirical science had become widely known.

Again, consider biologist Ernst Mayr's recent statement of the same general theme (1997, p. 227):

In most primitive cultures, Greek philosophy, and, conspicuously, the Christian religion, humans were considered to be entirely apart from the rest of nature. Not until the eighteenth century did a few daring authors call attention to the similarity of Man and the apes.

In my opinion, however, the conception of human nature and human history just described is both false and unjustified. To be more precise, I think that (i) unprejudiced examination of historical facts and texts does not support the idea that humans have a "primitive," perhaps even innately given, disposition to conceive of the world in a dualistic fashion. Furthermore, (ii) contrary to the idea that science is naturally opposed to all forms of dualism, I think it is more enlightening, as well as more historically accurate, to say that the notion of dualism has acted as a presupposition of, and foundation for, what we now think of as "modern empirical science." Still more concretely, I want to argue for the following two claims in this chapter: (i′) It is not true that, just by virtue of the fundamental nature of science, all scientific methods and results must be opposed to dualism. Rather, (ii′) considered from the perspective of human history as a whole, the special kind of science we now possess would not have come into existence at all, if humans had not learned—gradually, painfully, and over the course of a long development—to conceive of themselves and their world in a dualistic fashion.

What historical facts do I think of as substantiating the preceding claim (i)? (I do not intend to talk about the grounds for (ii) until later in the book.) A direct method of testing the truth of (i) would be to examine the artistic and religious ideas our ancestors developed at the time of the Upper Paleolithic Revolution—when humans first started thinking about things in a novel way that would prove remarkably powerful and effective. And then one could ask, concerning those ideas, whether there are reasons to suppose (in the manner of Mayr) that they were expressions of some sort of dualistic picture of the universe. Unfortunately, however, although it is easy to ask this question, we have no means of answering it. That is, we can speculate freely about the world-view that inspired, and is expressed in, the artifacts our Upper Paleolithic ancestors left behind (such as decorative objects; trade goods; pictures, marks, and signs on the walls of caves). But, in and by themselves, none of those artifacts provides a basis for drawing any firm and scientifically supportable conclusions about claim (i). Accordingly, then, to explore the question of whether humans have a natural, innately given inclination to think about their place in the world dualistically, we must look elsewhere. Accordingly, I suggest that our best available means of doing this is to examine the later (but nevertheless, still relatively early) human cultures of the Neolithic period—immediately after the invention of agriculture, government, writing, and recorded history.

In the words of Mark Lehner, "Ancient Egypt occupies center stage in popular imagination about the roots of civilization" (see his 2000, p. 69). Thus, it seems appropriate for us to begin by considering that case. In other words, the question I shall ask is this: Do the inscriptions, texts, practical objects, and artistic creations of the Egyptians show that those people divided the world between (at least) two basically different sorts of things? More especially, did the Egyptians think of the human soul, spirit, or mind as "disembodied," in the sense of being fundamentally different and separate from, and independent of, everything physical, prominently including their own bodies?

The answer is No. That is, in spite of the *a priori* historical assumptions of people like Dewey, Quine, and Mayr, there are no valid reasons to conclude that the ancient Egyptians conceived of things in terms of any such simple, two-part division. Still more specifically, examination shows that the Egyptians thought about the connections between the body on one side, and the mind, spirit, or soul on the other, in a much more complex and subtle fashion than any dualistic theory would be able to capture.

One proof of this last point is that the Egyptians did not suppose that each living person possessed (or consisted in) just a single soul. Instead, they surmised that every human had at least five souls, of quite different sorts. For example, Manfred Lurker (1980, p. 114) supplies the following list. According to him, the Egyptians maintained that, in addition to a body, every normal human being possessed a *ka*, an *ankh*, a *ba*, a name, and a shadow. Let me say a few words about each of these. First, they conceived of the *ka* as a certain sort of spirit double, or *Doppelgänger*. It supposedly was created at the same time as the person himself or herself, and after that, accompanied him throughout the course of his life. When the person died, the *ka* was not necessarily extinguished as well. But the fact that it was capable of living on after the death of its owner did not prove that it was in any sense eternal, abstract, or different in kind from everything physical. That is clear from the Egyptians' further idea that the *ka* could only survive the death of the person with whom it was associated, if, and for as long as, it was provisioned with food (or, in later periods, with clay replicas or wall paintings of food). Second, "*ankh*" was the name the Egyptians gave to a general life-force that some gods were graciously willing to supply to humans. Although the *ankh* had an intimate association with life and the living, it also was supposed to be able to assist the person who possessed it, in various ways, after he or she died (see David 1982, p. 79). Third, the *ba* was still another type of animating force, often depicted in paintings and sculptures as a human-headed bird. Its most distinctive characteristic was a power to leave the body and travel outside the tomb, so as to allow the dead owner of the tomb to visit places he had enjoyed during his lifetime (*ibid.*). Fourth, the Egyptians also considered a person's true name to be yet another part of both his personality and his being. During life, it was an important means by which a man or woman could receive either good or harm. For instance, one punishment judges sometimes meted out to a convicted criminal was to change his or her name from a positive and helpful one, to another that was negative and hurtful. Thus, as part of punishment for crimes, a convicted person might lose the name his parents gave him of *Ramose* ("Ra is the one who gave birth to me"), and instead acquire the new name of *Ramesedsu* ("Ra is the one who hates him"; see Taylor 2001, p. 23). After death, a person's continued survival as one of the "transfigured dead" required that other people—ones who were still alive—should remember his name, and occasionally pronounce it in the context of rituals of offering. This explains the care the Egyptians took to insure that the written form of the name of the deceased man or woman should appear in many places on the sarcophagus, on public parts of the tomb, in temples, on monuments, and so forth. Fifth and last, the shadow cast by a person's body also was supposed to have the power, under certain circumstances, to separate itself from that body, so that—similar to the case of the *ba*—it could move about freely and at will (*ibid.*, p. 24). Again, however, the Egyptians did not conceive of the name, shadow, *ka*, *ba*, or *ankh* as completely independent of all physical entities—or in other words, as disembodied. Rather, the point of all their elaborate funeral arrangements, in which they embalmed the corpse in such a way as to preserve it for eternity, was that the body should provide a resting place or focus, in which all of the souls of the sorts just mentioned could be reunited. By these admittedly artificial means, in other words, they hoped that something like the normal living person would be perpetuated once more after death.

Let us now turn to another example—the case of the ancient Greeks who lived in the heroic age described by the poet (or poets) we now call "Homer." This seems a good choice to focus on next, because (like Lakoff and Mark Johnson—note the subtitle of their book) I have a special interest in the European-based, "Western" intellectual tradition. And, quoting Richard B. Onians (1951/2000, p. xii), those people are "the earliest Europeans we really know." In other words, the Homeric Greeks count as precursors of the Western tradition, in a way the ancient Egyptians do not. And that in turn may entitle us to expect the thought patterns of the Greeks to be more similar to our own than those of the Egyptians. Nevertheless, it is still true that there are many important mental differences between the Homeric Greeks and ourselves. For example, neither Homer himself nor the people he described in his poems were literate. More specifically, although their Mycenaean ancestors had devised a system for writing the Greek language, that system had been lost and forgotten long before the Homeric Greeks appeared on the scene—during the Greek Middle or Dark Ages. In other words, the Homeric Greeks no longer had a means of understanding or employing any commonly agreed upon written language. (For this point, see Sourvinou-Inwood 1981, p. 15.) For example, Homer's poems were originally passed down entirely through memorization, followed by oral recitation (see Onians, p. 6 and n. 11).

In the introduction to his book, Onians mentions several other facts about Homeric Greeks which show that their intellectual characteristics were quite different from those of the vast majority of people today. To begin by mentioning a relatively trivial instance (p. 3), the manliest warriors among them often wept, copiously and unashamedly, in public. Another, perhaps more significant fact (*ibid.*) is that even the noblest and most heroic of the Homeric Greeks conducted themselves in battle with merciless cruelty and savagery. Another indication of the gulf between ourselves and them is that the Greeks of that time apparently agreed that women, after warriors had killed their husbands and killed or enslaved their children, were "an avowed aim and approved prize of war." Similarly, they considered piracy an honorable trade, and thought of thievery and perjury as admirable and enviable traits of character (pp. 4–5).

For our purpose, the crucial question is this: Do the words, thoughts, and activities of the people Homer described show that they conceived of the world in a dualistic manner? In particular, did they accept the notion of a disembodied soul that was fundamentally unlike, and separate from, anything physical? Again, the answer is No. Thus, consider the following short paragraph with which Jan Bremmer begins his book, 1983 (p. 3):

Modern secularization has made the salvation of the soul a problem of diminishing importance, but the prominence in Western society of psychiatry and psychology shows that we still care for our *psyche*, or "soul." Our idea of the soul has both eschatological and psychological attributes, and the borrowing of the Greek word *psyche* for modern terms implies that the Greeks viewed the soul in the modern way. Yet, when we look at Homer's epics we find that the word *psyche* has no psychological connotations whatsoever. And in Homer the *psyche* may fly away during a swoon or leave the body through a wound,

behavior now not associated with the soul. . . . Indeed, the Greeks of
Homer did not yet have "cognizance of any concept denoting the
psychic whole, of any notion that might correspond to our word
'soul,' as Bruno Snell has demonstrated in his epoch-making book
The Discovery of the Mind. (See Snell 1953/1960. Bremmer goes on
to attribute this particular way of interpreting Snell's thesis to Lloyd-
Jones 1971, p. 9.)

Thus, in respect of their general conceptions of the mind,
these earliest representatives of Greek and European culture seem
to have been more like the ancient Egyptians, than similar to
modern people like ourselves. More especially, they supposed in
an Egyptian-like way that there were not just one but several different kinds of souls present in each living human being. For
example, they drew careful distinctions between all the following
separate elements (selected from an even greater number of possible cases that also might have been mentioned): the *thymos*
(ϑυμο'ς), *phrenes* (φρε'νες) or *phren* (φρη'ν), *psyche* (ψυχη'), *nous*
(νους) or *noos* (νο'ος), *menos* (με'νος), *charme* (χα'ρμη), and
tharsos (θα'ρσος).

In fact, the Homeric Greeks maintained even more explicitly
than the Egyptians had done, that all the types of soul just mentioned should be identified with particular parts and functions of
the human body. What was the special organ of thought and feeling they called the *thymos*? According to Onians, Homer's language makes it clear that the *thymos* was a thing, rather than a
function. (See 1951/2000, p. 44.) More narrowly still, it was a
person's breath, in the sense of the vapor or steam that arises from
healthy, pumping blood. During life, the *thymos* was thought to
be physically located in the lungs (*phrenes*) or chest (*phren*).
Whenever the body was ill nourished, it diminished in strength
and power; but its strength could increase again, if and when the
body was well nourished (*ibid.*, p. 48). When the person died, the
thymos left—escaped from—the body altogether. (Onians suggests
that this idea was connected with the notion of thinking being the
same thing as inward talking, and talking in turn being identical
with breathing—as when a person says, "Don't breathe a word of
this to anyone.")

The *psyche* was the "life-soul," as contrasted with the "breath-
soul" (*ibid.*, pp. 93–95). According to Onians, this is shown by

the fact that the Greeks equated it with whatever it was that made life possible—the "life-stuff" (*ibid.*, pp. 109–116). They supposed it was contained in, or at least strongly associated with, the head (*ibid.*, pp. 95–122). It was responsible for consciousness in a very general and vague sense—but not specifically for wakefulness (*ibid.*, pp. 102–03, 116–17) or, as Bremmer remarked in the above quotation, for any other, specifically psychological attribute. The Homeric Greeks conceived of the *psyche* as the seat of all bodily strength (*ibid.*, pp. 195–97), and as the source of such things as quivering, throbbing, and itching (*ibid.*, pp. 197–99). They sometimes conceived of it as a shadow (*ibid.*, pp. 59–60), and sometimes supposed that it could take the form of a snake (*ibid.*, p. 122 n. 3, pp. 206–08). It was released by cremation (*ibid.*, pp. 261–62); and funereal libations were received by it (*ibid.*, p. 272).

The *nous* (which was to become more prominent in later Greek philosophy) was more narrowly associated with intelligence than were any of the other types of soul (see, e.g., *ibid.*, pp. 3 8, 56)—although it possessed dynamic and emotional aspects as well. The Homeric Greeks usually conceived of it as being located somewhere in the chest—(but two passages in the *Iliad* suggest a more specific identification with the heart in particular (see *ibid.*, p. 82, n. 5). However, Onians says the fact that *nous* typically was associated with a purpose, or act of conscious choice, suggests that, at least in origin, it was not identical with any specific bodily organ (see *ibid.*, pp. 82–83), but instead, was a formation, flow, or path of movement within purposing consciousness. For example, Homer's text shows that *nous* sometimes darted or rushed, but also sometimes was capable of being restrained and turned. And this shows in turn, according to Onians, that the *nous* was not strictly speaking identical with the *thymos*. Rather, it was present in it, and formed and defined the *thymos* in certain respects, in approximately the same way as a current consists in, but also controls or channels, a gas or fluid like air or water. More particularly, in Onians's view, the *nous* was that which separated intelligent and purposive consciousness on one side, from random and uncontrolled consciousness on the other. The basic reason for its association with intelligence and intellect was that it provided a "defining frame" for thinking and feeling. Because the Homeric Greeks supposed the "bronchial tree" of the lungs or *phrenes* performed a similar function, they also conceived of it as being either a thought or an organ of thought. But on the other hand, in contrast with the *phrenes*, the *nous* was not something obviously tangible. For example, it was not capable of being pierced by weapons.

Homer says at *Iliad* V, 296 (see Onians, p. 195 and n. 5), that when an advancing warrior is stricken, there "are loosed his *psyche* and his *menos*." What exactly is this *menos*? The answer is that Homer conceived of it as a special type of anger or fury that was capable of energizing men in battle and in other types of crisis. Nevertheless, he thought of it as something substantial and material in nature—presumably, as some kind of fluid or gas (Onians, p. 52). For example, Homer occasionally speaks of a god or goddess, like Athene, Apollo, or Hermes, as "breathing *menos*" into a hero or heroes or, alternatively, into horses or mules (*ibid.*, p. 51). And this process was assumed to be the god's literally filling up the lungs or *phrenes* of the intended subject(s) with gas, vapor, or liquid (see *ibid.*, p. 25, n. 5).

The proper translation of "*carme*" is "the spirit, joy, or lust for battle." That is, it is a name for the special sort of enthusiasm that comes along with the free play of all the warrior's instincts, energies, and powers—when "warring becomes sweeter than returning home" (*Iliad* II 453f; see Onians, p. 21, n. 4). Again, these early Greeks thought of *carme* as something that was physically present in the body—often as a result of divine intervention. For example, at *Iliad* XIII, 77 we read: "So they spake, one to another, rejoicing in the joy or lust of battle, which the god set in their hearts" (see Onians, p. 22 and n. 4).

Finally, the Homeric Greeks used the word "*tharsos*" to refer to a sense, feeling, or state of high spirits, boldness, and courage. This type or form of soul was not always present in a person. Rather, it was necessary for a god to bestow it on—or restore it to—a person at crucial times, by pouring it into his or her *phrenes*. Thus, at *Odyssey* IX, 380f. the poet says the comrades of Odysseus took their stand with him about the sleeping Cyclops and "some god breathed great *tharsos* into them" (see Onians, p. 52).

If the cases of the Egyptians and the Homeric Greeks are typical, what do they show? Again, one lesson they teach is that historical examination does not support Mayr's claim that dualistic thinking is natural and "primitive"—and perhaps innate—for human beings. Rather, our early ancestors' picture of the world in general, and of the soul or mind in particular, was not dualistic, but (in an important sense) was unified and monistic.

What "sense" am I talking about here? I suggest that, roughly parallel with the conception of the universe affirmed in sophisticated, scientifically informed circles today, there were not two worlds of thought in ancient times, but only one.[1] And because ancient people like the Egyptians and Homeric Greeks conceived of their world as a monistic system, I propose to call their view "ancient naturalism." Admittedly, the "nature" they recognized was not exactly the same as the nature that people talk about today. In particular, those ancient people thought about the universe around them in a very inclusive, non-discriminating way, since—as the preceding examples show—it contained many things that present-day, scientific thinkers no longer would recognize as real. For instance, neither the Egyptians nor the early Greeks drew any clear and consistent distinction between the divine and the secular; or between that which was magical and that which was mundane; or between the metaphorical and the literal; or between what was merely speculative, and what was tested, proved, and established.

2.2 The Path that Led to Modern Eliminativism: From Many, to One, to None

Assuming that the preceding suggestions were on the right track, for what reasons did people finally begin to conceive of the human soul, spirit, or mind as united and singular, rather than divided and plural? Jan Bremmer (1983, especially pp. 123–24) and Christiane Sourvinou-Inwood (1981) reject the idea that this conception of things was implicitly present from the beginning of our species, just by virtue of certain characteristics of our genotype. Instead, they argue that it was something that resulted from certain historical, cultural, and social changes. To be more specific, these authors say the change in question was a reflection

---

1. For instance, consider the first sentence of the Introduction of Searle 1995, p. xi: "We live in exactly one world, not two or three or seventeen."

of social and cultural circumstances that led people to feel an increasing sense of separation and alienation from the civil societies in which they lived. The first thing I propose to do in this second section of the chapter is to explain that point in more detail.

Bremmer divides his book into three main parts. The first is a short, introductory discussion of the Homeric notion of soul (or, more correctly, souls). Following that, he devotes most of the rest of his pages to a comparison between "The Soul of the Living" (Part Two) and "The Soul of the Dead" (Part Three). According to him, the early Greeks, like many other ancient peoples, conceived of the soul of a dead person mainly as an extension or continuation of the principal type of soul that was released from the body at the moment of death. As noted in the preceding section, the Greeks identified that type of soul with the *psyche*. (The *thymos* also was released at that time. But then it disappeared, never to be heard of again—presumably because its final fate was simply to dissipate and die. See Sourvinou-Inwood,1981, p. 18.)

In Bremmer's opinion, the most striking point that arises from comparing early Greek notions of the souls of the living, with that of the souls of the dead, is the extremely negative view these people had of the second. In almost all cases, for example, Homer described the dead as "witless shades" that were incapable of engaging in coherent thought or discourse. There were certain exceptions to that rule, on the rare occasions when some courageous living person contrived to pay a visit to Hades, in order to consult with a dead man or woman about some important matter. During those visits, according to Homer, the dead person's ability to speak and respond intelligently was temporarily restored. But as soon as the interview was finished, the person reverted once more to his usual state. That "usual state"—the customary nature and activity of souls of the dead—was to fly about quickly and aimlessly like bats, making shrieking or squeaking sounds devoid of any meaning. (This conception of the dead may have been connected with the Greek idea that the basic function of the *psyche* or "life-stuff" was simply to keep an individual alive, but not to assist him or her in the performance of any intellectual activities.)

Why did the early Greeks conceive of the souls of the dead in such hopelessly negative terms—as lacking (in Bremmer's words, see p. 124) "precisely those qualities that make up an individual"? The answer Bremmer gives focuses on characteristics of the special type of society in which this collective attitude towards the dead developed. He says (*ibid.*):

> Homeric beliefs reflect the life of the small, closely knit communities of the Dark Ages where the life of the community was more important than the survival of the individual. In these communities death was not yet so much the end of one person's life but rather an episode in the history of the community and the life cycle.

Later, however,

> the sweeping changes in Greek society in the eighth century [B.C.E.] and after promoted an individualization that created individual concern for death and survival. In the new constellation the representation of the dead as witless shades lost much of its influence but it never disappeared completely.

Although Bremmer was not concerned to say exactly what those last changes were, the crucial thing about them seems to have been a loosening of shared assumptions and obligations that previously had bound the members of society together. To be more precise, at that time, circumstances arose that forced individuals increasingly to fall back on their own initiatives and resources, as opposed (as once had been the case) to their being able to rely on, and trust in, familiar traditions associated with the group into which they had been born. And when that happened, it was natural for the people so affected to begin thinking in a new way about the souls that eventually would be left to them after death. They no longer were satisfied with a picture of those souls that was crucially dependent on "supports" supplied to them by society, so that any dying person would be bound to be radically and unhappily transformed as soon as those supports were removed. Instead, many eighth-century Greeks began to speculate (and to hope) that souls of the dead might be more unified, self-sufficient, and "normal," than their ancestors had assumed. To say the same thing another way, they now began to surmise that life after death would not necessarily be worse than this life, and might even be better.

A similar development also took place—at a much earlier
time—in ancient Egypt. This happened towards the end of the
Old Kingdom and beginning of the First Intermediate Period,
approximately between the years 2510 and 2040 B.C.E. For example, consider the following passages from Nicolas Grimal's *A
History of Ancient Egypt* (1988, pp. 150–54), describing some of
the events of that period.

> The theme of the individual confronting his death was new to the
> Egyptians, and it was linked with the development of the funerary
> role of Osiris. [For example, i]n the *mastaba* chapels the deceased is
> identified with Osiris by means of his pilgrimage to Abydos, where
> the bodily remains of the god were thought to have been reassem-
> bled. In the same way, the king is described in the Pyramid Texts as
> an Osiris, without calling into question his solar identity in the after-
> life: Osiris was an integral part of the great Egyptian cosmologies but
> he was above all a link in the chain that connected the creator-god
> with mankind. . . .
>   This was not the result of a revolution in Egyptian society, but
> simply the combined effect of two developments. The first of these
> was the disintegration of Memphite domination, while the second is
> often described as the 'democratization' of royal privileges
>   . . . . The increasing powers of the local dynasties also resulted in
> a certain degree of funerary independence. Local rulers ensured their
> own continued existence in the afterlife: rather than relying on the
> demiurge (of whom the king was still the only representative) they
> instead appealed directly to their local gods, whose importance grew
> in direct relation to the normarchs' own powers. . . .
>   When the king died, he was able to assume a place alongside Ra
> providing that he had correctly accomplished his earthly mission,
> which was to ensure that the equilibrium of creation was maintained
> during his lifetime. . . . private individuals would have been unable to
> use the same argument to ensure their own admission into the com-
> pany of the blessed. Their legitimacy in the afterlife was therefore
> broadly similar but transferred to a different level: it was simply nec-
> essary for each individual to have accomplished his or her specific
> role on earth without having disrupted society in any way. On this
> basis was created a system of morals, first expressed in the *Maxims of
> Ptahhotep* [, which] . . . was the Fifth Dynasty explanation of the
> individual's method of dealing with death. Anyone who did not fulfil
> his allotted role was a criminal in the eyes of the creator, who would
> then be obliged to exclude him from the cosmos after his death since
> he had refused to play his proper part during his lifetime.

[As yet another example of the same tendency, t]he greater awareness of the individual also emerged in the art of the First Intermediate Period, and this change can also be traced back to the weakening of central power. It is not possible to reconstruct the full history of the artistic school at Memphis, but it presumably declined at roughly the same rate as the central government.

An intellectual evolution of this type had a natural end or terminus. That terminus occurred at the point when people began to conceive of the souls of the dead as isolated from, and therefore independent of, *all* material things without exception. (This is what I meant by the words in this section's title, "from many to one.") Furthermore, it is clear from written records that this terminus actually was achieved—the process was "completed"—by various peoples, at different times in their histories. That completion is what I take to be the source of our present-day philosophical notions (i) of disembodied souls and (ii) of a dualistic universe.

Again if, as historical evidence suggests, our currently popular conceptions of dualism and disembodiment grew out of cultural sources in the way just described, then it follows that people could not have had those ideas from the very beginning of the human species. In other words, a dualistic picture of the world in general, or of humans in particular, is not something that is either simple or "primitive." Instead, it is complex and sophisticated. Thus, in place of describing the notion of disembodied souls as part of the intellectual equipment that belongs to every normal human at birth, it is more plausible to say that humans gained this conception through the labor, thought, and creativity of individuals who lived at specific times, and who operated in response to particular historical forces.

As far as the Western tradition is concerned, the first such "completed dualists" might have been those post-Homeric Greeks who followed the religious leader, Pythagoras. The "Pythagoreans" claimed that the most significant thing that occurred at the moment of death was that the soul was released from the prison of the body. According to them, in other words, the body usually had the effect of obscuring or even crippling the soul's natural qualities and powers. And therefore the process or transition of dying would not necessarily make souls worse, more confused, and more irrational. On the contrary, it was not just abstractly possible, but something to be positively expected, that—on average—souls of the dead would be more intelligent, serious, generous, loving, capable, etc. than those of the living.[2]

The Pythagoreans passed on many of those same ideas to Plato (again, see this last author's dialogue, *Phaedo*); and Plato passed something like them in turn to (other) Fathers of the Christian Church. For example, it was an obvious exaggeration for Nietzsche to say that Christianity amounted to nothing more than watered down Platonism. Nevertheless, it is clear to all informed people that the preceding claim contains a large amount of truth.

In some respects—again, relative to the Western tradition—the high-water mark of the movement of thought we are now discussing came during the declining years of the Roman Empire, when St. Augustine, bishop of the city of Hippo in North Africa (and a convinced Platonist), sat down to write his classic book, *The City of God*. Augustine's immediate inspiration for composing this work was his receiving the terrible, nearly inconceivable news, in the year 410 A.D., that Rome itself had been sacked by the Goths (see Starr 1991, p. 689). The main thesis for which Augustine argued in the book was that this event was not, as many had claimed, a punishment for the Romans' having abandoned their old pagan gods. Instead, he said it was a sign and means, through which the God, whose acts and thoughts were recorded in the Judeo-Christian Bible, proposed to teach humans a new lesson. That lesson was that it was always a mistake, based on a fundamental illusion, to put one's trust, sense of identity, and feelings of self-worth, in anything physical.

---

2. For example, Kirk, Raven, and Schofield say in the first chapter of their book, 1957/1987, p. 8: "Pythagoras was possibly the first Greek explicitly to treat the soul as something of moral importance." However, the Pythagoreans also maintained that how a person lived his or her life, made a difference to the eventual condition, fitness, and fate of his soul after death. Unless one had cared for, and tried to "purify" the soul during life, its state after death might be confused and unhappy. Plato expressed agreement with this idea in his dialogue *Phaedo* at (64C–70A, 72E–80C, 91C–95A), where he said: "The founders of the mysteries would appear to have had a real meaning, and were not just talking nonsense when they intimated in a figure long ago that he who passes unsanctified and uninitiated into the world below will lie in a slough, but that he who arrives there after initiation and purification will dwell with the gods." If the Pythagoreans had not added that point, their doctrine might have seemed to imply that the best and most rational course for any person to take was simply to commit suicide.

The most significant historical result of the new way of think-ing initiated by Augustine and like-minded individuals was this: In place of the old physical Empire, whose focus and center had been the city of Rome, European civilization now began to assume a form that, in a sense, was centered on nothing more than an abstract ideal. The ideal in question was what Augustine called the City of God, or in other words, the invisible, "moral" realm of Christendom.[3]

Let us now consider another, more recent intellectual revolu-tion in Western Society—namely, the movement of thought that ushered in what Bremmer refers to as "modern secularism." One source of inspiration for that new way of conceiving the world (a conception that continues to be powerful and important today) was science. More specifically, the type of science in question is the mathematically supported, rigorously empirical thinking and research that started in the Renaissance, beginning approximately with the fall of Constantinople to the Turks in 1453 (see Coles 1968, especially Chapter 1). To consider the matter historically, in place of the post-Platonic, Augustinian, two-part division between everything material, as contrasted with everything spiritual and divine, many people gradually came to believe, supposedly on the authority of modern science, that there was only one thing (or one kind of thing) that existed. That one thing was matter, or in other words, the physical and material, natural world, including all its contents. The reasoning by which secular materialists arrived at this conclusion was as follows: If it really were true, as science apparently indicated, that there was no supernatural realm, or any other exceptions to the general physical and material character of the universe, then one should divide things between that which was real (physical) and everything illusory—or to use a trivially different word for the same thing, that which was "noth-ing." (It is appropriate to refer to this more recent, anti-Platonist view, as "modern naturalism.")

Let me not exaggerate. Strictly speaking, it is not correct to say that this change in thinking came about through the influence of modern science alone, since it also was prefigured by parallel

---

3. This change in outlook was one of the factors that prompted William James to refer to St. Augustine as "the first modern man" (see Starr 1991, p. 690).

developments in religion. For instance, the first and longest part
of the Bible, *The Old Testament*, purportedly records many con-
flicts between Yahweh, God of the Hebrews, and other, less powerful, pagan, gods. A clear illustration is the story told in *Genesis*,
Chapter 7, verses 8–13. To impress the Pharaoh with the serious-
ness of their demand for release of the Hebrew slaves, and with
the dire consequences that would follow if that demand were
refused, the prophets Moses and Aaron performed the miracle of
turning a wooden staff into a snake. But the Pharaoh remained
unmoved. In fact, he called in his own magicians, who then
answered Moses's challenge by accomplishing the same thing.
More specifically, they threw down their own staffs, which then,
presumably through the powers of their own, Egyptian gods, also
turned into snakes. However—and herein lies the crux of the
tale—Moses and Aaron still triumphed in the end, because their
snake went on to devour all the other snakes that the magicians
had brought into being. This last event carried the implication, in
other words, that even though the Egyptians' gods were genuinely supernatural beings, the God of the Hebrews was more
powerful than any of them, or all of them together.

The New Testament, by contrast, contains much less talk about
a struggle between unequally powerful divine forces. Consider,
for instance, a point the apostle Paul made in Chapters 8–11 of
The First Letter to the Corinthians. The problem he was discussing
there was whether or not it was lawful for Christians to eat food
that had been sacrificed to pagan idols. In Paul's opinion, there
really was no issue here, because of the fact that the gods supposedly represented by (or identical with) those idols did not exist.
To say the same thing another way, there should not be any
grounds for offense in such cases, because the "beings" in question were nothing.

My thesis in this book is that we are not able to understand
the human mind correctly or adequately, unless we think of it as
having arisen out of certain particular historical circumstances. As
part of that project, I now point out that, as far as the topic of
mind is concerned, modern secular naturalism also has a natural
culmination, terminus, or "completion." Those theorists we call
"eliminative materialists" (more narrowly, "neurological eliminativists") provide a good illustration of what is involved in that ter-

minus.[4] According to them, recent scientific efforts to "clarify" the notions of mind, spirit, or soul have resulted in the disappearance of those notions, and their replacement by entities radically different from what people traditionally supposed the mind to be. (This is what I meant by the phrase in the chapter's title, "from one to none.")

Eliminativists think of themselves as making a contingent, empirically refutable prediction. They predict that, when scientists at last succeed in constructing a correct, detailed picture of the human central nervous system, no mind will appear in that picture. That is, nothing in the completed scientific picture of the brain will correspond to that which people now think of as the mind, or to any of the many items traditionally assumed to be its "contents." And therefore, future neurological discoveries will have shown that the mind is mythical, since it is neither something that scientists can clarify, by describing it more accurately, nor whose existence they can confirm experimentally. In particular, the notion of mind will be recognized to be misleading, since it is bound to waste the time and effort of researchers, by encouraging them to channel investigations in wrong directions—i.e. to look for items in the brain that could not possibly exist there.

Every concept proposed as having a hypothetical role to play in the completed body of scientific knowledge will finally meet one or other of two possible fates. Either further investigation will show that it is reducible to something simpler and more ontologically basic (which thereby "explains" it), or alternatively, it will be eliminated ("explained away") as something bogus and mythical. And whenever that happens, the most enlightened and responsible course is simply to dismiss and expel that concept from science altogether.

Here is a familiar, even hackneyed, historical example that is dear to eliminativists. "Earth," "air," "fire," and "water" are names we now give the four worldly "elements" that were widely

---

4. Radical behaviorist theorists like B.F. Skinner also proposed a second form of eliminativism, which envisioned mind-talk as being completely supplanted by behavior-talk (see Leahey forthcoming). But I do not propose to discuss that second form of eliminativism here.

accepted at the time of the Classical Greeks.[5] Of these four, only
water has survived to occupy a place in present-day science. What
does this mean; and why is it true? It means that researchers have
found a means of reducing water—but not the other three—to
more clearly empirically justified, "chemical" elements that scientists discovered in the eighteenth through twenty-first centuries.
In particular, we now identify water with H_2O, the compound of
two hydrogen atoms with one atom of oxygen. But similar developments never happened in the cases of earth, air, and fire. And
this justifies the conclusion that the Greeks were wrong to suppose that each of those last three was a single type of things. More
explicitly, we now have learned that what early philosophers
referred to as "earth" is really a hodge-podge of organic materials;
silicon; sulfur; metals and compounds of metals like iron, zinc,
aluminum, copper; and so on. What they called "air" is a mixture
of different gases like nitrogen, oxygen, hydrogen, and helium.
And what they named "fire" is not a type of objects at all, but a
loosely defined group of processes like combustion, electrical dis-
charge, phosphorescence, and so forth, each of which has the
property of emitting light or heat or both.

Eliminativists say the notion of "mind" is more like that of
"earth," "air," and "fire" than like "water"; more like "phlogiston" and "caloric fluid" than like "electron"; and more like
"demon" and "hippogriff" than like "giraffe." This is true,
according to them, because—for example—although the mind is
obviously and observably connected with purpose, meaning,
choices, reference, and other "intentional" phenomena, scientists
have not found any way of reducing such phenomena to simpler,
and more clearly physical terms.[6]

Consider another illustration. Medical practitioners known as
"phrenologists" operated in Europe and other parts of the world

---

5. This particular list of elements seems to have been introduced first by Empedocles,
and then popularized later by Aristotle.

6. Again, as noted when discussing Kim, in Chapter 1, Paul Churchland has pointed
out (1981, p. 67) that, as late as 1960, theorists' main worry was how the mind could produce or contain qualia or "raw feels"—such as patches of red, smells of roses, feelings of
cold. After that, however, they came to see it as a more important problem, how the mind
or brain was able to create or accomplish various expressions of intentionality, reference, or
meaningfulness. It seems to me (and Churchland) that most philosophers of mind still
hold that latter view today.

during the eighteenth and nineteenth centuries. In their view, it was possible for some familiar, common-sense words—such as "love," "hate," "jealousy," "anger," "greed"—to play essential roles in empirically confirmed, scientific theories about the brain and mind. The reason this was true was that traits of character, corresponding to each of those words, were localized in specific parts of the brain. In fact, whenever a brain was unusually well developed in one of those areas, a bump would appear on the person's skull at that same point. And therefore one could recognize someone who was especially greedy from the fact that he or she had a bump located at the greed area. One could identify a person who was particularly amorous from the fact that he or she had a bump at the love area. And so on. As a matter of historical fact, however, subsequent investigation did not succeed in confirming any of those phrenological claims (see Zadwidski and Bechtel, Forthcoming).

Eliminativists represent something like the reverse side of the phrenologists' coin. They say that if future scientists cannot show that what we now think of as the mind is identical with specific elements in living central nervous systems, then that will prove that the mind—analogous to air, phlogiston, demons, unicorns, and so forth—really is nothing. And even now, at the present point in scientific history, they add, there are good reasons for suspecting that "mind talk" is not a useful tool for explaining how the brain works. And thus we are justified in tentatively concluding that the mind is fictional.

Still another example of why eliminativists consider the notion of mind misleading is this: In common-sense contexts, we often assume that the means by which people and other animals succeed in remembering facts, events, names, directions, and so on is by "consulting memories." This last idea led the early twentieth-century, neurophysiological psychologist, Karl Lashley, to undertake an experimental search for the precise location, in the brains of recently trained laboratory rats, of their acquired memory-knowledge of how to run a maze (see Lashley 1960). But this investigation finally led him to conclude that, in fact, there was no single "memory-area" in the rats' brains that was functionally dedicated to performance of that particular task.

Let me explain this conclusion in more detail. He and his assistants surgically removed, in turn, each of several major brain areas from large groups of experimental animals (white rats). But, in cases where the operation left the rats still able to move, Lashley observed that the vast majority of them continued to run the maze in spite of their neurological loss. Furthermore, this was true no matter which area of their brains had been removed. For example, imagine for the sake of simplified illustration that the rats' brains contained four major areas, A, B, C, and D. (Again, I am not claiming this is true, but am only proposing an imaginary situation to clarify the experiment.) First Lashley removed area A; and the rats still could run the maze. He then removed B from another group; and this second group of rats still could do it. He then removed C from a third group; but they still completed the maze successfully. *Ex hypothesi*—by a process of elimination—he now felt justified in predicting that the memory must be located in area D. But the next experimental step completely destroyed the plausibility of Lashley's original hypothesis, because, after D had been removed from a fourth group of rats, those rats were *not* prevented from running the maze, but continued to do so.

Since Lashley's time, other investigators have extended and further confirmed roughly the same point. For instance, the neuroscientist, David Gaffan (1997), in a review of a collection of papers about scientific reduction and elimination compiled by R. Llinas and P.S. Churchland (1996), writes as follows:

> The idea that mental activity is brain activity has retarded research in neuroscience. We have gone into the brain expecting to find such things as memories and percepts waiting there to be discovered, and systems for attention, action, and so on—all corresponding to traditional mental events or faculties. The better we understand any of the brain processes we study, however, the clearer it becomes that they do not correspond in any sense to mental activities in folk psychology. . . . for example, the concept of "attention" for a neuroscientist is, at best, an intuitive label for a set of questions whose answers in the end are given by reference to a general account of cortical competition, an account that goes far beyond the topic of attention. The search for an attention system or an attentional mechanism in the brain has hindered, not helped the finding of these answers. Similarly, the search for memory systems in the brain, and the idea that cortical plasticity will instantiate the associationism of folk psychology, have hindered progress. This hardly seems surprising if one considers that the claim to remember an event is not a description of one's brain, but rather a move in a rule-governed social game carry-

ing, for example, the implied promise that one can supply further details about the event if requested. So I am skeptical about the idea, presented in [P.S.] Churchland's chapter, that neuroscience is simply an improved version of folk psychology and that folk psychology is nothing more than neuroscience-in-waiting. Rather, the two are parallel activities with different aims, a situation that one could tendentiously describe as: "the posit of a radical discontinuity between the mental and the neural" but more properly is described as common sense. (Gaffan 1997, p. 194)[7]

To be even more specific about this matter, eliminativists say that because we conceive of minds as intentional or meaningful entities, it is appropriate to suppose that beliefs and desires are their most basic and least dispensable components. In fact, we regularly think of minds (or of the people who have them) as, in a phrase proposed by Steven Stich, "believing-desiring mechanisms" (see his "map of the mind" in Stich 1983, p. 75). In other words, minds are supposed to work the following way: Perceptual experiences, combined with subsequent chains of reasoning, create beliefs in human subjects. And these, in turn (when acting in concert with desires) lead subjects to engage in various behaviors. However, modern neuroscientists cannot "find" beliefs or desires in the brain. In particular, they have not been able to locate relatively unified, inner effects of outward perceptions—or inner causes of outward behaviors—that it would be remotely plausible to identify as referents of those terms. And therefore it is appropriate to reject that picture.

Eliminativists say the job of "folk theories" is to guide thinkers in the first few steps along the long path that eventually might lead them to theories of a different sort—ones that are scientifically significant, defensible, and empirically justified. But having taken those steps, eliminativists say, would-be scientists cannot make any further progress, unless they abandon all such intuitive, folk, and common-sense considerations, and replace them with something quite different. Consider a simple case: Early theorists tried to account for the fact that apples fall from trees by arguing in something like the following fashion:

---

7. This quotation was pointed out to me by Thomas Leahey. It appears in Leahey forthcoming.

(1) Apples are mostly composed of the element, earth.

(2) The proper place or "home" of earth is lower than that of air.

And therefore:

(3) Any apples that happen to become detached from trees fall towards the ground, because the ground "wants" them more than the sky also does.

(Analogously, they claimed that apples float whenever they fall into the river, because they are partly constituted by air as well as earth, and the natural place of air is above that of water.)

But in order to obtain genuine scientific knowledge, one must reject, and move beyond, all such common-sense, anthropomorphic notions as "home" and "wanting." For example, the laws of gravitation and buoyancy, in terms of which present-day science now accounts for the falling and floating of apples, do not appeal to any notions of that type.

More generally, then, according to eliminativists, scientific physics replaced folk physics, scientific chemistry supplanted folk chemistry, scientific biology and genetics displaced folk accounts of those subjects, scientific medicine was a substitute for folk medicine, and so on. They now pose the further question: Will psychology be an exception to this same historical pattern? That is, will folkloric generalizations about attention, memory, pain, believing, desiring, etc. show themselves to be crude approximations to the truth? Or, like the other cases just mentioned, will such generalizations need to be replaced, rather than sharpened and extended? Eliminativists' answer is that we already have convincing grounds for believing that psychology is *not* such an exception.

2.3 Eliminativism Revisited, then Reversed[8]

In my opinion, opponents of eliminativism—present-day theorists who maintain, and try to prove, that the mind is non-mythical,

---

8. An earlier version of some of the material in this section appears in D.M. Johnson 1997.

real, and existent—have not done a good job in defending their position. For example, many of their views about the nature, operations, and origin of mind are vague and poorly defined. And even the relatively few accounts that are clearer and more substantial typically grant a point that seems to give away far too much to eliminativists. This is the point, namely, that an appropriate test and support for concluding that the mind is real—in fact, the only conceivable such test—is brain researchers' finding mind "physically instantiated" in the brain. Thus, the dispute begins with the question of whether physiological investigators someday will establish the mind's unreality. Eliminativists answer Yes; their opponents say No. But is it necessary (or wise) for non-eliminativists to accept this way of formulating the controversy, in the first place?

A pair of instances will help show what I mean. The first is the view of Jerry Fodor and Zenon Pylyshyn (1981). They say that eliminativism is mistaken because, contrary to the claims of its adherents, examination shows that the folk-psychological ideas of belief, desire, and other "propositional contents" are capable of playing substantive roles in the laws of a scientific psychology after all. But then these authors go on to interpret everything they just said in terms of the brain. That is, they maintain that the brain operates in terms of a "computational architecture" that has important, presumably non-coincidental analogies with the meaningful reasoning that takes place in everyday logic and language (also see Fodor 1994, p. 24).

The second case is the view of Horgan and Woodward (1985). I think these authors start in a promising direction, because they apparently reject the idea, shared in common by eliminativists and most of their opponents, that only future brain research can establish the non-existence of mind. But how exactly do they propose to criticize and undermine that notion? The answer is that they do it by saying it counts as a bit of common knowledge to suppose that mind is part of the "natural equipment" with which every normal human is, and must be, born. In other words, they remind readers that we would classify anyone who lacked a mind as damaged, incomplete, and abnormal—in fact, as not a genuine human at all. Nevertheless, then, despite their hopeful beginning, it turns out that Horgan and Woodward also grant the crucial point, since they say that the "natural equipment" constituting the human mind must be something that exists in the brain. Accordingly, it seems to me that they are not entitled to claim there is any "necessity" in the case in question. In other words, it is nothing more than a contingent fact that minds somehow exist in brains—if they really do exist at all. Thus they also seem to agree that brain researchers are the only people qualified to answer the question of whether minds exist, and therefore it is premature, and probably also presumptuous, for philosophers to try to anticipate whatever those researchers eventually will discover.

The reason the two ways of opposing eliminativism just mentioned are misguided, in my view, is that both rest on a single, common mistake. More specifically, none of the preceding authors gives sufficient weight to a point Gilbert Ryle made a long time ago (see his 1949), which still strikes me as important. Ryle said that common-sense talk about beliefs, desires, memories, moods, and so on neither presupposed nor implied any explanatory hypotheses whatever about the design and workings of the central nervous system. And the reason for this in turn (as Gaffan also hinted) was that the purpose or point of mind-talk was very different from that of brain-talk. Still more narrowly, although the second was primarily concerned with inner, neural conditions and causes of outer behavior, the focus of the first was behavior itself. (Thus, I think at least some aspects of the supposedly discredited views of behaviorists like Ryle, John Watson, B.F. Skinner, and J.L. Austin are *not* wrong-headed after all.)

It is possible to generalize the preceding point as follows: The reality of the mind (itself) does not depend on whether or not the notion of mind is able to play a useful role in scientific explanations. Rather, both (i) the mind, and (ii) the concept of mind, are items that we "find" in our concrete, lived experience, and which at least some of us then undertake to try to understand and explain more clearly. In short, we are entitled to think of the mind as an *explanandum* rather than an *explanans*. And because of this, my basic reply to eliminativists is parallel to the answer G.E. Moore once gave to metaphysical skeptics who claimed to doubt the existence of all material objects, including their own hands. Moore said the existence of the supposedly doubtful items in question was a more obvious, familiar, and well-known fact of daily life, than any considerations that a philosopher might propose as premises for an argument designed to establish their nonexistence. (I owe this way of interpreting Moore to William Lycan; see his Forthcoming. Also, consider the analogous claim that Owen Flanagan makes—in his 1992—about the often puzzling notion of consciousness.)

However, as Shakespeare said, it is necessary to give the devil his due. Contrary to the opinion of Horgan and Woodward, it seems to me that eliminativists made an important conceptual advance, when they insisted that there was nothing contradictory or impossible about the idea of genuine, normal human beings without minds. Before eliminativism appeared, many theorists took it for granted that virtually everything people did and said counted as expressions of their minds, since humans were obviously "minded" creatures who acted in "mindful" ways. But this idea was not an illuminating one, if only because it rendered the word "mind" so trivial, vague, and empty as to be virtually meaningless. What, then, can we put in place of that approach?

Consider a crude analogy. Imagine a determined, Zeno-like skeptic who sets out to defend the intuitively implausible proposition—on one ground or another—that "Everything (really) is green." For example, he devises clever arguments to "prove" that ripe apples in fact are (reddish) green, ripe bananas (yellowish) green, and so on. Philosophers in the tradition of Plato, Augustine, and Descartes maintain that one always can refute such skeptics by detecting contradictions in their positions. But I am not as optimistic about this as they are, and do not know of any good reasons for agreeing. Nevertheless, even if we cannot ferret out formal fallacies implicit in the skeptic's reasoning, we still can attack his claims in an effective way by appealing to certain facts from ordinary experience. In particular, it is a familiar point that people discriminate colors by locating each of them within a larger and more general system of colors. Accordingly, one could argue that the idea of *everything's* being green would make nonsense of both the word "green" in particular, and the concept of color in general.

Can we rethink the issues surrounding eliminativism along similar lines? For example, can we construct a plausible defense of the paradoxical claim that eliminativism has clarified and bestowed substance on the word "mind," by rescuing it from vacuity? My tentative answer is Yes. (I think the principal trouble with eliminativism is simply that its adherents interpreted the notion of mind in *too* narrow and rigorous a way, and thereby rendered it clear but incoherent.) More precisely, we should conceive of mind as a "believing-desiring mechanism," and should stick to that same conception, even if eliminativists' predictive claim, that scientists cannot locate beliefs and desires in the brain, turns out to be true.

What then does it mean to say that mind, so conceived, really exists? And how could one substantiate that assertion scientifically? My answer to those questions depends on the expository technique of "temporalizing" eliminativism. That is, (1) I maintain that eliminativists are right to say that (a) the notions of humanness and mindedness are not the same; and (b) there are no "logical" or "empirical" connections between them. Nevertheless, I also believe that (2) virtually all present-day people have minds. How is it possible to reconcile (1) and (2)? My proposed way of doing this is to affirm the further point that (3) although humans did not possess minds during the majority of the millennia of our species's past, they have them now. To be more specific, beginning with the Upper Paleolithic Revolution, and then through a reassertion, confirmation, and "solidification" of that same event that took place at a later, *historical* date, certain humans developed a set of culturally inspired "tricks" that allowed both them and other people to acquire minds. As a matter of contingent historical fact, almost all the people alive today count as cultural and intellectual descendents of those same long-past individuals. And because of that, it is also appropriate for us to say that present-day humans have minds.

2.4   Although the Mind Is Natural and Physical in Terms of Its Ontology, from the Viewpoint of Society and Culture, It Is *Not* Part of Nature

Philosophers known as computational functionalists—such as Hilary Putnam (1967), Ned Block (1978), and David Armstrong (1981b)—often made the following point. They insisted that the question of ontology (of what did and did not exist) was only one, and frequently not the most important, of the concerns of disciplined, scientific investigation. And because of that, they said, it was wrong to suppose that the only possible scientific means of justifying *prima facie* knowledge of mental entities like beliefs and desires was to reduce those entities to others that were ontologically more basic. To be still more precise, functionalists maintained that the most significant properties of beliefs and desires were behavioral, epistemological, and performative in character. And thus it made little difference to a correct, adequate, and scientifically legitimate account of those entities, to specify exactly what they happened to be "made of."[9]

A simple analogy will throw light on this point. If a man buys a circus, he does not thereby purchase some specific set of sub-atomic particles. Of course, as part of the transaction, the buyer acquires trucks, wagons, tents, animals, and so forth, all of which are obviously composed of such particles. But this is only one small aspect of the sale, and other things involved in it are far more important. For instance, the new owner acquires the right to use a certain name and title, and the right to refer to—and locate himself and some of his actions within the boundaries of—a particular history. Furthermore, the purchaser enters into contractual relations with various (human) employees, who thereby promise to put some of their talents and skills at the service of the organization. Are those skills composed of sub-atomic particles? Are the contractual obligations? Are the special history and the name? Even if, in some sense or other, it is necessary to admit that the answer to all these questions is Yes, the sense in question is hardly an insightful or illuminating one. The reason this is true is that thinking of a circus as composed of particles does not provide any means of accounting for what is most distinctive and characteristic about it.

Similarly, eliminativists are forced to leave out of account certain crucially important aspects of mind—considered as a culturally situated, believing-desiring mechanism. In particular, believing and desiring also have something like a moral, as opposed to physical, dimension. And we typically express this

---

9. At one stage of his career, Ned Block tried to go beyond that basic idea, by also claiming that psychology was different from all other sciences by virtue of the fact that its subject matter was abstract and general rather than concrete and particular. But this last idea is not a plausible one, since (and here I agree with Chomsky 1997a, pp. 29–30) its main effect would be to undermine naturalism and replace it instead with some unjustified and objectionable form of dualism.

moral aspect of mentality in behavior (and language)[10] that presupposes a sharp distinction between the minded person (and the
species to which he or she belongs) on one side, and everything
else on the other. That is, people constantly act and speak as if
their minds, and they themselves, were significantly different from
all (other) natural entities.

Consider an instance. A group of hikers stumbles upon the
ruins of a house in a forest. Their use of the word "ruins" to
describe what they see indicates that they conceive of this situation in terms of a three-part scheme. First, they presume that all
the objects now before them "began" as ordinary parts of nature,
unaffected by any human influences. For instance, a certain stone
might have been formed as a result of volcanic action, or by pressure exerted over a long period on layers of sedimentary
deposits.[11] Next, for a limited time, those same objects were influenced in ways dictated by various human values, plans, and purposeful actions directed towards the future. For example, one or
more people explicitly shaped the stone mentioned before, by giving it flat surfaces and square corners, and then either they or others moved it to its present location to form part of the foundation
of a building. Finally, the observers assume that the objects in
question reverted to being expressions of entirely natural, non-
human processes once again. For instance, the stone now has
weathered, so that its corners no longer are square.[12]

Here is another, similar case. We usually talk about, and classify, all extra-human influences on the earth's atmosphere (such as

---

10. Behavior and language are closely related. In fact, for many purposes they are
interchangeable. Thus, consider a parallel. Are hummingbirds shy, timid, retiring little
creatures, whose first instinct is always to flee and hide from danger? Or are they assertive,
daring, and quarrelsome? Someone who watched hummingbirds visit her feeders over the
course of many years once provided a quick and elegant summary of her views on this
question, by saying that if those birds had a vocabulary of 100 words, at least 40 of them
would be swear-words.

11. There may be exceptions even here. For example, a plank of wood may have
begun as an internal part of a tree of a species that never would have existed, except for a
program of breeding and splicing carried out by human farmers, or a program of genetic
engineering undertaken by human biologists.

12. Does this same three-part distinction apply to a bear's scratching tree, a prairie-
dog town, a bird's nest, or a termite hill? That is, can we say that these last-mentioned
objects also count as having been removed from nature for some part of their history?
Later (especially in Chapter 4) I shall return to the issue of what it is appropriate to say
about the "mentality" of non-human animals. But for the time being, readers need to bear
in mind that humans like us, and their artifacts, always provide the clearest and least
ambiguous examples of what I call "non-nature."

storms, volcanoes, or forest fires started by lightning) as parts of the "course of nature." But we do not speak the same way about human-induced changes (such as increased CO_2 from automobile discharges) that also helped create our planet's present mix of gases and airborne particles.

This manner of thinking and speaking has characterized our species—and perhaps even some of our ancestors—for a very long time. For example, whenever archeologists uncover remains of past human activity and habitation, they often find evidence that indicates that these creatures took steps to try to distinguish and separate themselves, in various ways, from everything around them.

If readers will forgive a personal digression, this point once led me to accept a mistaken idea. When I first became interested in the early history of our species, I was fascinated for a time by an argument that the popular writer, Robert Ardrey, formulated in support of the so-called killer ape hypothesis of Raymond Dart. As Ardrey explained in his book, *African Genesis* (1961/1972), Dart was a professional anthropologist and anatomist who excavated a certain cave in the Makapan valley in the northern Transvaal of South Africa in the 1920s. Dart proposed the following interpretation of various clues he found at the Makapan site. He claimed that during the Villafranchian period, three quarters of a million years earlier, this cave had been a dwelling place, over many generations, for a group of comparatively large, upright and bipedal, carnivorous, hunting primates. The name he gave those creatures was "australopithecines" or "southern apes." Furthermore, Dart maintained that those same primates also might have been ancestors of modern humans like ourselves.

In his book, Ardrey composed and collected a long list of arguments in defense of Dart's theories, and against the views of Dart's detractors. One of the items on this list struck me as especially attractive (perhaps, in part, because of my background as a student of philosophy). It was that which Ardrey called (1961/1972, pp. 305–08) "the evidence of the yellow stain."

Before Dart's arrival in 1924, miners and limeworkers in the employ of a toothpaste manufacturer already had finished excavating the Makapan cave in order to obtain its limestone. Since the breccia beds, or those parts of the limestone that contained a high concentration of fossilized bones, were worthless for the miners' purpose, they had removed them to get at the pure lime under-neath, and piled the resulting debris nearby. When anthropolo-gists arrived at the same site later, looking for fossils, they focused their attention on those piles of debris. Furthermore, as Ardrey stated the matter, in a very few cases, Dart and his associates found breccia that were discolored with a deep yellow stain. Ardrey said that those distinctively marked rocks turned out to be crucially important for the purposes of anthropologists, because "as a rule, they were the ones that contained australopithecine remains." What was the explanation of the stain? Dart's answer was that it was the result of a chemical reaction that had occurred whenever organic material came into contact with the dark dolomite rock that formed the original sides of the cave, as it existed approximately 750,000 years before. And, after having examined the evidence in more detail, he concluded that a general pattern was present in all these data. In particular, Dart thought that, typically speaking, the bodies of the primates had not been left to lie among remains of animals of the many other types that also littered the cave's floor. Instead, something or someone had removed those bodies in a fairly systematic manner, and set them back against one or another wall of the cave, where eventually they combined with the dolomite to produce the yellow stain. In the opinion of both Dart and Ardrey, it was unlikely that preda-tors of other types, like hyenas, lions, or leopards, would or could have separated the australopithecine corpses from the remains of the other creatures. And thus the yellow-stained rocks provided still another good reason for believing that the hunters who brought slain prey animals into the cave were the human-like aus-tralopithecines.

This is a pretty tale. But evidence now available (for instance the fact that no stone weapons ever were found at the site—see for example Tattersall 1993, p. 85; Mithen 1996, p. 28; Stringer and McKie 1996, pp. 29–31) has led the great majority of more recent commentators to reject it. In particular, most commenta-tors now affirm the probable truth instead of the hyena-leopard hypothesis. In other words, a more likely explanation of the fact that there were fossilized bones of extinct animals in the cave is to say that, not australopithecines, but predators of another sort, either dragged or dropped prey into that hiding place—including the bodies of the australopithecines themselves. But if this last hypothesis is correct, then it follows that the "pattern" Dart thought he had detected in the bones contained in the yellow stained rock was nothing more than a product of his own imagination.

Gullible amateurs like me at least have one good excuse for having found the preceding story appealing. The excuse is that it is an obvious fact that present-day humans tend to think of themselves and their fellow species-members as special. (Of course, this tendency of thought is neither sharp, unambiguous, nor entirely consistent.[13] Nevertheless, it seems to be something that every person intuitively recognizes.) For example, modern funerals, as well as laws against "perpetrating indignities to a corpse," are signs that humans regularly extend this "exclusivizing" conception of things, even to the bodies of their dead conspecifics. Thus, it is at least somewhat plausible to speculate that our pre-human ancestors also might have participated in something like this characteristically human pattern of behavior.

The ways of thinking and acting that I am talking about here are not just expressions of an unrealistic, wishful sense of self-importance, on the part of human beings. Rather, there really are substantive respects in which humans have proved to be different from all the other things and creatures in their surroundings.[14] Consider the following "circumstantial" proof of that point. Biologist E.O. Wilson lists four main revolutionary events that were crucial to the entire history of life on earth. (Wilson 1992, p. 186.) The first was the spontaneous origin of life itself from pre-biotic organic molecules, which took place about 3.9 to 3.8 billion years ago. The second was the origin of eukaryotic or "higher" organisms—life-forms whose DNA is enveloped in membranes—around 1.8 billion years before the present. The third was the so-called Cambrian explosion that happened 540 to 500 million years ago, "in which newly abundant macroscopic animals, large enough to be seen with the naked eye, evolved in a

---

13. In certain circumstances, people stop extending the category of humanness to some of their fellow species-members, and begin to treat them as if they were parts of nature. For instance, this frequently happens in war, where soldiers are taught not to think of enemy combatants as people like themselves, but rather as targets.

14. Terrence Deacon says (1997, p. 23) "Biologically, we are just another ape. Mentally, we are a new phylum of organisms." But it seems to me that even that radical claim is a vast understatement of the truth.

radiative pattern to create the major adaptive types that exist today." Finally, the fourth revolutionary development was the "origin of the human mind in the later stages of evolution of the genus *Homo*, probably from a million to 100,000 years ago."[15]

Why does Wilson include this last event in his list of the most fundamental changes that happened in the history of life on earth? In order to answer this question, let us set it against the background of still another set of historical facts Wilson mentions. He says there have been six major extinctions of species during the roughly 4 billion years in which life has existed. The most recent of these—one that still is going on at the present time—is almost certainly connected with the activity of humans. To be more explicit, human beings apparently have introduced some new and unprecedented type of causal factor into the history of life. And, because the operations of this factor have not yet "settled down," or arrived at a state of sustainable equilibrium, an (unintended) result of that change has been to create a great deal of environmental damage, including the extinction of an enormous number of species.

In summary, it seems to me that many accounts of mind proposed by present-day theorists put a misleadingly large emphasis on the themes of physicalism and naturalism. And because of that, those accounts are in danger of overlooking what is important. For example, recall the absurd idea, discussed before, that it is possible to obtain a complete understanding of the commitments, contractual obligations, and skills of circus employees, just by the method of examining patterns of cells, molecules, atoms, and sub-atomic particles in the muscles, nerves, and brains of those people. One reason this notion is absurd is that, while these are procedures an omniscient God might employ, they are of absolutely no practical or theoretical use for people like us.

There is a more general point that lurks in the background here. It is that the notion of "mind" does not take its sense from sophisticated scientific conjectures, hypotheses, or theories. Rather, it is a concept that is—and remains—firmly grounded in

---

15. Again, of course, I do not agree with Wilson that the human mind (narrowly conceived) came into existence nearly as recently as that.

everyday, common-sense, normatively significant experience. (In this respect, it is like the term "species," which also is essentially a common-sense idea, rather than a technical concept that has arisen out of specialized scientific work. See the comments Hilary Putnam makes about Ernst Mayr in Putnam's 1997, pp. 40–41.) In particular, one point it would be disastrous to omit from a proposed theory of mind is the cultural and historical fact that humans—the creatures who are most obviously possessors of minds—habitually think of themselves as falling outside the boundaries of the (more general) natural world. In other words, in the course of their daily, practical, social lives, humans have learned to suspend, set aside, and reject the various presuppositions of both ancient and modern versions of naturalism. Thus it follows that, in terms of ontology, the mind counts as one instance of a fairly ordinary type of natural, physical entities. Nevertheless, relative to the concerns of society, history, and culture, it also is true to say that we are not entitled to think of it in terms of ontological categories at all.

2.5   The Place of Reason in History

There is still another misunderstanding that seems implicit in the way certain recent theorists conceive of the mind. The authors I am talking about say the mind is the "controlling part" of a human being—i.e. that which allows and enables him or her to behave in an orderly, acceptable, and effective fashion. Furthermore, a central aspect of the special kind of order associated with mind is the set of rules (procedures, standards, methods of assessing, etc.) that we now call "reason." (See for example Damasio 1994, and the passage from Lakoff and Mark Johnson quoted in the previous chapter.) The supposed centrality of that last notion should—but rarely does—inspire cognitive scientists to ask precisely what reason is. For example, is acting reasonably simply the "nature-given" procedure of comporting oneself in a healthy, sane, and efficient manner? Or, by contrast, are there significant and coherent alternatives to reason, in addition to breakdown and insanity?

Here is another personal digression: Shortly after beginning my formal study of philosophy, it seemed to me that the answer to the question just asked had to be No. Why? The reason was that I could not think of any convincing reply to a comment that occurred in one of the texts assigned in my introductory philosophy course—namely, Bertrand Russell's, *The Problems of Philosophy*. That book contained a brief but fascinating discussion of the so-called "laws of thought." Russell distinguished three such laws: (a) "the law of contradiction," according to which nothing could both be and also not be; (b) "the law of excluded middle," which said it was necessary for everything either to be or not to be; and finally (c) "the law of identity," that whatever was, was (1912/1964, p. 72). He then remarked in an off-hand manner, as if it was nothing more than an obvious fact, that the traditional name bestowed on those laws was misleading, since they were not really descriptions of general ways in which humans and other creatures thought. Instead, he said, they were general descriptions of the behavior of things themselves. It struck me at the time that if Russell was right about this, then reason—understood as including not just the three laws just mentioned but much more besides—could only have one possible form, since any other form would fail to correspond to the behavior of things.

Soon afterwards, I went on to read Aristotle's *Metaphysics* in another course, and was surprised to find that author saying things about the law of contradiction that seemed completely at odds with Russell's view. In particular, Aristotle gave a long list of arguments designed to defend the law of contradiction against certain unnamed Sophistic critics. But, if Russell were right, any such defense should have been impossible or, at the very least, superfluous and unnecessary. According to Russell, any person (like one of Aristotle's Skeptical opponents) who seriously undertook to reject the law of contradiction, and expel that law from his or her thinking, thereby would have rendered himself unable to argue, reason, or even to live. The reason this would be true is that any such program of thinking would bring it about that none of his thoughts or actions would be able to "mesh" with reality.

In addition to philosophy, my other main love as an undergraduate student was the study of Latin, classical Greek, and the history of the ancient Mediterranean area. That seemingly irrelevant interest led me—years later—to begin thinking about the above problem concerning reason in a different way. For example, one thing that pushed me in that new direction was reading, *Before Philosophy*, written by Henri Frankfort and several other authors (1946/1954). That book (and especially its first chapter) made me suspect that Russell's claims might be wrong, because they were based on nothing more than a narrowly ethnocentric, twentieth-century prejudice. More especially, I found myself asking: "How would things look, if one assessed the possible truth of Russell's comment, against the backdrop of the historical fact that, in Aristotle's world, what we now call 'reason' was not common, but rare?"

Not many recent philosophers and scientists recognize the point just mentioned. One main reason for this is that hindsight leads present-day people to imagine that Aristotle, and others like him, were far more influential in their own time and place than actually was the case. For example, historical records of the period (which very few recent theorists of mind have bothered to examine) show that, during most of Aristotle's lifetime, the vast majority of inhabitants of the Mediterranean-Persian Gulf area did not consider Athens, Macedonia, or any other place in the Greek sphere of influence to be the center of their world. Rather—as far as political, military, and economic power were concerned—they were much more likely to locate that center in the Persian cities of Susa and Persepolis, from which the King of Kings, his military officers, and his civil court, administered their powerful, enormous, and still comparatively stable empire. Similarly, with respect to intellectual, religious, artistic, and architectural matters, Egypt was far more important than either Greece or Persia. (This was so, despite the fact that Egypt, by that time, unlike most of the Greek city-states, had become part of the Persian Empire.) Accordingly, most Mediterranean people were not willing to bestow the prestige associated with wisdom, wealth, and power on Aristotle and his ilk, but instead reserved that status for people like the Persian King, the Egyptian Pharaoh, and certain wise and capable individuals who served those monarchs.

What makes these remarks relevant to the problem of deciding how modern theorists of mind ought to think about reason? One answer is that it helps us make sense of the otherwise puzzling fact that Aristotle did not consider it a waste of his time to construct a long and complicated defense of the law of contradiction against its detractors. Why was he willing to do this? I suggest that one of the most important reasons was a historical one—namely, that the general patterns of thought the great mass of his contemporaries then earnestly were trying to cultivate in their own lives, were not the same as those he himself recommended and exemplified. Still more explicitly, the majority of people living in the Mediterranean area (including the Greeks) were perfectly capable of reasoning in a style that Aristotle would have approved. But in spite of that, they had made a more or less conscious decision *not* to adopt Aristotle-like thinking, because they were not impressed with it. Instead, they admired the sort of thinking and behaving that, for example, had assembled the vast empire of the Persians; that had helped organize the ancient system of farming along the Nile, Tigris, and Euphrates rivers; that had overseen the construction of monumental buildings like the King's Palace at Susa, the temple of Amenhotep III at Luxor, and Khufu's Pyramid at Gizeh; and that had guided the creation of works of art like King Tutanhkamun's funeral mask. Yet none of these last-mentioned thought patterns were "reasonable," in the Aristotelian sense, since they did not include a commitment to the "laws of thought."

As a means of starting to make this last comment clear, let me quote what H. and H.A. Frankfort said about one minor, incidental, but arguably typical, example (1946/1954, 30-1).[16]

In Egypt the creator was said to have emerged from the waters of chaos and to have made a mound of dry land upon which he could stand. This primeval hill, from which the creation took its beginning, was traditionally located in the sun temple at Heliopolis, the sun-god being in Egypt most commonly viewed as the creator. However, the Holy of Holies of each temple was equally sacred; each deity was—by the very fact that he was recognized as divine—a source of creative power. Hence each Holy of Holies throughout the land could be identified with the primeval hill. Thus it is said of the temple of Philae, which was founded in the fourth century B.C.: "This (temple) came into being when nothing at all had yet come into being and the earth was still lying in darkness and obscurity." The same claim was made for other temples. The names of the great shrines at Memphis, Thebes, and Hermonthis explicitly stated that they were the "divine emerging primeval island" or used similar expressions. Each sanctuary possessed the essential quality of original holiness; for, when a

---

16. As befits what I take to be the importance of this case, I have mentioned it in another place as well. See Johnson 1987.

new temple was founded, it was assumed that the potential sacred-
ness of the site became manifest. . . .

But this coalescence of temples with the primeval hill does not
give us the full measure of the significance which the sacred locality
had assumed for the ancient Egyptians. The royal tombs were also
made to coincide with it. The dead, and, above all, the king, were
reborn in the hereafter. No place was more propitious, no site
promised greater chances for a victorious passage through the crisis
of death, than the primeval hill, the centre of creative forces where
the ordered life of the universe had begun. Hence the royal tomb
was given the shape of a pyramid which is the Heliopolitan styliza-
tion of the primeval hill (also see Tobin 1989, pp. 41–42).

As mentioned before, I consider it a contingent fact of history
that anyone likely to read this book will have inherited an Aristotle-
like mind.[17] Therefore, the probable first reaction any such reader
will have to the preceding passage will be to say the Egyptians
described by the Frankforts were guilty of a contradiction. In other
words, these ancient people should have realized (but somehow did
not) that all their claims could not be true at the same time. This
point is obvious, these modern readers will say, for the following
reason: The tombs and temples on whose walls were written the
inscriptions described by the Frankforts were many, but the precise
spot where a mound of earth first appeared out of the primordial
water (temporarily assuming its reality for the sake of argument)
was, and only could have been, one.

However, the Egyptians would not have been swayed by these
comments. In fact, they would have dismissed all such criticisms
out of hand, on the grounds that they were insensitive, impious,
vulgar, and fundamentally un-Egyptian. As the Frankforts go on
to say (*ibid.*):

To us this view is entirely unacceptable. In our continuous, homogeneous space the place of each locality is unambiguously fixed. We

---

17. I am speaking of cultural rather than biological inheritance here. Thus, I do not
accept a Lamarckian view of evolutionary mechanisms, but am merely referring to a
familiar fact of everyday life: in addition to acquiring genes from biological predecessors,
and passing them on again to biological descendents, humans, through teaching and
learning, are able to receive and bestow culturally determined items like languages, traditions, values, and attitudes, from (and to) people with whom they have no close biological relationship.

would insist that there must have been one single place where the first mound of dry land actually emerged from the chaotic waters. But the Egyptian would have considered such objections mere quibbles. Since the temples and the royal tombs were as sacred as the primeval hill and showed architectural forms which resembled the hill, they shared essentials. And it would be fatuous to argue whether one of these monuments could be called the primeval hill with more justification than the others.

Skeptics will claim it is not appropriate for the Frankforts to talk about the Egyptians' thinking as if it were strange, exotic, and exceptional, because something much like it often still occurs in society today. Thus, imagine a present-day man whose job it is to sell automobiles, houses, insurance policies, or Caribbean vacations; or a woman who desperately wants to avoid provoking her boss or landlord; or a mother trying to get a small child to take his medicine, or to convince her teenage daughter to stop smoking; or a man wooing a haughty, suspicious, and capricious woman. Wouldn't all those individuals be likely to make fanciful, extravagant claims at the beginning of their negotiations, but later, if it was advantageous to do so, be fully prepared to revise, reassess, or even contradict what they said before? Such cases, objectors will say, show that the modes of thinking and reasoning typical of the ancient Egyptians were not fundamentally different from ours. Still more particularly, even if people of that time and place sometimes seemed to "deny the law of contradiction," this might only have been a matter of their superficial, outward, and merely verbal behavior, but not of what they inwardly, fundamentally, and actually believed.

The first response I want to make to this objection is to note that it begs the question. In other words, it assumes a certain answer to the point at issue, rather than arguing for that answer. Simple examples of this fallacy often occur in battles between pro-choice and pro-life political activists. The first say it is obvious that any woman should be allowed to control her own body, when the question they were supposed to be addressing is whether a fetus *is* part of her body, or whether it is someone else's body. Correspondingly, the second say it is obvious that killing a person is wrong, when the question at issue is whether a fetus is a person.

Can I propose a means of breaking the deadlock between the objector's position, and that of the Frankforts and myself? In particular, are there further reasons for supposing that the gulf between the thinking typically employed today and that characteristic of the ancient Egyptians really is different from, and much wider than, the separation between present-day librarians, computer programmers, and physics professors on one side, and lovers, used-car salesmen, and religious fanatics on the other? As a means of convincing readers that the answer is Yes, consider the following.

Anyone who seriously studies the religion of ancient Egypt soon becomes familiar with the notion of "syncretism." This is a word scholars have invented to describe cases where—often as a means of resolving political disputes—two or more gods became so closely connected in the thought and allegiance of their worshippers, that they finally merged into a single god. (In Egypt, for example, this was true of Amon-Re, of Ptah-Tatenen, and of Ptah-Sokar-Osiris). Furthermore, despite the fact that modern people would consider this illogical, because of its failure to comport with "laws of thought," Egyptians did not conceive of the new gods that resulted from syncretism as "mixtures" of the old ones from which they had been derived. Rather, they thought of them as entities with new identities and properties, in approximately the same way that table salt has different properties from those of the elements—sodium and chlorine—from which it is compounded.

A simple instance is this. The Egyptians often portrayed their pharaoh, in painting and statuary, as a falcon. One reason for doing this was that they expected him to achieve immortality after death, by rising into the sky to occupy a prearranged place among the stars. Furthermore, an obvious way of making that happen was for him to be transformed into a falcon, the bird that flew higher than any other (see Grimal 1992, p. 127). A second reason was that the pharaoh's main responsibility during his lifetime was to oversee the affairs of the entire land of Egypt. And comparing him with an all-seeing falcon was a good expression of that important administrative role. But there also was a third reason that simply stemmed from a historical accident. From Egypt's earliest period, the human-like god, Horus son of Osiris, had been strongly associated in public perception with the royal family in

general, and the pharaoh in particular. But at some time during
the second dynasty, Horus became syncretized with Soped, an
obscure, local god that (as it happened) had the shape of a falcon
(see *ibid.*, p. 54). And this last event, motivated by nothing more
than developments in local politics, was a major contributor to
the connection the Egyptian public felt there was between the
pharaoh and a falcon.

Here is a second example.[18] Egyptologist Erik Hornung tells
us that a certain curse-formula on a Ptolemaic stela or grave head-
stone, now located in a museum in Leiden in the Netherlands,
says that a violator of the tomb in which it was placed will, like
Apopis, "not exist" (1971/1990, p. 158, n. 57). What does that
mean? Is it a promise that anyone penetrating into the previously
sealed tomb will be simply snuffed out, by being transformed
into nothingness? If so, it was a silly and idle threat that could
not have had the power to frighten away any potential tomb
robbers.

But this is *not* what it means. The interpretation just mentioned is a typical expression of modern thinking, and fails to
reflect what the Egyptians understood by the notion of existence.
Hornung's reference to Apopis provides a better clue for understanding the curse formula. Who or what was Apopis? And why
was it appropriate to mention his name in connection with the
curse? The answer is that even though the Egyptians regularly
spoke of Apopis as "not existing," this did not mean they thought
of him as a merely fictional character like Sherlock Holmes,
Mother Goose, or The Little Man who Wasn't There. Instead,
they conceived of him as a "being" with an important—albeit
negative—role to play in determining the fate of the universe. To
be specific, the Egyptians pictured Apopis as an enormous snake
who lived in, and who also represented, the endless, chaotic ocean
of *Nun*, or non-existence, out of which the existing world originally had arisen, and which continued to underlie, surround, and
interpenetrate the existing world, ever since its creation. Each day,
the crew of the divine ship of the sun or, "solar bark," was forced
to do battle with Apopis during their journey across the sky. And
every day, they finally succeeded in killing this dangerous enemy,

---

18. For further details about this case, see D.M. Johnson 2000.

thereby driving him back into non-existence. But this victory was only temporary, since Apopis, whom the Egyptians also referred to as "the destroyed one," had no beginning and no end, and therefore was always able to reappear in full strength the next day to challenge them again.

For our purposes, the significance of this mythical story is this: Unlike us, the Egyptians did not think of existence as an all-or-nothing affair. Instead, their basic understanding of it was as a type of order—a kind that was capable of defeating, or at least holding at bay, the various powers of chaos. For instance, one popular visual image they used to represent the existing, ordered world was that of "Apopis bound"—a picture of a large snake held aloft in a rigid position by comparatively small, stiff threads, rods, or ropes distributed along its body, which extended up from the earth below. (An example of this picture appears on p. 159 of Hornung's 1971/1990.) Thus, the Egyptians' way of thinking about existence versus non-existence was quite different from ours. And there is no natural means of making their conception fit together with any, some, or all three of the Aristotelian-Russellian "laws of thought." For example, the Egyptians would not accept the idea that nothing can both be and not be; nor would they agree with the notion that everything must either be or not be.

I do not claim that the preceding comments and illustrations have proved these points conclusively. Rather, I have only begun to argue in favor of the idea that ancient thinking and our own are importantly different—and that taking that difference into account can help us develop a more adequate conception of mind. I intend to continue that same argumentative program later, especially in Chapters 3 and 5.

The final point I want to make in this chapter is a methodological one. Many philosophers who take scientific thinking as a model for their own work assume it cannot be correct to appeal to facts of history as a way of trying to gain a better understanding of our own species, because historical inquiries do not count as legitimate scientific research. In particular, they say that history merely records "surface phenomena"; and therefore it cannot reveal any of the fundamental workings of the world in general, or of the human species in particular. Still more narrowly, some of those same critics say that history always repeats itself. This idea is implicit, for instance, in the statement attributed to former U.S.

president Harry Truman that: "The only thing new in the world is the history you don't know."

Still another example of the same general idea occurred in a speech I once heard the late, well-known British theologian Malcolm Muggeridge deliver, in which he explained what first led him to become interested in religion. He said that as a young man he worked for several years as a professional journalist. But it gradually dawned on him that no matter how long, faithfully, and accurately someone followed the various twists and turns of the events recorded in the daily news, information of that sort never could help one make sense of life in general. Surely, he thought, there must be a better means of addressing the problems that really mattered. This "better means," he at last decided, lay in a study of the words, acts, and commandments of God.

Muggeridge's skepticism about the significance of events reported in the news seemed to be based on the idea that events of that sort were bound to occur over and over again, in a way that ultimately would show itself to be meaningless and uninformative. And the reason for that in turn was the fact that humans themselves—the creatures whose actions generated the news in the first place—were, and always would be, basically the same. Accordingly, the only way to get out of this circle was to stop paying attention to humans and what they did, and ask instead about the God who had created them, and who could provide a meaningful "background" for their lives.

I agree that the attitude of Truman and Muggeridge is justified when one contemplates human affairs over a time-span of days, weeks, or even centuries. But if one thinks about human affairs on a still larger scale—the major intellectual changes that have taken place over the course of the whole history of our species—then I no longer believe their conclusion is appropriate. In particular, historical reflection of this sort shows that humans have *not* always been the same. (*A fortiori*, it also proves that "merely" historical facts *can* play a significant role in empirical and scientific inquiries into the nature of our species.)

What major revolutionary events have occurred since human beings first appeared? As mentioned before, I think the Upper Paleolithic Revolution was the most important of those events. Another, somewhat similar occurrence was the beginning of the Neolithic Age, roughly 10,000 years ago, when group-supported agriculture, and the settled way of life required to sustain it, were first invented (see Starr 1991, pp. 18ff., and Lemonick 1992). Since that time, one also should mention the transition between the Ancient world and the Middle Ages (in Europe), and that between the Middle Ages and the Modern period (again, starting mainly in Europe). Still more recently, humans have seen the inauguration of the industrial era, and the beginning of the present, "post-industrial" period, where information exchange has become a dominant focus not just of production, but of civilized life in general. Has the human mind remained essentially unchanged through all these upheavals? More particularly, has reason, as a method and ideal that regulates the procedures of mentality, also remained constant?

When someone first begins using computers on a regular basis, he or she often starts to develop clearer and more rigorous habits of thought in other areas of life as well. This is a simple case where not just narrowly intellectual conditions, but also material ones, have proved able to foster certain changes in the workings of peoples' minds. Of course, this is only a minor, relatively unimportant case, since the changes we are talking about are only matters of degree. In other words, a novice computer user learns to sharpen distinctions that once were vague, and learns to define and classify things that previously were obscure, in crisper, more explicit, and more exhaustive terms. But the important question is this: Did any of the great revolutions of history affect patterns of human thinking in such a deep way that they brought about changes of kind rather than degree?

I argued at the end of the first chapter, that this was true of the Upper Paleolithic Revolution. And now I also claim that something similar (though far less fundamental) also happened in connection with the change mentioned by the Frankforts—namely, the transition from the quasi-mythical or magical thinking that was common among the ancient Egyptians, Babylonians, Persians, and so on, to the new style of thought introduced in connection with what I call "the (pre-Classical) Greek revolution."

Of course, neither I nor anyone else "owns" the word "mind." And therefore people are entitled to use it in any way they see fit. Nevertheless, as noted previously, we tend to think of the mind today as having certain properties. In particular, we assume (1) that it centrally involves the notion of objective belief (belief capable of being true or false), and the idea of objective or non-personal standards of evidence. Furthermore, we suppose (2) that it is something that is separated, or which stands apart, from everything (else) in the natural world. Finally, we also tend to believe (3) that the mind is closely connected with "reasonable"—for example, internally consistent—thought and behavior. My project in the rest of this book is to argue that mind, in this sense, was effectively unknown before the pre-Classical Greeks. And because of that, we are justified in saying that the Greek intellectual revolution *created* the modern mind.[19,20]

---

19. This will recall the title of Merlin Donald's book, *Origins of the Modern Mind* (1991). But even though there is an obvious parallelism between his position and mine, there are also important differences. For instance—to mention just one trivial point—the two of us propose to define and understand the words "modern" and "origin(s)," in quite different ways.

20. Why do I choose to argue in favor of my theory of mind by appealing to long-past historical examples? One central reason for doing so is the fact that modern, mass-information media largely have brought it about that there now exists only a single, world-wide human culture. Furthermore, the existence of that culture has prompted many other recent theorists to conclude—mistakenly—that: "As far as mentality is concerned, all the people who ever lived were approximately the same as us—they had essentially the same set of intellectual and moral characteristics as we do now." One of my main projects in this book is to avoid making that same mistake.

Chapter 3

Mind As a Product of the Greek Revolution

History is philosophy teaching by examples.

—DIONYSIUS OF HALICARNASSUS

If we knew history better, we would find a great intelligence at the origin of every innovation.

—EMILE MALÉ

3.1 Did the Hebrews Prefigure What the Pre-Classical Greeks Introduced Later?

Nietzsche says somewhere that the great events of human history are the great ideas of history. I do not think of that statement as having a merely poetic or metaphorical meaning. Rather, it seems to me that—at least in some respects—it is literally true. Accordingly, I reject the view of many recent theorists that the only way to construct a legitimately scientific account of the mind is to begin from the presupposition that mind is a more or less ordinary, natural object, state, fact, or function. Instead, in the rest of this book, I shall defend the following two propositions: (i) the mind is one of those few great ideas that have managed to change the overall course of human history; and (ii) nothing stands in the way of one's being able to take scientific account of that fact, and to assimilate it into the general body of scientifically confirmed knowledge. To be still more specific, I maintain that it is misleading to conceive of the mind as a narrowly physical entity that scientific observers simply "find," and then go on to describe in objective and impersonal terms. And the main reason for this is that it is basically cultural in nature. Thus, I am willing to admit that the mind counts as part of physical nature—in a broad sense of the word "is." But I also insist that its way of belonging to nature is quite different from the way that applies to (say) an oxygen atom, a stone, a gravitational field, the fact that water boils at 100 degrees Centigrade, the process of crystallizing a salt from solution, a galaxy, or a human brain. As contrasted with cases of the sort just mentioned, I consider it more correct and insightful to conceive of the mind's nature and existential status as similar to those of the items on the following list: the invention of bifacial stone tools, the founding of the Persian empire, Caesar's crossing the Rubicon, Jesus's Sermon on the Mount, the Norman Invasion of England, the introduction of digital computers.

Let me now say, more precisely, what I take to be the great idea that constitutes the modern human mind—or in other words, mind as the vast majority of people now have come to conceive of it. In my view, that idea is an extension, continuation, or "completion," of the culturally motivated separation of humans from their natural surroundings that began at the start of the Upper Paleolithic. However, that idea only assumed its relatively final and most developed form at a much later time—during the historical rather than pre-historical period. To be specific, I shall argue in the present chapter that this relatively final adjustment and completion of the idea of mind began at the time and place of the pre-Classical Greeks.

As mentioned before, my view is somewhat similar to that of Lakoff and Mark Johnson since, like them, I also am interested in certain connections that exist between the mind (including reason) and "Western Thought." But that is where the similarity ends. Those authors' general program is negative. They first propose to expose and criticize, and then also to reject the validity of all those connections, on the grounds that many of the assumptions and presuppositions associated with Western Civilization make it difficult or impossible for us to gain a proper understanding of the mind. In particular, according to them, the assumptions in question have led us to conceive of mind as abstract, God-given, and disembodied, rather than as something concrete that has been produced in a natural way by parts, aspects, and properties of the human body. In my view, however, most attempts to correct "misconceptions" along these lines do more harm than good. In other words, many of the efforts of people like Lakoff, Mark Johnson, Pinker, Chomsky, and the Churchlands to clarify the concept of mind have instead undermined, deformed, and distorted it. Why do I believe this? The basic reason is that what they say has had the effect of returning us to a time before the mind was invented. More especially, they have reintroduced (in a modern, "scientific" form) something like the same monistic, naturalistic system of the universe that existed in pre-historical and ancient eras. But I think naturalism, in either its ancient or its modern version, obscures and hides the culturally motivated separation of humans from the rest of the world that is the key to a correct understanding of mind. In fact, it seems to me that the whole of the intellectual tradition we now commonly refer to as Western Civilization began with—and continues to be based on—the invention of mind, in the sense just mentioned. And that which prompted certain individuals to invent mind (and thus also, Western Society) in the first place, was their desire to expose and reject the mistakes implicit in ancient naturalism.

Let us now pass on to another point. Historical movements and themes—a political idea, an ethnic group, a social class, a profession, a religious institution—often become increasingly amorphous and difficult to discern clearly with the passage of time. But it is sometimes possible to get an insightful perspective on such a theme by asking how matters stood at the time when, from small beginnings, it first appeared on the stage of history. One can call the particular method just mentioned, that of "tracing back to origins." Here is a simple case of it. The most numerous and influential group of people living in the Middle East and North Africa today are the Arabs. However, they are split into a confusing welter of more or less separate streams, factions, and sub-divisions. Furthermore, many individuals who regularly identify themselves as Arabs, also deny that they belong to any of those sub-groups. Thus, does it really convey specific information to describe some particular person as an Arab? Or does this name simply connote the fact that the person in question lives (or more precisely, that his or her ancestors lived) in a certain geographical area, without implying anything further about his cultural background, the attitudes he is likely to have, the modes of thinking in which he probably will engage, and so on? Most historians take an optimistic view about issues like these, and would give the respective answers Yes and No, to the preceding two questions. In particular, historians would say this group had a relatively clear, distinct, and cohesive set of attitudes at the time (742 B.C.E.) when—as far as we now know—someone first noticed them and mentioned them in a text (see Grimal 1994, p. 341). And even now, it is still a useful means of trying to understand the values, actions, and tendencies of thought of present-day Arabs, to keep in mind those same characteristics. For example, one can assume that even secular, modern-day Arabs are still influenced to one or another extent by the exploits, judgments, commandments, and so forth, of early historical figures in their tradition, like Abraham and Mohammed.

Are similar considerations able to throw light on the notion of "Western Civilization"? In particular, I said before (Chapter 2, note 20) that, because of the influence of mass information media, there are some respects in which virtually all humans alive at the present moment count as members of this same one cultural and intellectual group. If it is appropriate to refer to that single, worldwide tradition as "Western Civilization,"[1] does that also imply that this last phrase now has become so general and vague as to be almost meaningless?

The first sentence of an old, quasi-popular text by Stewart C. Easton runs as follows (1965, p. 1):

> Western civilization, to which most readers of this book probably belong, is the creation of the men and women who succeeded to the inheritance of the Greeks and Romans in the fifth century A.D.

Easton goes on to identify the particular fifth-century men and women in question as, in Western Europe, mostly Teutons—people the Romans thought of as barbarians—and, in Eastern Europe, mostly descendants of the ancient Greeks themselves. However, if my suggestions about the way it is appropriate to think about Western Civilization are on the right path, then this cannot be an illuminating description of its origin. The reason is that, even if it were in fact the case that the historical agents mentioned by Easton were important in certain respects, it also is clear that those people were not the originators of the intellectual tradition they followed, but were merely preservers and elaborators of something they had received from others.

Easton also says (*ibid.*, p. 2) that a second, less important source for what we now think of as the Western tradition—a factor that had nothing directly to do with either Greece or Rome—was the legacy of religious thinking that came from the Hebrews. I want to continue my discussion of the origins of Western Society by considering a problem connected with that second, lesser source. The problem is this: Was the contribution that the Hebrews made to Western Civilization in fundamental agreement with the other, more major contribution made by the Greeks and Romans; or were these two sources so radically different as to be

---

1. This way of talking is at odds with another conception recently popularized by Harvard political scientist Samuel P. Huntington (see his 1996, especially the picture of the world—Map 1.3—that appears on pp. 26–27). Huntington understands the phrase "Western Civilization" as the name of the particular cultural tradition common to Western Europe and North America, excluding Mexico. Nevertheless, the contrast between Huntington's use of the phrase, Easton's definition of it (see the following paragraph), and my own, much broader proposed meaning for the same words, need not lead to confusion, if readers bear in mind the different intellectual goals that stand behind each of these three programs.

inconsistent with one another, and thus necessarily in conflict? This is a question that both scholars and laypeople have debated for many centuries. For example, Tertullian, one of the early Fathers of the Christian Church (born in Carthage in North Africa about 155 A.D.), claimed that the second rather than first alternative was true. For example, in one of his polemical treatises (following a path marked out earlier by the apostle Paul), he posed the following rhetorical question: "What indeed has Athens to do with Jerusalem?" (Tertullian's words are quoted in Quasten 1958, p. 320.)[2] On what grounds did did he consider that question rhetorical; and why did he present it as such? The reason was that he took it for granted that any informed, right-thinking person already would know that the correct answer was: "Nothing at all." And even today, many reflective people still maintain that the world-wide civilization we now have developed is constantly in a state of "creative tension" between its Hebrew and its Greek foundations. In fact, some of these same commentators claim that the only function the Hebrew tradition continues to perform in today's world is to challenge, check, and thereby "soften" the rigorous logic and robust sense of reality that we have inherited from Greece and Rome.

However, this Tertullian-like view of the fundamental conflict between the two historical precedents of the West is problematic, because it leads to paradoxes. For one thing, it fails to explain why our cultural ancestors should have chosen to affirm and preserve the Hebrew conception of religion, as opposed to any of the large number of alternatives they might have chosen instead. Thus—to consider just one particular location and period—in the area of the eastern Mediterranean Sea, at roughly the same time as the Jews were living in their small, obscure states of Israel and Judah, there also existed many other, non-Greek cultural groups that each had its own special religion. For example, it is possible to

_____

2. More fully, what he says is this: "What indeed has Athens to do with Jerusalem? What concord is there between the Academy and the Church? What between heretics and Christians? Our instruction comes from the porch of Solomon, who himself taught that the Lord should be sought in simplicity of heart. Away with all attempts to produce a mottled Christianity of Stoic, Platonic, and dialectic composition. We want no curious disputation after possessing Christ Jesus, no research after enjoying the gospel! With our faith we desire no further belief. *De praescriptione haereticorum* 7 ANF 3. Quasten 1958, pp. 320–21. (I owe this reference to Glen Nelson.)

distinguish the religion of the Phoenicians, of the Syrians, the Assyrians, the Babylonians, the Medes, the Persians, the Elamites, the Urartuians, the Phrygians, and the Egyptians (see Table 9 in Grimal 1994, pp. 344–45.) Why did none of these other religious traditions go on to become a foundation for Western civilization, in place of the religion of the Hebrews?

The answer, I suggest—building on a theme introduced in the previous chapter—is that all those other religions were based, in one way or another, on various natural, more or less intuitive, ways of responding to the world. But this was not also the case with respect to the Hebrew religion. Compared with those others, it was more deeply reasoned; and it stood in a relation to the sensible world that was far more indirect. One historical indication of the distinctive status that belonged to the religion of the Jews is this: By the time of the cosmopolitan Hellenistic and Roman periods, the vast majority of the followers of other religions had allowed themselves be persuaded that the gods their ancestors had worshipped were the very same as (but merely had different names than) the gods that all other nations worshipped as well. Notoriously, however, a majority of the Hebrews refused to go along with this friendly, sophisticated, civilized, and by then, otherwise almost universal manner of thinking. Instead, they insisted that their God, whose acts were recorded in one special set of scriptural writings, was different from all the others. (In fact—recalling our previous discussion about St. Paul's *First Letter to the Corinthians*—it also became embarrassingly clear to everyone who took an interest in such matters that, in the opinion of the Jews, their God was the only one that really existed. See Wright 1974, pp. 311–12.) The particular way the Jews proposed to sum up all the preceding ideas was by proposing a single name—"paganism"—to refer to all the other, "homogenizing" religions. By means of this title, they drew a sharp and careful line between themselves on one hand, and what they considered to be a vast, single, alien, and erroneous tradition on the other.[3]

---

3. As noted before, the Egyptians—like the Hebrews—also had a talent for making careful, even pedantic, distinctions in the field of religion (see again, for example, Hornung 1990, p. 185). But unlike the Hebrews, the Egyptians were never led by this practice to adopt a theological principle, according to which all things were supposed to fall into one or other of two mutually exclusive, and conjointly exhaustive, categories—namely, the divine and the secular.

Vincent Tobin mentions one aspect of the cultural difference we now are discussing, in the following passage:

> In the mind of the ancient Hebrew, only his God, Yahweh, was immortal, and man could not expect to share in that immortality, for there was too great a distinction between God and man. Such was not the case for the Egyptian. For him there was not this great gulf fixed between himself and the gods. (1989, p. 129)

Again,

> In the Hebrew myth the deity did not originate within the waters, but, due to the more sophisticated theological level of the period of its composition, was totally other than and outside of the creation. Hence, in the Hebrew myth the action of the deity was expressed as one of speaking . . . [But, by contrast,] creator and creation merge in Egyptian religious thinking. (*Ibid.*, p. 74, note 22)

My comment on all this is that I am not able to see any good reasons for agreeing with Paul, Tertullian, and all the modern-day people who continue to think of things in a way similar to them. That is, superficial appearances to the contrary, I believe the crucial reason our cultural forebears chose to combine the Hebrew conception of religious truth, with Greco-Roman patterns of thought, to constitute the complex, living tradition we now refer to as "Western Civilization," is that they saw those two elements as basically similar, and mutually supporting. To be still more explicit, the similarity between those two elements lies in the fact that both are ways of rejecting the undifferentiated, quasi-naturalistic view of the world that, as explained in the last chapter, was an almost universal feature of ancient thought before the advent of Western Society.

Later, in a manner roughly parallel to what the Hebrews already had accomplished, certain Greek thinkers—as I shall explain more fully in the next section—appealed to the distinction between *nomos* (law) and *physis* (nature), as a means of dividing everything that had to do with the meanings, intentions, morals, decisions, and stipulations of human beings (including the Greeks' own, human-like gods), from non-meaningful and non-reasoning natural things (including the human body). Later still, other, more synoptic thinkers contrived to bring together, or combine, the two sides of this dichotomy. And as a result of their putting together these two, apparently contrasting and mutually irrelevant conceptions of things, they created Western culture as a single restless, developing, and dynamic cultural entity.[4]

What makes these historical observations relevant to the central topic and problem of this book—namely, the being, status, and characteristics that belong to mind? The quick answer, as noted in section 2.4, is that, despite recent theorists' apparent overthrow of all forms of dualism, we are still strongly tempted to think about the mind, not as a part of nature, but as outside it. For example, things in the natural world are not able to operate in terms of logical notions like "all," "none," "strict implication," and so on. Therefore, it is plausible to locate the source of the distinction just mentioned in some set of culturally determined rules, stipulations, or definitions of the sort that only human beings can propose and employ. (Recall Nietzsche's saying— 1887/1969, p. 80—"Only that which has no history is definable." That claim is parallel to the basic argument offered in this book, despite the fact that Nietzsche uses the word "history" here in a different way than I do.)

Neither scientific nor metaphysical considerations lead us to conceive of the mind as something that lies outside nature. Rather, our reason for doing this is the simple, not very mysterious fact that mind has the status of being an invented, social institution. More concretely, it seems to me that the mind, as we now conceive of it, originated from a single, broad human culture which, in various respects, was different from any that had preceded it. In particular, that society—Western society—had the power to bring mind as we now know it into existence, because it resisted the previously universal idea that it was necessary to assimilate all existing things into the same one general category, called "nature." And the reason it resisted that idea, in turn, was that its members found it inconceivable that God (or Law) and, by analogy, all God-like (or Law-like) things like thoughts, mean-

---

4. Still another, subordinate means some of the founders employed to bring about this fusion was to appeal to a certain idea or story from the Judeo-Christian religious tradition. The story is this: Although humans had been created by the Hebrew God, and therefore were completely dependent on Him—were part of creation rather than part of the Creator—they still counted as relatively different from all the rest of created world, by virtue of the fact that, unlike other things, God had formed them in His image.

ings, values, morals, etc. could be items that had exactly the same status, and type of existence, as trees, boulders, oceans, mountains, and thunderstorms.

3.2 The Greeks' Intellectual Version of Anti-Naturalism, Expressed in Their New Interpretation of "Childishness"[5]

What is child-like behavior? The answer one proposes to give this question depends in a fairly direct way on how one also conceives of adulthood. For example, some people would say it was not just unfriendly and bad-tempered, but also childish, for anyone to disapprove of, resist, and denounce things apparently accepted by the great majority of his or her fellow citizens. By contrast, others take a different outlook and claim that, at least under certain circumstances, behavior of that same sort can be evidence of sound judgment, moral courage, and emotional maturity. The incompatibility of those two ways of looking at things stems from the contrasting ideals of adulthood that each presupposes. More specifically, people who hold the first opinion think the most important thing it means to be an adult is that the person in question should cultivate the kind of flexible, non-judgmental attitudes that allows him or her to be sensitive to the values, desires, and feelings of others. On the other hand, people who think the second opinion is correct believe the crucial factor is that one should be truthful, responsible, consistent, and courageously independent. For example, the warning, "For Mature Audiences Only," sometimes appears at the beginning of movies on television. Some individuals think this really should read: "For Childish—that is, Rebelliously Perverse—Audiences Only." By contrast, others would claim that cultivating such a stubbornly hostile, dismissive attitude towards contemporary popular culture can only be an expression of bigoted self-righteousness. Which of these two views is right? There is no means of answering this question. Instead, it is inevitable that each person will lean in the direction of either the one or the other answer, depending on the

---

5. Earlier versions of some of the points made in both this and the following section appear in my paper, 1987.

particular conception of adulthood he or she already is inclined to accept.

Robert O. Fink, the teacher who first introduced me to the history, language, and culture of ancient Greece once said that he considered the pre-Classical period in Greece to be a decisive turning point in history, since only in that place and time did humans succeed in advancing beyond the childhood of the species. I discovered later that this was not just an idiosyncratic opinion of his alone, but was the more or less "standard" view to which the great majority of modern scholars of the ancient period also subscribed (for example see Tobin 1989, p. 169).[6] Furthermore, many of the ancient Greeks themselves took this same view of their society's place in the history of the world. Thus, Nicolas Grimal reports (1994, p. 2) that early Greek travelers in Egypt "clearly regarded Egyptian civilization simply as a stage in the development towards the perfect Greek version." Similarly, Erik Hornung provides a list (in 1990, pp. 15–16) of many supercilious and negative references to Egyptian culture, art, and practices, which occur in surviving Greek literature.

Do I also accept this same conception of human intellectual development? No. In other words, I do not consider it either fair or correct to describe Greek-like thinking as "mature," and all other forms of thought as "primitive"—such as the Egyptians' tendency to affirm and deny the same statements ("Temple A stands on the same spot as the first mound," "Temple B stands on the same spot as the first mound"; "Apopis exists," "Apopis does not exist"). Rather, this idea strikes me as superficial and narrow-minded, because it fails to take account of an important source of relativity. In particular, we can distinguish several, fairly independent varieties of childishness—and therefore also, several different conceptions of what it means for someone to overcome childishness, or leave it behind. For example, the ancient Greeks were especially interested in denouncing the kind of blind denial and wishful self-deception that mildly spoiled children often display. (To repeat a homey case from a situation once witnessed by Fink: "I did *not* spill the milk! I was *not* spanked! I was *not* sent to my room!") By contrast, members of Egyptian society were more

---

6. However, Henri Frankfort is someone who does not share this frequently expressed attitude (see Frankfort 1954, pp. 19ff).

concerned to point out—and overcome—the sort of egocentric, selfish rejection of long-established conventions and traditions that also frequently separates attitudes of children from those of adults. ("I don't need you or anybody else to tell me what to do!" "What I think is true right now, and doesn't depend on anything that happened before!") However, neither the Greeks' way of looking at these matters, nor that of the Egyptians, is a God-given expression of precisely what it means to be an adult, since nothing forces us to choose between these alternatives.

Accordingly, I think the classical scholars mentioned before should have been content to make a humbler and more qualified claim than they did. Instead of taking it for granted that the Greeks were right and the Egyptians wrong about what separates childhood from maturity, they should merely have noted that today most people tend to agree with the Greeks about these matters, and disagree with the Egyptians. Thus, to express the same point in slightly different terms, it seems to be true that all the major cultural groups in today's world have adopted more or less Greek-style patterns of thinking, and are *not* interested in accepting the special kind of thought that was typical of the Egyptians. This situation is largely an accident of history, and has not resulted from any necessary or inevitable laws of development. We can easily imagine another, contrary-to-fact situation where the opposite was true—a scenario where history took a different turn from the one with which we now have become familiar.

Still another problem with the currently popular view of the Greeks' role in history is that it has a close association with the old-fashioned, and now discredited, "diffusion theory." (For popular expressions of this theory—in the "classic" form confidently affirmed by grade school text books of my generation—see for instance Wernick *et al.* 1973, pp. 26–28; and Edey *et al.* 1975, pp. 22, 24.) According to that theory, most of the major cultural innovations with which humans have been associated—domestication of animals, cultivation of grain, the founding and building of cities, the invention of government, of the wheel, of war, of writing, and so on—came from the same source. That source was the so-called Fertile Crescent of the Near East (more especially, the societies of Sumeria, Akkadia, and Egypt), during the period from fifteen thousand to ten thousand years ago. Following that time, according to the theory, news of all those discoveries gradually spread—diffused—to the rest of a previously undeveloped and uncivilized world.

However, it is now clear that the view just mentioned is false. (For a recent skeptical discussion of the diffusion theory, see Larsen 1989.) For example, in even as old and as popular a book as Knauth *et al.* (1974), we read (p. 16) that

> recent archeological evidence clearly demonstrates that agriculture and writing were independently discovered by different groups of people living thousands of miles from each other.

Also, because of the corrected time-scale of Carbon 14 dating,[7] researchers now have established that quite a few early architectural monuments, like the passage graves in Breton, France, and the temple complexes in Malta, are considerably older than anything built in Sumeria. (Again, see Wernick *et al.* 1973, p. 32.)

Nevertheless, are there at least a few, narrowly defined respects and cases, where the old diffusion theory has turned out to be correct after all? Percy Knauth and his fellow authors claim that knowledge of how to smelt and refine metallic ores like copper, gold, and silver was one such exception. They say (1974, p. 16) that

> in the case of metallurgy, it now appears that, because of the sophisticated technology required, the craft's development did diffuse from the Cradle of Civilization through the Old World. From the Near East, knowledge of metallurgy flowed not only westward into the European continent and from there to the British Isles . . . but also eastward into the Indian subcontinent and perhaps by some unknown route into China and Southeast Asia.

But these are highly suspicious claims. China is a long way from Iraq and Egypt. Furthermore, Chinese history shows that the early inhabitants of that country were knowledgeable, patient, questing people who easily could have discovered independently how to smelt metals, by experimenting with various ores. Also, the above passage fails to explain the apparent fact that inhabitants of the New World learned to smelt metals like

---

7. For a simple account of this, together with other, more sophisticated forms of scientific dating, see Zimmer 2001.

gold and silver long before coming into contact with any people, or indirect influences, from the Middle East and Europe.

In spite of points like these, however, quite a few present-day authors continue to believe that Greek-like *thinking* really did diffuse to the rest of the world, from a source in the ancient Mediterranean area. In particular, many have argued that the ancient Greeks played a crucial role in the invention and dissemination of literal and evidential, as opposed to mythical, habits of thought. For example, Robert Wenke says (1999, p. 16):

> As far as we know, the ancient Greeks were the first people to think profoundly . . . about the problem of cause and effect in a supposedly divinely directed world. "We are all Greeks," it has been said, because so much of modern Western thought is ultimately traceable to ancient Greece. Some scholars feel that the Greeks were more deeply in debt to other cultures than we commonly suppose [here he mentions, in a footnote, Martin Bernal 1987], but in many ways it seems as if the Greeks simply thought about the world differently from their predecessors.

Are there good grounds for agreeing with authors like Wenke, that this is a legitimate exception to the usual denunciations of the diffusion theory? On this point, I am more sympathetic. Of course, there was nothing "magical" about the intellectual contribution the Greeks made to world-culture. Other cultural groups living in different places at different times might have made the same, or an equivalently similar contribution instead, if various "predisposing" conditions had been different. But, as a matter of fact, it seems true to say that those conditions were *not* different. And because of that contingent fact, Greeks of the pre-Classical period did seem to have started something new. Furthermore, analogous to the manner of the earlier Upper Paleolithic Revolution, that new element was not something that "ripened" over a long period. Instead, it seems to have burst into the arena of history in a remarkably quick and dramatic way.

Let us now pose the question of whether it is true (or even meaningful) to suppose that, starting from a source in Greece, that intellectual innovation spread to all the rest of a previously unenlightened world. Furthermore, even if we tentatively agree that this diffusion really did take place, why and how did it occur?

One important consideration is that the "Greek intellectual revolution" seems to have been the spark that eventually led to the conflagration we now think of as "modern science." What makes that point especially important? The answer is this: Present-day humans have become almost universally dependent on technological devices associated with science of that type. And as a result, they are all familiar, at least indirectly, with the special sort of thinking that created, and now continues to support, that technology. For instance, most people have no exact idea of how telephones, refrigerators, and television sets work. But they are aware of the kind of thought that probably was required to invent such devices in the first place, and which is still needed to maintain, repair, and improve all the devices of that type that already exist.

Let me elaborate a little further. We can distinguish three technological transformations through which human society has passed (see Kates 1994, especially p. 116). The first was the discovery, by our primate ancestors, of how to make and employ stone tools, how to control fire, and how to seek or construct shelters. Those technological achievements led to an increase in the number of members of the group, *Homo,* who before then— as Wilson notes somewhere in 1992—had been remarkable for their scarcity.) The second such transition was the inauguration of agriculture, which took place roughly between 15,000 and 8,000 years ago, and which we now think of as providing the dividing line between the Mesolithic and the Neolithic periods. (Perhaps because of the more dependable food supply this change made available, it soon was followed by another dramatic increase in human population. One estimate, for example, is that about 86.5 million humans lived on earth six thousand years ago, which was eight times as many as there had been two thousand years before that (see Lemonick 1992, p. 53). Finally, the third transition was the development of fully-fledged industrial techniques of production, which were based on various earlier discoveries made by pioneers of modern science. (This last event led to still another—and this time enormous—increase in human numbers.[8])

---

8. There obviously were many other important technological changes in human history besides those just mentioned—for example, the transition from producing bifacial stone tools to producing flake stone tools (see Grimal 1994, p. 19). As mentioned before, I consider the most important of all those developments the Upper Paleolithic Revolution

In this book, the type of thinking in which I am primarily interested is connected with the third, rather than the first two, of the changes just listed. That is, I am principally concerned with the advent of modern science and its associated methods of production. More particularly, I conceive of modern science as a recovery, after a long period of neglect—what some historians refer to as "a thousand year sleep"—of a way of thinking that had its beginnings in pre-Classical Greek society. Still more precisely, this special type of thought probably first appeared on the Greek mainland, during the Greek Middle Ages that separated the Mycenaean from the Classical periods, between 1100 and 750 B.C.E.[9]

What conditions allowed thinking of that type to come into existence at that time and place? I intend to give a fuller account of my answer to that question in the final Chapter 5. But it will be helpful to give a preliminary sketch of those ideas here. Historians say that the temporal and spatial location of the early Greeks gave them a unique set of cultural opportunities. For instance, their "nation" was geographically situated at a crossroads between several older and more sophisticated civilizations—Babylon, Persia, Assyria, and Egypt. But the Greeks never were conquered by, or assimilated and incorporated into, any of those older civilizations. Those physical conditions left them free to observe and emulate the achievements of those other societies, in a fairly independent way.

The mountainous terrain of Greece also might have been a contributing factor. This is a plausible idea, if only for the trivial reason that ethologists have noted the fact that similar types of terrain often have analogous effects on other, non-human creatures. For example, whenever sage grouse in the western United States (Wyoming and Montana) live in open, flat areas without

---

itself, which (among other things) provided humans with the new mental technique of the "detailed visualizing." of things (see White 1989).

9. According to the traditional story, the ancient Greeks believed that "the first philosopher" was an individual named Thales, who lived in the basically Greek city of Miletus, on the coast of Asia Minor, in and around the year 585 B.C. (the year of an eclipse of the sun that Thales predicted). But some stories characterizing Thales as "a typical philosopher"—see for example Kirk, Raven, and Schofield (1957/1983) pp. 80–81—show that he could not literally have been the first person to have thought in the way that eventually led to modern science and the industrial revolution, since those stories describe him as just one among many similar people, and thus as one more case within a long process of previous development.

much vegetation, they tend to follow a "lek" system of breeding, where only one or very few of the dominant males mate with all the females in the flock. But in other, forested areas where there is more cover—trees, bushes, gullies, ravines—more of the male birds are able to mate (see Wiley 1978).[10] Taking this as a parallel, one can speculate that the mountains of Greece may have made it harder for kings, dictators, or warlords to force people who lived there to accept any single set of religious, political, or cultural "truths." And this in turn might have made it comparatively easy for Greeks (as contrasted with other people) to devise new, more individualistic ideas of exactly what it means for statements and claims to be acceptable, justified, and true.

(Some scholars say the beginnings of a similar intellectual cultural movement occurred at a much earlier time in Egypt. According to those people, this happened between 1348 and 1338 B.C.E., in connection with the monotheistic religious reforms inaugurated by the pharaoh, Akhenaton. See for example Hornung 1990, pp. 244ff. In particular, many works of art created during Akhenaton's reign, or the so-called Amarna period—including the famous head of Nefertiti, now located in Berlin—were more realistic in style than the traditional Egyptian paintings, statues, and reliefs that both preceded and succeeded them. And this has prompted modern commentators to suppose that, during the Amarna period, there also was a movement towards relatively objective and less mythological thinking in general. But even if all these last speculations are correct, the scholars in question are still forced to admit that Akhenaton's revolution did not have the same profound and lasting effect on the world— or even on Egypt itself—as the cultural movement inaugurated by the Greeks. Egyptian society was a very conservative one, especially concerning religious matters. And, consistent with that sociological and historical fact, there was a violent, very widespread reaction shortly after the death of the pharaoh Akhenaton, against everything he had tried to establish during his lifetime. Furthermore, in the course of that counter-revolution, nearly all

---

10. More precisely, Wiley says (*ibid.*, p. 121): "Polygynous grouse that live in forests do not form leks; the individual males occupy large territories and perform their displays at widely dispersed locations. In open country, however, the males of all polygynous grouse species display in aggregations."

traces of the intellectual legacy he proposed to bestow on Egypt—
in so far as the subsequent history of Egypt itself was concerned—
were destroyed.)

The Egyptian people only came to accept modern, Greek-like
thinking at a very late stage in their history. To be precise, this
happened when, after the Assyrian and Persian occupations
already had brought Egypt's long isolation to a close, the country
was forced to respond to various cultural influences from—and
later still, to military invasion and occupation by—the Greeks. As
Grimal expresses the point:

> Egypt opened up increasingly to the outside world during the fifty-
> four years of Psammeticus' reign [664–610 B.C.]. Foreign merchants
> arrived on the heels of foreign soldiers, and diplomatic relations
> between Egypt and Greece evolved on a distinctly economic basis:
> Egypt exported such commodities as grain and papyrus and in return
> allowed the first *Milesian* trading posts to be established at the
> mouth of the Bolbitinic (Rosetta) branch of the Nile. This period
> also saw the appearance of a professional body of Egyptian inter-
> preters who guided Greek intellectuals around the great shrines . . .
> Gradually, almost unavoidably, Egypt became involved in the mas-
> sive Mediterranean trade network that was developing from Asian
> Minor to the Aegean region. (1994, p. 355; italics added)

Who exactly were the Milesians, and what factors made those
people commercially important? Miletus was a city-state located
on the southern coast of Asia Minor. It had a basically Greek population, but also included a wide mixture of many other ethnic
groups. I want to make the speculative suggestion that the
Milesians' successes in the areas of exploration, sea-faring, colonization, and trade were partly a result of a certain style of thinking common among inhabitants of that city. In particular, the
type of thinking characteristic of them was one that avoided, or at
least minimized, magical, poetic and mythological elements, and
instead promoted recognition and acceptance of literal, objectively justified facts.

Let me now give one minor, and two comparatively substantive examples of what it means to say that the Egyptians' failure to
develop a style of thinking similar to that common among the
Milesians, put the Egyptians at an economic, political, and military disadvantage, as compared with these new competitors. The

trivial case is this: In the Egyptians' view of things, cats were not just pleasant, occasionally useful, house-pets. Instead, they thought of those animals as having certain divine characteristics and powers. As a direct result of that assumption, the Egyptians spent a great deal of time, money, and labor that they might have devoted to other pursuits, mummifying and entombing the bodies of literally millions of these animals. The nineteenth-century British, colonial rulers of Egypt found they could obtain at least some economic benefit from this ancient practice, by using mummified cats as ballast for one of their ships, and later grinding up that same cargo to use as fertilizer (see Newman 1997, p. 72).

The first of the more important examples is the following: According to the Egyptians, the powers and authority that belonged to the pharaoh, his court, and his armies were—again—largely products of divine and magical forces. Nevertheless, as later historical events were to show, these magical forces were not able to provide them either with consistently good government, or with a military establishment that was effective and successful. For example, the pharaoh's supposed authority among the gods proved incapable of stemming the rising tide of military attacks from outside their borders (see Grimal 1994, p. 352).

The second of the two weightier examples is this: It apparently was the case that the country had no permanent, written legal codes, until after it was conquered first by the Persians, then also later by the Macedonian army under Alexander the Great (see Tobin 1989, p. 82). If this in fact was true, the probable reason for it was that the Egyptians thought of their pharaoh as a living god—one who "owned" both all the land in the country, and all the people who lived on it. Thus, they also conceived of each pharaoh's succession as a completely new beginning (see Morenz 1973, p. 76). And this meant in turn that there could be no possible guide to what was lawful and illegal, right and wrong, at any given moment, apart from the actions, decrees, and speech of the particular person who then happened to occupy the throne of Egypt. As Tobin remarks:

> The Pharaoh was the sole effective means whereby Ma'at [justice, truth, righteousness] was maintained on the earth and in the state. . . . [He was] an integrating symbol, drawing together and actualizing within his person all aspects of existence, the earth, the sky, the polit-

ical realm, human society and nature itself. He was the embodiment of the order of Ma'at which was in all of these. (1989, p. 100)

Do instances like these show that the Egyptians' characteristic mode of thought was silly and childish, and therefore also that it was something every sensible, adult person alive today ought to avoid? Mothers, psychiatrists, history buffs, religious leaders, and other social conservatives might be inclined to answer No. But on the other hand, almost all scientists, economists, military leaders, judges, legislators, and leaders of nations all would say Yes. Furthermore, for better or worse, people of the second sort are—and have been for a long while—a much more potent force in determining the course of human history than representatives of the first group.

A still more basic explanation of the pre-Classical Greeks' commercial and political advantages over competitors like the Egyptians is that these first people had attained an insight parallel to that which the Hebrews had already discovered, but which operated in another, "parallel" dimension. To be specific, this insight of the Greeks was not about the way humans were related to the divine, but about the way that humans had to relate themselves to the natural world, in order to know it. The typical means by which the Egyptians tried to understand nature was to attempt, in one or another respect, to merge themselves with it. (This is what I take to be the basic epistemological method associated with the view I call "ancient naturalism".) By contrast, the Greeks proposed to think about the world on one side, and human knowledge about the world on the other, as clearly different and separate. This last idea carried the implication that, only in so far as a person conceived of himself or herself as different from nature, would he also be in a position to examine, describe, and account for nature successfully.

3.3 Mind, Belief, and Desire Presuppose *Our* Conception of Truth, and Thus, Strictly Speaking, Are Limited to the Western Tradition Alone

The notion of belief—or, to speak more correctly, one specific version of that notion—has played a pivotal role in determining that which people now think of as the mind. As mentioned before, it seems to me that Steven Stich's diagram (p. 75 of his 1983) purporting to represent the mind's general structure and workings, provides an especially clear expression of what I am talking about. In that diagram, every part of the mind is depicted as related, either directly or indirectly, to two central files, repositories, or "boxes." Those boxes respectively contain (i) the subject's current set of beliefs, and (ii) his or her current set of desires. Stich says that the first and most important step that has to take place for thinking to occur is that perceptions need to trigger certain brain processes that lead in turn to various beliefs being created. Second, he says inferential mechanisms then come into play, which generate new beliefs from old ones. The third step is that subjects go on to employ methods and mechanisms of practical reasoning, in a more or less conscious way, in order to create desires—sometimes from beliefs that they already have, and sometimes from beliefs combined with still other desires. (An illuminating means of thinking about desires is to interpret them as beliefs that subjects conceive of and employ in certain special ways—in particular, in ways that accomplish practical or "action-directed" purposes.) Fourth and finally, Stich maintains that subjects attempt to get their desires realized in the environment outside their skins, through "action control mechanisms" that connect those desires with the muscles of the body.

Even though I do not agree with everything Stich says about the detailed workings of the mind, I think he is right to presuppose that beliefs and desires are centrally important to everything the mind is and does. Thus a plausible first step towards obtaining a proper understanding of the mind (as people now conceive of it) is to become clear about what does and does not count as a belief. Let me begin by reviewing three main types of theories of belief proposed by various authors in the recent past. First, some say that beliefs are identical with certain patterns of observable behavior, or with inferentially known internal states that dispose and cause subjects to engage in such behavior. For example, John McCarthy once claimed (1983) that ordinary, two-metal strip thermostats had a limited number of simple beliefs, on a limited set of topics, just because they consistently initiated changes of certain types, in given circumstances. Thus, McCarthy might say that, thirty minutes ago the thermostat in his dining room had a literal belief that his house was too warm, as shown by the fact that it then responded to the temperature of the surrounding air, by turning off the furnace. And now, thirty minutes later, that same thermostat just has acquired the new belief that his house has become too cold, as proved by the fact that it has responded to current air temperature by turning the furnace back on. Second, defenders of the "interpretive stance" position say there are situations where (for example) someone could improve his chance of winning a chess game against another human, or a computer, by attributing various beliefs and desires to his opponent. And in every case where something like that is true, the human or machine in question really does have the particular beliefs and desires so attributed to him, her, or it (see Dennett 1981/1990). Finally, a third way of conceiving of beliefs is to identify them with a "correct fit" between assumptions a subject makes, and the objective situation in which he finds himself. For instance, Hilary Putnam says that his (true) belief that water is wet presupposes, and is partly constituted by, the fact that he happens to be located in an environment where genuine instances of water (H_2O) are present, which therefore can act as referential objects for some of his words, expectations, and behaviors (see Putnam 1975b.)

Does each of these three types of theories contain a certain amount of truth? Even if the answer is Yes, our previous discussion of the history of Greek-like thinking shows that none of them can be completely adequate. The reason is that none of them has anything to say about the idea that attributing a belief presupposes that the subject in question can assess the value and soundness of propositions, attitudes, and behaviors against the standard of objective, literal, and consistent truth. Accordingly, it seems to follow that neither of the following two ideas is true: (a) that beliefs are simply identical with subjects' acting in certain ways, in certain circumstances, and with certain results; and (b) that the ability to believe is part of the intellectual equipment that belongs to every human being innately. Instead, I shall defend the view in the following pages that (in the strict sense) beliefs and minds did not begin to exist, until a relatively recent date in human history. More exactly, this did not happen until one or more members of the Greek cultural world invented the notion of objective, consistent truth, and began using that notion to assess the truth and epistemological adequacy of statements and actions.

The idea of the early Greeks' having created the human mind is not original with me. (See for example Snell 1953/1960.) Nevertheless, my proposed new contribution to that idea is to situate it within a much wider scientific, philosophical, and historical context than any of my predecessors have done.

What sort of defense can I offer for the preceding claims? Consider the following. Nowadays, whenever people say of an individual I that he or she believes the proposition that O is F, one principal assumption they make is that I is under an impression that there is an arrangement of objects and properties present in the world, which renders all of I's thoughts and sincere assertions that O is F true. Furthermore, the truth of the thought, assertion, sentence, or gesture in question is independent of anything subjective or personal. For example, people now deny that the truth of any given proposition depends on the fact that some human being of high social standing, or great moral authority, or who performs a religious function, or who holds a significant political office happens to accept, affirm, or agree with that proposition.[11]

Is this conception of truth trivial and uninformative? One proof that the answer is No, is to note that the ancient Egyptians did not share that conception. For instance, the Egyptians considered every word uttered by their pharaoh to be a source of Ma'at—justice, rightness, decency, and truth. Accordingly, they regularly affirmed the correctness of claims, just because of the fact that the pharaoh accepted those same claims. At the present time, however, we do *not* expect intelligent, educated, moral, and responsible people to follow such a policy. And this shows that our notion of truth is not the same as the Egyptian's concept of Ma'at, despite the fact that French scholars regularly translate this Egyptian word as "*verité*," Germans translate it as "*Wahrheit*," and English speakers translate it as "truth."

Why is it more difficult for scholars to produce accurate, non-paraphrased translations of ancient Egyptian texts into modern

---

11. Some such idea may have been one of the sources of the grandiloquent (but misleading) philosophical principle, accepted by Parmenides, Plato, and Descartes, that "truth is the same as being."

languages, than for them to translate the works of ancient Greek and Latin authors? To give a "feel" for the difficulty I am talking about, let me provide a few examples.[12] Consider a more or less randomly selected list of English translations, by R.O. Faulkner, of the so-called Pyramid Texts (spells inscribed in early pyramid tombs, starting about the year 2350 B.C.):

Utterance 352: "A vulture has become pregnant with the King in the night at your horn, O contentious(?) cow. Your papyrus-plant is the green of the turquoise of the stars, your papyrus-plant is the green of the King, (even as) a living rush is green, and the King is green with you." (Faulkner 1969, p. 112)

Utterance 404: "the King is greater than Horus of the Red One, the Red Crown which is upon Re, the King's green eye-paint consists of the papyrus-head of your eye which is in the heat(?), and the King is sturdy with you." (*Ibid.*, p. 132)

Utterance 502A: "Sothis goes forth clad in her brightness(?), she senses the bright ones(?) who are among them. The striking powers of the city are quiet, the region is content. I have prepared a road that I may pass on it (?), namely(?) what Meref foretold in On." (*Ibid.*, p. 178)

Utterance 514: "Endure(?) [. . .], endure(?), O Tadpole; this [. . .] who presides over Khem with his life-amulets on his neck. Your (fem.) seat [belongs to] your son, [your (masc.)] seat belongs to your son, and Geb has summoned(?) [. . .]." (*Ibid.*, p.189.)

In some cases, Faulkner simply gives up, and labels certain passages partly or wholly incomprehensible. For example:

---

12. Cognitive scientists like Noam Chomsky, Jerry Fodor, and Steven Pinker are critical of the argumentative technique to which I am now proposing to appeal. The technique in question (associated with the linguist Edward Sapir and his student Benjamin Lee Whorf) is that of arguing for the non-equivalence of different types of human thinking, by appealing to examples of ways of speaking that occur in special cultural contexts. One main reason these critics oppose this idea is that they assume that all human thinking must be basically the same, because of the fact that it takes place in a universal, species-specific, "language of thought" or "Mentalese," analogous to the "machine-" or "computational language" of (a given type of) computers. See, for example, Fodor 1975 and Pinker 1994, pp. 59ff. But I am less suspicious of this mode of arguing than they are, because I see no good reason to believe the language of thought hypothesis is true.

Utterance 235: ". . . you have copulated with the two female guardians of the threshold of the door . . . (untranslatable at both beginning and end)." (*Ibid.*, p. 56)

Utterances 281 and 502B: (wholly untranslatable). (*Ibid.* pp. 85, 178)

Utterances 286 and 292: (wholly incomprehensible). (*Ibid.*, pp. 86, 87)

These are strange examples. And it does not strike me as a promising project to spend a great deal of time and energy trying to explain away this strangeness, for the following reason. Experts tell us (see Morenz 1973, p. 1) that the basic reason modern people find it hard to translate ancient Egyptian texts accurately is not that they are puzzled about certain aspects of the grammar and vocabulary of the Egyptian language. In the two centuries since Napoleonic soldiers unearthed the Rosetta Stone, scholars effectively have mastered all the idiosyncratic details of that language, as well as the hieroglyphic system the Egyptians used to write it. Instead, the principal problem faced by modern translators lies in the simple fact that the Egyptians thought and reasoned in ways that we find unfamiliar, alien, and thus also unintuitive.[13] Apparently, for instance, Egyptian texts indiscriminately mix reliable, historically confirmable facts on one side, with mythical-magical references and themes on the other (see Faulkner 1969, viii). Thus, in inscriptions on coffins and tomb walls that scholars now refer to as the Mortuary Texts, the dead man frequently claims to be identical with one or more gods like Osiris,[14] Ptah, or Amon; or the dead woman maintains that she is the very same person as one or several goddesses like Isis or Mut. Presumably, those magical invocations were meant to be means by which the deceased could share in the creative power and relative permanence that belonged

---

13. Morenz's exact—translated—words (*ibid.*) are these: "The difficulties encountered in translation are as a rule not of a graphical or grammatical nature but stem from the fact that the Egyptians had a mode of thinking very different from our own.

14. Cf. Morenz, 1960/1973, p. 211: "The idea of 'becoming Osiris's was the antithesis of the idea of divine judgment upon the dead. According to this the dead person was absorbed into the substance of the deity; the (Heliopolitan) idea that he ascended to heaven and that he accompanied the sun-god on his journey had the effect of elevating him to a plane as durable as the created world itself.

to the gods mentioned in them (see Morenz 1960/1973, p. 231). A concrete case of this—involving the king rather than a subject— is Faulkner 1969, pp. 46–48, Utterance 219.[15] Accordingly, the "truth" that Egyptians associated with assertions of this sort was vague rather than sharp, vacillating rather than consistent, partial as opposed to complete, and revisable as contrasted with settled and final. But today (at least in formal contexts, and when "reasoned belief that" rather than "belief in" is in question), we put people under a great deal of pressure to make sure that any claim they designate as "true" is something that is sharp, consistent, whole, and final.

Here is still another argument against the philosophical idea that believing is nothing more than a certain type of physical event, state, or process. Leibniz claimed in the seventeenth century that there were no sharp divisions in nature. A trivial example of what he had in mind is this: Are all male white cats deaf? Although many present-day people affirm the truth of this proposition, knowledgeable informants—such as veterinarians—tell us that white male cats (who, by the way, must be pure white and have blue eyes) are deaf in only roughly forty percent of cases. This example, like an infinity of others that might have been mentioned instead, reminds us that—at least on levels higher than basic physics and chemistry—Leibniz was right to claim that nature does not operate in terms of "all" or "completely," but in

-----

15. At least some of our difficulties in translating these texts stem from the fact that Egyptian culture was primarily an oral rather than written one. Because of this, for example, whatever words the authors wrote were meant to have a secondary, merely derived status, compared with what the authors and others did and said in their ordinary (non-literary) lives. For example, Egyptian texts and inscriptions contain a great number of hints, allusions, and plays on words. And therefore modern readers cannot interpret (as opposed to translate) those texts in cases where the presupposed stories, traditions, historical incidents, socially determined norms, and so forth, have become lost to us. (Robyn Gillam pointed this out to me, during one of my visits to the Egyptian Section of the Royal Ontario Museum.) Consider a parallel: Imagine a future archeologist who, drawing on philological research based on scattered fragments of writing, succeeds in learning the vocabulary and grammar of twentieth- and twenty-first-century English. This person then discovers a partially preserved copy of James Joyce's novel *Finnegan's Wake*, and in it reads the sentence, "Wait one eye-gone-black!" Sophisticated readers of our time recognize this as a humorous comparison with the German phrase, *ein Augenblick* (one moment or "eye-blink"). But even if the archeologist suspects that this sentence is an expression of some punning joke, if no examples of the German words, *"Augen," "Blick,"* or *"Augenblick"* have survived into his era, then he would not be able to interpret this English sentence correctly, in spite of the fact that he knows English. (On the crucial role of puns in Egyptian texts, see the discussion and example provided in Morenz 1960/1973, p. 223.)

terms of "some" and "partially." There is also a roughly analogous point to be made about time. For instance, astronomers say the collapsing of a gigantic star into a supernova explosion is something that happens very quickly. In fact, the small fraction of a second this event takes would appear instantaneous to observers like us, since we have no observational means of detecting that such an event took any time at all to happen. Nevertheless, there are empirical and non-a priori reasons (reasons that do not just appeal to the notion that "instantaneous event" is self-contradictory) for believing that any natural process cannot literally take place in an instant.

By contrast, these same points do not apply to some cultural transitions. How fast, how completely, and at exactly what moment does a defendant become a convicted felon; does a buyer become the owner of a car; or does a crown prince assume the title, responsibilities, and authority of king? Legally speaking, I suppose one could say that this happens when the foreman of the jury finishes saying, "We find the defendant guilty," or when a purchaser has completed signing the last letter of his name on a contract, or just after the archbishop has intoned, "I now pronounce you king by the grace of God." But it is nothing more than a superstitious mistake to assume that any of the occurrences just mentioned amounts to some special sort of natural event. As Søren Kierkegaard often observed, the essential thing that all magic and mythology involves is a hopeless attempt to submerge, obscure, or ignore the otherwise obvious gap that exists between items that are (solely) natural on one side, and those that are cultural on the other.

According to the story I am telling in this book, then, beliefs and believing are not natural entities, but cultural ones—human artifacts. If I am right about this, then it follows, for example, that it is senseless to ask whether person P acquires some new belief B more quickly or slowly than a flea is able to jump the distance of thirty centimeters, or than a particular star can complete its collapse in a supernova explosion. Still more generally, it is nonsense, strictly speaking, to try to divide believing into precise parts; or to ask how rapidly, or how completely it takes place; or to try to determine exactly when some instance of believing began and when it ended, and so on. Furthermore, if—as Stich supposed—beliefs and believing play a central role in all the workings of

mind, then it is possible to make points of the same sort, not just
about belief, but about the mind as a whole as well. Thus, as contrasted with the view of "naturalized epistemologists" like Quine
(see his 1969b), it is not true that minds exist in the same manner
and sense as all other parts of the natural world. For instance,
there are no natural entities that spring into existence simply
because of the fact that humans make certain decisions, stipulations, or inventions. Nevertheless, something of precisely that sort
regularly creates our beliefs, and also was that which first brought
into existence what we now think of as the mind in general.[16]

Thus, the basic reason it is easier for us to translate Greek and
Latin texts than Egyptian ones is that our minds are intellectual
descendants of those that belonged to the Greeks. On the other
hand, our minds have *not* descended from the styles and recipes
for thinking characteristic of the Egyptians. To say the same thing
in less metaphorical terms, many of the Egyptians were intelligent, educated, cultured people, who managed their practical
affairs efficiently and effectively. Furthermore, on average, they
were just as emotionally stable and mature as the majority of people alive today. But in spite of these facts, the Egyptians neither
employed nor presupposed the same ideals of literal truth that we
do now; and therefore they also did not have minds, in the strict
sense of the word we now employ. Still another expression of the
same point is to say that the Egyptians lacked what we now refer
to as "common sense," or what some philosophers call "folk psychology." (If I am right, it follows that common sense and folk
psychology are far more special, more determinate, and more
dependent on our own particular cultural situation than most
philosophers have supposed.)

3.4   Frankfort, Jaynes, and the Concept of Infinity

Some scientific theories (and philosophical theories inspired by
science) take the form of comparisons, analogies, or parallels
between a puzzling *explanandum* on one side, and a relatively

---

16. This point shows the sense in which I at least partly agree with the theories of
belief—discussed earlier in the section—proposed by Dennett and Putnam.

clearer, less problematic *explanans* on the other. More especially, many thinkers have tried to shed light on the human mind by comparing it with various familiar things. For example, Plato said the mind was like a lump of wax, on which other objects were able to leave their impressions. Descartes tried to improve on that image later, by comparing mind instead to a piece of wax melting by a fire (see his 1641/1985). This was part of an argument designed to prove that the mind was an unchanging substance that underlay a series of changing, perceivable properties. Still later, certain early twentieth-century theorists proposed to compare the mind with a telephone exchange. And others, in that century's last half, said it was like a digital computer.

The thesis I am defending is that a good but neglected means of understanding the mind is to consider it from the viewpoint of history. As mentioned before, one thing that led me to adopt this view was reading Henri Frankfort's description, in *Before Philosophy* (1954), of the transition from "mythopoeic thought" to "rational thinking." According to that author, all human civilizations employed the first of these—including special conceptions of space, time, and causality that differed systematically from the corresponding modern notions—before the date of approximately 1000 B.C.E. Frankfort maintained that the idea of causality, as the ancients thought of it, recognized and allowed for the possibility of all sorts of magical and miraculous creations and transformations. Similarly, early people also conceived of space and time as capable of being influenced by such things as dreams, wishes, attitudes, promises, and curses. However, in addition to simply describing this change from one way of conceiving the world to another, Frankfort also proposed a speculative account of the general nature of ancient thinking. He did this by comparing ancient mythopoeic thinking on one side with modern aesthetic awareness on the other. For example, he said (p. 11):

> The thought of the ancient Near East appears wrapped in imagination. We consider it tainted with fantasy. But the ancients would not have admitted that anything could be abstracted from the concrete imaginative forms which they left us.

Frankfort admitted that it probably was more difficult for ancient thinkers than it is for artists alive today, to pass at will from aesthetic contemplation to more literal and realistic ways of considering things. Nevertheless, aside from that one difference of detail, he insisted that, in most respects, the special sort of imaginative thinking typical of modern artists, and the "everyday" thinking in which all ancient people engaged, were closely similar. Furthermore he claimed that, by virtue of that similarity, it is now appropriate for us to employ our own aesthetic awareness as an explanatory parallel, model, or "key" to help us grasp the workings, properties, and status of ancient, mythopoeic thought.

But I suggest that Frankfort underestimated the width of the gap that separates the two items he took to be illuminatingly parallel. In fact, it also seems to me that even a relatively superficial knowledge of ancient history is enough to confirm this point. Consider an example. Are there good grounds for believing, as Frankfort evidently did, that the basic reason Old Kingdom Egyptians went to the trouble of planning and constructing the Great Pyramid of Giza, was that they wanted to create an aesthetically pleasing structure of impressive size, beauty, style, and symmetry? If one answers Yes to this question, then another one immediately arises, in its place, of why those people should have been willing to devote so much thought, effort, patience, and expense to creating details of construction that were invisible to observers. For instance, the builders took great pains to ensure that the four sides of the pyramid's base were closely aligned with the points of the compass—North, South, East, and West. And they also spent a lot of time constructing a foundation for the building that was extremely level and flat.[17] But neither of those features could make any direct contribution to the aesthetic experience of viewers, since it is not possible to detect either of them, just by looking at the pyramid. By contrast, the Greeks who built the Parthenon temple in Athens made many deviations from what they knew to be straight lines, right angles, and so forth, in order to ensure that anyone who looked at this building always would have pleasingly aesthetic visual impressions, from his or her perspective.

---

17. Thus, Lionel Casson *et al.* say (1965, p. 135): "To assure this level foundation the pyramid builders erected an extensive system of water-filled trenches about its base. Then, using the water level as a standard, they were able to lay out the 13-acre site so evenly that experts using modern instruments have found that the southeast corner of the pyramid stands only half an inch higher than the northwest corner.

Is it possible to defend Frankfort's position, by claiming that the observers the Egyptians were most concerned to please were their all-seeing gods, rather than partially-seeing human beings like themselves? The trouble with that idea is that it would have the effect of seriously disrupting the particular analogy Frankfort proposed, because it is very clear to us that the aims and practices of modern artists are aimed at humans rather than gods. In other words, the intentions of present-day artists are much more like the ones that motivated the Greek builders of the Parthenon, than like the intentions of the Egyptians who built the Great Pyramid.

To summarize the point, the examples I just mentioned—and others I might have chosen instead—ought to warn us against adopting too simple a view of what ancient thinking was like. In particular, cases of this sort show that there is more than just a superficial difference between the methods, goals, programs, and standards of thought our ancestors employed, and those which people habitually use today.

Let us now consider a theoretical comparison proposed by another author which, in my opinion, went too far in the opposite direction. In other words, this second comparison depicted ancient and modern thinking as more different from one another than they really were. I am talking about the theory of the late psychologist, Julian Jaynes (1978), according to which, ancient thinkers were not analogous to normal adult humans living in the present era, but instead were like certain modern-day people with epilepsy or schizophrenia. What motivated Jaynes to adopt such a view? The answer is that his main reason for talking this way, was that he thought that both of the two groups just mentioned shared the status of being what he called "unconscious automata."

Let me explain this last remark. Jaynes believed it was possible to see, from a careful and unbiased examination of documents like Homer's *Iliad*[18] and the earlier parts of the Old Testament, that

---

18. Parallel to a statement already quoted from Richard Onians in the previous chapter, Jaynes said (1978, Chapter 3) that the reason he chose to model much of his theory of mind on descriptions of thought and action found in the Homeric poem, *Iliad*, was that he considered this work to be "the earliest writing of men in a language that we can really comprehend" (p. 82).

the supposedly conscious actions of the individuals described in those documents were results of a set of causal processes that were very dissimilar to those that are usually effective in today's world. More especially, he claimed that the great majority of modern people did whatever they did by a process of (i) consulting their own beliefs and desires, in order to formulate certain intentions and plans, and then (ii) setting about to realize those plans in action. But in ancient times, by contrast, the process by which individual human beings determined their actions was by responding to, and attempting to obey, certain commands they heard pronounced by "inner voices." Furthermore, Jaynes said, in virtually all such cases, the people in question took the words spoken by the voices they heard to be commands that issued from the mouths of the gods that they worshipped. As a matter of fact, however, Jaynes said the actual source of those voices was neither divine nor external. Instead, all the messages originated from their own, relatively isolated, non-dominant (usually right) cerebral hemispheres, which these individuals (or, to be more specific, their dominant, usually left brain hemispheres) had not yet learned to recognize as ordinary, non-divine parts or aspects of themselves.

Jaynes then claimed that the greatest intellectual accomplishment of what both he and I call "the Greek revolution" was the following fact: At that time and place, he said, certain people discovered how to create a "self-symbol," or "analogous I." And, from that moment until the present day, that symbol has continued to provide a focus around which humans have been able to forge informational connections, which have bound together their two, formerly separate cerebral hemispheres. Jaynes referred to the historical change just mentioned as "the breakdown of the [previous, ancient] bicameral mind." According to him, that event also made it possible, for the first time in history, for humans to become (completely) conscious beings. To say the same thing another way, ever since that date—but not previous to it—humans have possessed an inner life of introspective awareness, in addition to an outer life of direct action and experience.

These ideas strike me (as they also have struck many other people) as interesting and provocative. But I consider Jaynes's background theory, which was the source of—and the intended justification for—all those ideas, to be implausibly complex, strange, and esoteric.[19] Furthermore, it seems to me that the theory in question runs far beyond any conclusions that the textual, historical, and physiological data to which he appealed were legitimately capable of supporting. My opinion, to be more precise, is that Jaynes's explanatory account of mind is fundamentally mistaken, for at least the following four reasons. First, nothing forces us to accept the truth of his principal hypothesis about the occurrence of some massive, historically induced change in the basic way the human brain was organized, which then led to a corresponding revision in the way humans thought. This becomes clear when we reflect on the point that there is an alternative, much less controversial thesis available, which also is capable of explaining the phenomena in question, in at least as plausible a fashion as the theory that Jaynes endorsed. Second, even if what Jaynes said about the occurrence of hallucinatory voices, and ancient humans' responses to them, was a correct description of a few unusual and atypical cases, there are no good reasons to suppose that absolutely all the people who lived in the ancient period heard and obeyed such voices. Third, it seems to me that Jaynes's account of mind may rest on his having confused, or run together, a well-known ancient literary convention on one side, with an ordinary and plain statement of fact on the other. Finally, I think Jaynes (along with many other theorists) made the mistake of failing to distinguish the mind in general, from consciousness in particular.

I shall postpone discussion of the fourth and last reason just mentioned, until the next chapter. But it will be helpful to make a few remarks about each of the first three points here.

(1) What precisely is the alternative, less complex, more intuitive, and less contentious hypothesis that seems to me to be capable of explaining the special mental phenomena with which Jaynes was concerned? There is a simple expression of it at the end of one of the stanzas of John Greenleaf Whittier's famous poem (which also has been set as a hymn), "Dear Lord and Father of Mankind." In particular, what I am thinking of is the place where the poet refers to a "still small voice of calm." I suggest, in other

---

19. At one point (1978, p. 84) Jaynes himself ironically referred to his own account as a "preposterous hypothesis." (This remark puts me in mind of Kierkegaard's claim that one insightful definition of irony is "pretending to be bad, in order to be good.")

words, that it is possible to make sense of passages in ancient documents where, according to Jaynes, gods "speak" internally to their subjects, without accepting his hypothesis that ancient brains were differently "wired" (had a basically different physiological organization) than our own, by the following means. Some ancient people may have been under an impression that their gods were speaking to them, in approximately the same way as many normal, non-schizophrenic people continue to suppose that God, Jesus, Allah, or Vishnu speaks to them today. This "way" is that the man or woman in question can attend to a silent, imagined voice—but not therefore one that also counts as hallucinatory. Many examples in ordinary life (our own lives, as well as those we read about in books) make it clear that voices of that sort often can produce states of mind like comfort, inspiration, conviction, or resolution. And they also can motivate or induce people to perform various actions. But in spite of that, voices of this sort do not involve any sort of pathology nor any experiences that are literally hallucinatory.[20]

(2) At least some references in ancient documents to gods "speaking" to their subjects may be genuine descriptions of particular past individuals who suffered from schizophrenic-like, aural hallucinations. But even if that is true, it still does not provide support for the more general conclusion that *all* ancient people were, or must have been, like that as well. In every past era about which we possess a reasonable amount of information, we know that there were individuals who heard inner voices of the kind that present-day medical experts would describe as hallucinatory. Nevertheless, people of that description are always relatively rare

---

20. Modern thinkers tend to accept the methodological principle that William of Ockham proposed towards the end of The Middle Ages—namely, that one "should not multiply entities beyond necessity." This means that if an explanation is available in a certain case, which posits the existence of a fewer number of items, but which nevertheless has as much or more explanatory power than another that posits a greater number of things, then one should prefer the first over the second. I am appealing to a similar explanatory ideal here. That is, if one can explain historically documented claims about ancient gods "speaking" to their subjects, by appealing to relatively simple and familiar psychological notions, then there is no justification for accepting Jaynes's account of those same claims, which presupposes a complicated and unusual theory about brain physiology. Thus, I agree with Jaynes in rejecting "the modern idea that men have always been the same" (p. 186). And I also agree that he was approximately correct about the time and place of the appearance of the first modern minds. But I do not accept his further claim, that the basic difference between ancient and modern humans lies in the general structure and workings of their brains.

exceptions. For example, even Joan of Arc's "friends" considered her such an odd, puzzling, and therefore suspicious person that, after she was captured and held for ransom by the English invaders, they apparently found it easy to convince themselves that she was expendable. Furthermore—a point Jaynes seems not to have noticed—ancient documents show that much the same situation also existed in Homeric and Mosaic times. For instance, on at least one occasion in the career of the biblical prophet, Jeremiah (1976, Chapter 43, verses 1–4; p. 859), certain members of the crowd of witnesses who had gathered to hear one of his prophecies accused him of lying. More precisely, those witnesses claimed that some of the supposedly prophetic words Jeremiah was speaking to his audience that day were, in fact, not opinions and instructions he had received from God in an honestly passive, merely receptive way. Instead, they claimed that those words were expressions of his own personal views. If Jaynes really were correct to suppose that at this early stage of human history, there did not yet exist any such thing as personal thoughts and desires, then how could the people in question possibly have made this accusation?

At one point in his book, Jaynes tried to blunt the force of an objection like this one by insisting that, rather than a sharply defined historical event, the breakdown of the bicameral mind was something that took place gradually, over a comparatively long period. For instance (see his pp. 273–76) he said that, although the *Iliad* was a completely bicameral book, the *Odyssey* was only partially of this character, because by the time the second work was composed, many individuals already had learned to think (at least for some purposes and on some occasions) in the new, conscious, independent, and active style. Accordingly, Jaynes might attempt to explain away the preceding example about Jeremiah by claiming that, during that particular period, although some people continued to think in the old-fashioned way that once—for example during the lifetime of Moses—had been characteristic of every human without exception, others had learned to think in a more modern style.

However, there are two replies I want to make to any such defense. The first is that it is suspiciously difficult to detect and describe the supposedly crucial change between earlier ("completely bicameral") and later ("only partially bicameral") ancient texts, which this defense presupposes. The Bible tells us that certain Israelites became so discouraged about the exodus from Egypt, that they eventually lost faith in the idea that God really had commanded this event in the first place, or at least that He still was willing to continue to direct and support it—see for instance *Exodus*, Chapter 14, verses 10–13. Those people then expressed approximately the same doubts about the truth and legitimacy of Moses's prophecies, as the others were to do later, about the prophecies of Jeremiah. Second, Jaynes's hypothesis that the breakdown of the bicameral mind was accomplished gradually might be impossible in principle to refute on empirical grounds. But if that is true, then it seems to follow that Jaynes was not justified in supposing that his theory had scientific import. For example, he was not really entitled to describe himself—as he did, for instance, on p. 76—as a "psychohistorical scientist."

(3) What did I mean when I said before that what Jaynes took to be a type of thinking constantly employed by all people during the ancient period might have been nothing more than a literary convention characteristic of that same period?[21] I meant this: Whenever the authors of the *Iliad* and Old Testament spoke about less prominent, "background" characters, or about important characters doing things in unimportant situations, they seldom talked about what these people did, decided, thought, desired, felt, or concluded as being prompted by or from a divine source. The writer of the *Book of Daniel* did not represent the anger of the Babylonian king, Nebuchadnezzar, directed at his subjects, Shadrach, Meshach, and Abed-nego, for their having refused to worship his golden idol (Chapter 3), as having arisen from a god. Instead, it was apparently assumed that this anger had arisen just from Nebuchadnezzar himself. The author's reason for representing things this way was that the anger in question (a) was quite predictable in the situation; (b) did not have any special or distinctive characteristics; and (c) did not play any significant role in determining the course of events still to come. By contrast, why did the writer of the *Book of Exodus* explicitly claim that the stubbornness and anger of the Egyptian pharaoh (arguably identical with Ramesses II) towards Moses, and the various things Moses was

---

21. Jaynes discussed this objection to his theory very briefly (pp. 78–79). But, to my way of thinking, he did not do so adequately.

demanding, had issued directly from the will of God or Jahweh? ("But the Lord made Pharaoh obstinate; as the Lord had foretold to Moses, he did not listen to Moses and Aaron"; 1976, Chapter 9, verse 12; p. 63). The answer is that this was a commonly accepted, dramatic means of emphasizing that the pharaoh's anger was crucially important for achieving some of God's purposes.

Instances of approximately the same "divine emphasizing" convention occur in modern, as well as in ancient history. For example, Napoleon I of France frequently drew a distinction between those things he did and said, which were nothing more than expressions of his own personal whims, desires, ambitions, and so forth, and statements and actions dictated by his "destiny." According to him, all of the first were unimportant, and could be safely dismissed and ignored. But the same was not true of the second. Similarly, Roman Catholics recognize a roughly parallel division between that which popes say in casual conversation, and what they say when speaking "ex cathedra."[22]

If arguments presented so far in this last section of the chapter have provided grounds for concluding that neither Frankfort nor Jaynes succeeded in proposing an adequate, historically based account of the human mind, what do I think is a better account of this type? My ambitions concerning this matter are much more limited than those of the other two authors just mentioned. I do not pretend to have given a key for explaining every instance of, or every property that belonged to, ancient thinking. Rather, my only concern is to describe what (from our present viewpoint) seems to be the single most important difference between our usual style of thought and theirs. In fact, I have already mentioned several times what I take this particular difference to be. I did this when I said that—in the strict sense, and as far as we now know—no human being who lived before the Greek Middle Ages possessed what we now understand as a mind, for the following (three-part) reason: (i) Minds as we conceive of them today centrally presuppose the presence and operation of beliefs; (ii) beliefs are essentially connected with the notion of objective evidence and truth—(in other words, anything one believes must be either true or false, in a way that is independent of all personal considerations); and (iii), before the

---

22. This second example was a suggestion of my wife.

time just mentioned, people had not yet invented the notion of objective belief.

Is my own theoretical account open to the same objection as the one I just brought against Jaynes—namely, that it cannot explain certain things written in the ancient documents themselves? More precisely, modern translations of the *Iliad*, the Old Testament, and similar works, contain many references to people believing certain things and not believing other things. If one takes this way of speaking at face value, it follows that what I said about ancient people having had no beliefs must be false. As an example, consider another case recounted in the *Book of Jeremiah* (1976, Chapter 40, verses 13–16; pp. 857–58). A delegation of men came to visit Gedalia, son of Ahikam, whom Nebuchadnezzar, king of Babylon, had appointed governor of the conquered country of Judah. These men warned Gedalia that the king of the Ammonites had sent Ishmael, son of Nethaniah, to assassinate him, and advised him to have Ishmael killed before he was able to carry out his mission. But, the author reports, "Gedalia . . . did not believe them." In fact, he even said to the members of the delegation, "'Your story about Ishmael is a lie.'" This turned out to be a tragic mistake on Gedalia's part, since later events showed that their warning had been justified after all.

The way I propose to reply to this objection is to invoke a parallel from the history of mathematics. How long have human beings possessed the related set of concepts expressed by the words "infinity," "eternity," "endlessness," and similar expressions? At first, one might be tempted to say that humans have been familiar with those ideas almost from the beginning of settled, civilized life—and especially since the development of literacy—since there seem to be many implicit references to them in many mythological stories. For example, consider again the Egyptian myth discussed in Chapter 2 about the giant snake, Apopis, who supposedly was present in the original chaos that preceded the creation of the world. According to that story, Apopis was an enemy of the gods—in particular, the god or gods who first brought the world into being. Furthermore, he had a fundamentally different nature from them, and from everything else that existed, by virtue of the fact that he had no beginning and no end (see Hornung 1990, p. 158). Thus, as Erik Hornung says (*ibid.*):

He [Apopis] is already there at the creation of the world and must be defeated for the first time by the creator god and driven out of the ordered world of existence. From then on he continually opposes the sun god in his path and threatens the deceased in the underworld. Every day and every night powerful magic is necessary to repel him from the solar bark [i.e. the divine sun conceived as a ship]; he is burned up and "destroyed"—but he is always there again. His existence cannot be extinguished.

. . . [O]nly for a moment can his threat be countered. The sun god and the other gods are indeed there all the time, but in a different way, in the alternation of death and resurrection, not in the unchanging *endlessness* that is the lot of Apopis as a power of chaos. (Italics added)

Examples like this apparently provide a conclusive proof that humans have known about the idea of infinity from the earliest historical times. Furthermore, they also seem to show that all it was necessary for people to do in order to acquire that idea was to imagine certain objects existing, and never going out of existence, or to imagine a series of events taking place repeatedly, without ever coming to an end. For instance, they might have acquired the concept of infinity by imagining a large snake that had no beginning in time, and also no end. Or they might do so by picturing the sun rising in the morning, then setting in the evening, through an endless number of days. Or they might have learned the meaning of the word "infinity" by imagining a spatial distance so vast, or an extent of time so enormously long, that no matter how far one imagined himself traveling along or through it, he never encountered any terminus or outer limit.

But the trouble with all the preceding suggestions is that they fail to address the question of proof. For example, exactly how large, and how long lasting, is our universe—or, more correctly, the universe as one conceives it to be? No matter how many trillions of light-years of cubic space someone imagines as being included in it, and no matter how vast a number of millennia he or she pictures it continuing, or extending into the future, by what right can one also claim that the picture conjured up is sufficiently extensive and coherent to guarantee that the universe imagined actually has no end? We humans are obviously limited and fallible creatures. And therefore our imaginative capacities also must be limited. Thus, could it not be the case that our imaginations are simply too weak—or that they are not instruments of the right sort—to allow us to devise a correct, coherent, and defensible conception of endlessness?

What would a "proper proof" of the possibility and correctness of the notion of infinity be like? Some historians of mathematics (such as A.W. Moore) say that none of the vague, intuitive notions that appear in the works of early authors, like the "endlessness" of Apopis, or the notion of the "unlimited," which figures in the metaphysics of the Greek-Milesian philosopher, Anaximander, is the same as the concept of infinity we recognize today. Strictly speaking, in fact, no human being possessed a correct and defensible concept of infinity, until a particular (later) historical date. The date in question is when certain Pythagorean thinkers devised a *reductio ad absurdum* proof (a proof which, by the way, they personally found distasteful and repulsive) of the proposition that the side and diagonal of a square were incommensurate. This proof began by making the unproved, hypothetical supposition that the side of a square *was* commensurate with its diagonal. In other words, it started by assuming that there was some way of relating the two lengths just mentioned, by means of an expressible ratio of numbers. For example, a ratio of the right sort might take the form of the numerator and denominator of a fraction that is capable of being written down on a finitely large piece of paper. The proof then proceeded by showing that no such ratio or fraction possibly could exist, since the very idea that there was one implied a contradiction. To be precise, the proof was that, if the side and diagonal of a square were commensurate, then it also would have to be the case (*per impossibile*) that a certain number was both even and odd. The following passage is A.W. Moore's statement, explanation, and illustration of this proof (1990, p. 22):

> Suppose that there *is* a pair of natural numbers such that the square of one is twice the square of the other [which—as we know from the so-called Pythagorean theorem—would have to be the case if a square's side were commensurate with its diagonal]. Then there must be a pair with no common factors (the number 1 does not count as a factor here): for obviously we can, where necessary, divide through. Let p and q be such a pair. Then $p^2=2q^2$. This means that p^2 is even, which means, in turn, that p itself is even. So q must be odd, otherwise 2 would be a common factor. [(Moore's) comment: It is not

surprising that the Pythagoreans should have noticed this, given that odd and even occurred in their table of opposites.] But consider: if p is even, then there must be a natural number r such that $p = 2r$. Therefore $p^2 = 4r^2 = 2q^2$. Thus $2r^2 = q^2$, which means that q^2 is even, which means, in turn, that q itself is even, contrary to what was proved above. There cannot after all be a pair of numbers such that the square of one is twice the square of the other. (Also see Lloyd 1970, p. 35)

What this proof shows, then, is that the correct mathematical expression of the relation that holds between the side and diagonal of a square must include a literally infinite number of digits (such as decimal points). For instance, if the length of the side of some given square were 1 meter, then its corresponding diagonal would be the square root of 2—or in other terms, 1.414213562373 . . . (continuing on for a literal infinity)— meters long.

Thus, my suggestion is this: If it really is true to say (as Moore does) that human beings only succeeded in obtaining the concept of infinity as a result of a particular discovery that certain people made at a definite time and place, then—by analogous reasoning—it cannot be entirely absurd to propose something similar for the case of belief as well. The reason this is not absurd is that the idea of belief, as we now understand it, involves and presupposes certain definite elements or factors. But the analogous, roughly corresponding notions the ancients employed (the notions of "opinion." "assertion," "claim," or "inclination to say and do such and such") did not involve those same factors. Let me explain this in still more detail. It is easy for casual, not very well informed readers to slip into the idea that the ancient people they learn about in books held many different beliefs about many different topics. And in the light of that sociological fact, whenever scholars translate accounts of the thoughts and activities of ancient people from tongues like Egyptian, Chinese, Hebrew, or Babylonian, into modern languages, they find it convenient to use the English word "believe," the German word "*glauben,*" the French word "*croire,*" and so on, for this purpose. Nevertheless, more considered and sober reflection ought to tell us that "believe" is not really a word applicable in such contexts, because our present use of that word presupposes certain things that ancient peoples' usage of corresponding words in their languages did not. In particular, our concept of belief presupposes a commitment to the ideal of objective evidence and truth.

Of course, any person pedantic enough to insist that no translations of ancient documents ever should include either the word "infinite" or the word "believe" would be rightly dismissed as a crank. However, even though pedants are silly and tiresome (this, after all, is what the word means), what they say is often correct. For example, despite the fact that scholars regularly translate Anaximander's Greek word "*apeiron*" with the English word "infinite," we now know that Anaximander could not have had exactly the same thing in mind as modern mathematicians do whenever they talk about infinity. Similarly, although we often encounter the word "believe" in English translations of the Old Testament, the *Iliad*, the Egyptian *Book of the Dead*, and so forth, that does not prove that the individuals described in those documents had beliefs, in precisely the same way and sense as we do now. In particular, modern people habitually assume that any belief has to be either true or false, with no "wiggle room" between these two alternatives. But that was a quite untypical way for people living in the "pre-Greek period" to think. In fact, many of them would have found this notion, not just strange and alien, but also childishly rebellious and offensively vulgar. That cultural difference implies, in turn, that ancient people did not really have what we call beliefs at all, but intellectual states that in various ways were merely analogous with beliefs, or parallel to them.

Accordingly, I claim that, at the moment some now unknown person in the pre-Classical Greek world first got the idea of measuring his or her opinions, and those of other humans, against the standard of objective and impersonal truth—an idea destined not to disappear in the future, but to spread to the ends of the earth—what we now refer to as belief came into existence. Similarly, this same innovation also gave rise to the more general notion—and entity—of mind. Thus, it is wrong to think of either of these as referring to some type of physical or natural entities. Instead, both belief and mind are cultural objects that are firmly associated with Western Society, but not with any other cultural group.

The last task I want to accomplish in this chapter is to reply to still another objection that was suggested to me by one of my colleagues.[23] It is this: My basic claim in this book is that there is an important difference between the kind of thinking associated with those humans who were influenced by the cultural revolution that took place in pre-Classical Greece about 1000 B.C.E., and the thinking of all other people—in particular, those who lived before that date. I also have argued that this difference was significant enough to justify the idea that the "Greek revolution" created what we now understand as the human mind. However, the arguments I have given do not really add up to a proof that we are entitled to distinguish ancient and modern thought in this way, since all of them are merely focused on the familiar, general distinction between religious thought on the one side and non-religious, secular thinking on the other. Furthermore, the objection continues, people still are just as likely today, as the Egyptians were many years ago, to lapse into superstitious, magical, and irrational modes of thought, whenever they begin to consider matters in personal, emotional, or religious terms. Thus the distinction that I conceive of as providing a sharp dividing line between one main period of human intellectual history and another, is really something that always has been, and always will be, present and recognized at all times and in all places alike.

My first point in response to this objection is to remind readers that I do not think of the Greek intellectual revolution *(à la* Jaynes) as, or as involving, some dramatic, inner, physiological transformation of the human brain. Rather, what happened in Greece at the time just mentioned was simply that someone thought of—invented—a novel pattern, goal, or ideal for thought. It is implicit in the nature of this or any other such ideal that people sometimes are able and willing to observe and "live up to" it, and sometimes not. In view of that point, it is almost certainly correct to speculate that many Greeks who were alive at the same time as Aristotle (and who spoke the same language as he did), continued to think about many issues and topics—especially ones involving love, sex, war, politics, and religion—in essentially Egyptian-like terms. Admittedly, furthermore, it is also an undeniable fact that we still are able to find many instances of that same type of thinking in our society today. To consider a

---

23. Henry Jackman.

famous instance, Pope Pius X once issued the command to church members that they should give "external and internal assent" to decrees of the Pontifical Biblical Commission, such as that woman had been formed out of the body of the first man (see *Time Magazine*, December 30th, 1974, p. 41).

But in spite of the points just mentioned, I continue to believe that people today do not think in the same way as the ancient Egyptians did—even about emotional (for instance religious) matters. The reason I say this is that, beginning with the Greek revolution, a change in society (as opposed to the brain) gradually spread or "diffused" to all the rest of the present-day world. And as Putnam reminds us by means of his hypothesis about a "twin earth," the thought of every person who lives in a particular society (or in fact, even in a particular physical environment) inevitably is influenced by the fact that he or she lives there. And this is true, irrespective of whether or not that person explicitly chooses to be so influenced, and whether or not he or she is aware of being influenced. Thus, my claim is that what happened in pre-Classical Greece now provides every present-day human with an opportunity to think in a systematically rational way—an opportunity that was not available to people who lived before that time. Furthermore, the availability of that new possibility counts as having changed us in a fundamental, but not—at least directly and primarily—a physiological, respect.

Another way of saying the same thing is that humans now are able to employ a set of intellectual tools that allows them draw a clear line between entirely rational thought, and relatively irrational, dramatic, emotional—for instance, religious—thinking. But ancient thinkers did not have that opportunity. And therefore, at the time and in the environment in which these last people lived, it was easier and more natural for such categories to "bleed into" one another. (For example, ancient Egyptians would have been in a much better position to follow the above-mentioned command of Pope Pius X, than Catholics living today.) This is still another illustration of what I meant when I said before—contrary to Frankfort—that the transition from mythological to rational thinking was a larger and more profound change than just imposing certain restrictions or limits on certain types of ordinary, modern thought.

Chapter 4

Reintroducing
the Mind
into Nature

4.1 Finishing the Job: Mind in the Wide as well as Narrow Sense

Igor Stravinsky once said of his fellow composer, Ludwig van Beethoven, that he had been born with every musical gift except one—the gift of melody. When I quoted that remark to an acquaintance, who was relatively unsophisticated about music, she rejected the whole idea as nonsense. Everyone knew, this person insisted, that Beethoven's music was full of melodies. In fact, she added, every bit of music Beethoven wrote consisted in nothing more than one melody after another. Then she proposed to prove the correctness of this last claim by whistling several representative passages. Politeness kept me from expressing strong disagreement. (After all, this was nothing more than a casual, friendly conversation.) Nevertheless, it seemed to me then—and still seems to me now—that my friend's indignant response was based on, not just a verbal, but a substantive, misunderstanding. To be specific, her way of talking implied that a melody had to be present in every musical passage without exception, simply because every such passage was composed of notes, and some of those notes—usually those of highest pitch—were bound to strike listeners as more prominent than the others. However, this was not an appropriate reply to Stravinsky, since he was trying to make a quite different point. For example, part of Stravinsky's purpose was to say that anyone unable or unwilling to set aside the popular, loose way of speaking that my friend employed, in favor of another, stricter definition of the word "melody," would lose an opportunity. That is, he or she no longer would be able to see or appreciate an important division between musical styles—one that separated composers like Beethoven on one side, from others like Tchaikovsky, Bellini, and Borodin on the other.

In roughly similar style, I also have been arguing for a Stravinsky-like thesis in this book. It is this: The narrow, strict sense of the word "mind" that I have introduced in preceding chapters is not something arbitrary, idiosyncratic, or mad. Instead, it can be understood as the kernel of the particular conception of mind that virtually all people actually recognize (or at least presuppose) at the present time.

As opposed to the thesis just stated, some cognitive scientists favor a wider, vaguer, and more "objective" conception of mind.

In particular, the people I am talking about tend to picture the mind as a large, random, rather untidy collection of "contents." Furthermore, according to them, all of those contents qualify as equally good instances of "mental entities," in spite of the fact that some classes of them are markedly different from others, and play very different epistemological roles.[1]

Consider a simple example. One traditional but still popular such nomenclature dictates that it is appropriate to classify the mind's contents in terms of the following three categories. All the thoughts, beliefs, hypotheses, and so forth that one would naturally express in terms of "matter of fact" language count as the mind's "cognitive" contents. Next, desires, wishes, hopes, volitions, and other intellectual states that have the status of goals to be pursued, or projects to be accomplished, belong in the second, "conative" category. Finally, feelings that we are able to locate and describe in a general way, but which have no inner contents capable of being given direct linguistic expressions (such as bodily sensations; visual, aural, gustatory, smell, and touch perceptions; and so forth), belong to the third category of the "sensitive." (Some who follow this last approach say it is also possible to distinguish intermediate cases. For instance, they think of emotions as complex mixtures and combinations of cognitive, sensitive, and perhaps even conative elements.)

Why do I not accept the kind of theoretical picture just mentioned—one that depicts mind as a "bag" of entities (objects, facts, processes, procedures, and so forth), all of which have the same—and an equal—right to be called "mental"? The reason is the following: I believe it amounts to a more sensitive, informative, and realistic picture of the way people actually talk and think today to draw a distinction between the mind's "center" (mind considered in the narrow and proper sense of the word) and its "outskirts" (mind understood in a looser, wider, and less stringent way). Furthermore, reflection on certain aspects of Western history has convinced me that our ancestors began to make this particular distinction only at a comparatively recent (historical rather than pre-historical) time. To repeat what I already said several

---

1. A relatively old example of this general approach, with which I am contrasting my own view, is James 1890/1950. A more recent instance is Pinker 1997.

times before, it first began when some now-unknown individual invented the sharper, more explicit, more exact standards of correctness and adequacy (true versus false; satisfied versus unsatisfied) that we now associate with the notions of belief and desire.[2]

If what I am suggesting is on the right track, then it follows that it is wrong to think of the mind as a natural organ with which every normal human being is equipped at birth. Instead, it is more useful and accurate to say that the mind is just another, more or less ordinary, culturally determined invention. Even more concretely, I agree with those computational functionalist theorists who say the mind is like "software," whose job it is to channel, direct, and guide various workings of the "hardware" of our innately inherited nervous systems and brains. However, I disagree with the further assertion many of the same people make that minds themselves are also innately given entities, in addition to the physical brains they influence and control. As opposed to this last idea, I believe the best and least misleading way of talking about the nature and ontological status of mind is to compare it with items of the following sort: Arabic numerals; the nursery rhyme "Bah, Bah Black Sheep," double-entry bookkeeping; the literary device of footnotes; the children's game of Snakes and Ladders, the "approximating" mathematical techniques of differential calculus. In other words, it is not something innate, but an invented intellectual device, routine, procedure, and set of standards, that virtually all adult, normal people now have mastered and learned to use correctly. (In this last respect, the mind is more like Arabic numerals, and less like calculus, since the first have become familiar to almost everyone today, but the second is still only employed by an elite.) The main practical result of that invention has been to allow us to use our brains in a more organized, efficient way than we otherwise could have done. This particular invented procedure is what I propose to identify with mind in the strict, narrow, and proper sense of the word.

Thus, I do not locate the division between minded and unminded creatures at the boundary between "higher" primates and other, "lesser" animals. Nor do I draw that distinction between humans and all other organisms. Instead, I divide (strict)

---

2. For a somewhat different perspective on similar issues concerning mental classification, see van Gelder forthcoming.

mind on one side, from non-mind on the other, *within* the boundary of our species, at the line that separates our own, Greek-based civilization from the various (past) cultural traditions that once belonged to many of our fellow, equally normal, equally intelligent, human beings.[3]

As a means of approaching the subject from a slightly different angle, let us now consider the question of whether our galaxy contains any intelligent, extraterrestrial life. One popular argument in favor of spending time, effort, and money in support of organized searches for such life is this: If we were able to discover radically exotic ways of thinking about mathematics, physics, biology, and other such areas, the instructive contrast that this would provide would allow us to gain a better knowledge both of ourselves, and of many other matters that we already claim to know scientifically. However, I do not believe that argument is a good one. My reason for being skeptical about it is that the past record of our society shows it probably would be very difficult for people like us to make that kind of use of any such discovery. In fact, it seems to me that we already have—without needing to spend money searching for it—a good contrastive means of gaining perspective on our own characteristic patterns of thinking. What I am talking about is the fact that we already are in a position to compare our present habitual ways of considering and assessing things with the different styles and patterns of thought that people used in earlier historical times. However, not many of our society's intellectual leaders have chosen to take advantage of this last-mentioned opportunity. In fact, they typically ignore all the differences just mentioned, or deny their existence altogether, because of their habit of assuming that all past human beings must have thought about the world in essentially the same terms as we do now.

Thus, imagine that our search for intelligent extraterrestrial life finally proved successful. Imagine further that the beings we discovered turned out to be understandable, friendly, moral, non-exploitative, and willing to help us. Even so, the inhabitants

---

3. I again emphasize that what I say here does not imply that those other traditions were necessarily inferior to our own. In fact, disinterested historical research might provide good reasons for concluding that, in some respects, various ancient civilizations were more developed, cultured, moral, subtle, emotionally mature, and so on, than ours.

of earth probably would prove incapable of making a contrastive intellectual use of the newly discovered race of beings, for the following reason. Sooner or later, they would find themselves under a great deal of political pressure to begin supposing that all the aliens were "basically like us," and therefore that all their cultural achievements also were "basically like ours." By that means, the hard-won and very expensive chance to gain increased perspective on our own status, nature, and accomplishments would have become lost. In particular, after a time, people most likely would start to think about those aliens in approximately the same way as most of them now conceive of the ancient Babylonians, Egyptians, Chinese, and others who preceded us on this planet. That is, they would assume that those creatures could not really be mentally different from us in any significant respect.

The attitudes I am talking about are ones that present-day humans often adopt for reasons that seem to them to be good, ethical, righteous, and "democratic." For example, what are the average people like who live in London, Tokyo, New York, Moscow, Lima, or Toronto today? More particularly, what do they consider to be involved in recognizing the dignity, worth, intelligence, and genuine humanity of long dead members of our own species? The answer, I suggest, is that they assume that part of this desirable way of thinking is for them to make the generous assumption that all the past individuals in question contemplated the world in roughly the same, "scientific," "rational," "enlightened" way as we do now. Despite these good intentions, however, I suggest that this is a mistake—the mistake of putting one thing in place of another. The error I am talking about strikes me as similar to one the French aristocrat, Alexis de Tocqueville, pointed out a little over two hundred years ago. During the French Revolution (largely for his own safety) this person paid an extended visit to the then newly founded American Republic. Later he wrote a book (*Voyage to America*) in which he recorded some of the general impressions he had formed of the people who lived there. One of de Tocqueville's remarks in that book was this: What the Americans honored above everything else, and desperately wanted to achieve in their own lives, was Freedom. But in this respect, he said, they rarely managed to get what they wanted, because they repeatedly confused Freedom on one side with Equality on the other, and sub-stituted the second for the first.

All this having been said, it now is time to turn our inquiry in a new direction. Let us look once more at a problem first men-tioned in Chapter 2, namely: How can it be consistent for me to maintain (as I did, for example in section 2.4) that the mind is something cultural rather than narrowly physical, and yet also claim (see for instance the end of 1.1) to reject dualism and all other forms of magical supernaturalism? To state the same diffi-culty another way, what exactly do I think is the relation between mind in the narrow, strict, culturally relative sense, and mind in the wider, physical, and physiological meaning of the term, which people like Chomsky, Pinker, Lakoff, and Mark Johnson accept?

As a first step in untangling this knot, let us now consider, once again, a simpler version of the same problem. Ethologists, zoo keepers, hunters, pet owners, and others say it is clear from the behavior of many non-human animals that those creatures have, and operate in terms of, something very much like our own beliefs and desires. But if this is true, and if it was right for me to say before that beliefs and desires play a centrally important role in the mind considered generally, then it apparently follows that all the animals just mentioned also must possess something like minds. *A fortiori*, it seems that the same must be true as well, of all the talented, subtle, cultured, non-Western, human thinkers who lived in ancient Assyria, China, Egypt, and other earlier cul-tures. Furthermore, it is very unlikely that this parallel between our behavior and that of other creatures (including non-Western humans) is nothing more than a cosmic—for instance, an evolu-tionary—coincidence. Therefore, contrary to what I said before, doesn't the presence of those similarities amount to a proof that mind in the narrow sense must be some sort of natural phenome-non, rather than something cultural, after all?[4]

The way I propose to deal with this question is to adopt a viewpoint that is parallel in some respects to the one espoused by so-called "new dualists" (See for example Reynolds 1981, pp. 13–18 and Burkert 1996, p. 2). The intellectual movement that

---

4. By the way, I do not deny that some animals have—and all ancient humans had—*something like* minds. I am only concerned to dispute certain conclusions some theorists are prepared to draw from that idea.

goes by this name began as a response to "sociobiological" accounts of mind. Sociobiologists predicted that scientists some-day would be able to account for absolutely every human cultural practice and institution, by showing that it could be understood as an evolutionarily selected survival strategy. Furthermore, each strategy of this sort did not just apply to human beings alone, but—at least potentially—to a much wider group of animals as well. For instance, consider the following programmatic declaration made by Hahlweg and Hooker (1989, p. 23):

[Human] knowledge development is a direct extension of evolutionary development, and the dynamics of the two processes are identical.

In contrast with this, new dualists say sociobiologists have conspired to ignore the familiar fact that there is an important, systematic difference between two types of things. Those two types are: (a) human cultural traits (being of a certain religion, having a certain nationality, being politically biased, and so forth) and (b) characteristics it is possible to explain in terms of physical factors alone (such as having blue eyes, being of a certain race, being left-handed, being athletically talented). In particular, new dualists remind us of the biological fact that, while narrowly physical properties are determined by separately specifiable, inheritable factors ("genes"), this is not true of cultural attributes. (For example see E. Leach's comments about Lumsden's and Wilson's book, 1981, in his review, 1981.) Still more narrowly, it is wrong to suppose that the great majority of human cultural developments could have come into being just through blind, Darwinian-style variation and selection, because they are products of conscious, directed, purposeful thinking—thinking organized in terms of learning as opposed to inheritance. On the basis of this and similar points, new dualists say that, in place of the old, Cartesian distinction between body and mind, it is better to think of the semi-opposed elements that combine to make up the world in general, and humans in particular, as "nature" and "culture."

It should be obvious from what I have said so far in this book that I am more likely to be sympathetic to opponents of monistic naturalism (including sociobiological versions of that doctrine) than to any form of monistic naturalism itself. But does that mean that I also am willing to accept some form of new dualism? To be more precise, am I prepared to assert that (i) minds, in a broad sense of the word, are natural and physical entities—in accordance with the view (loosely associated with modern science)[5] that everything that exists is physical? But then do I also qualify the preceding assertion by adding that (ii) minds, when considered in a narrower sense, fall outside nature, (a) because they are cultural entities, which therefore are underlain and instantiated, but not literally constituted, by existing things; and (b) because, even if it is true to say that products of culture and of (for example) natural selection sometimes are analogous to one another, it is wrong to suppose that the two are identical, since they operate according to "dissimilar rules"?

The answer is No. Admittedly, the new dualism strikes me as being a step in the right direction. But it is only a small and rather feeble step, in my opinion, since it boils down to nothing more than a sketch of a theory, as opposed to a developed position. To be more precise, I think this is true because of its characteristic vagueness and negativity. Supporters of this view often appear to be more interested in appealing to various "brute facts," than in trying to explain ("unbrutalize") those presumed facts. Although some of them denounce the idea of "reducing" mind to its physical underpinnings, they have nothing clear or substantive to say about exactly what they think the relation is between mind one side and the body-brain on the other. But my goal in this book is to accomplish something like that last-mentioned, positive task.

4.2   A Platonic Conception of the Universe, and Species' "Adaptive Tricks"[6]

As a means of setting out to do what I just proposed, let me now introduce several bits of "metaphysical machinery." The first of

---

5. I am indebted to my student Pavel Davydov for reminding me of the looseness of the connection between these factors, or in other words, of the fact that we have no good reasons for supposing that modern science has "proved" the correctness of the idea that only natural and physical things exist. Rather, this last idea is merely a working assumption that many practitioners of modern science have found it convenient (and perhaps also fruitful) to make.

6. Earlier versions of some of the points in this section appear in my papers, 1990 and 1988.

them is this: I accept it as a working hypothesis—based partly on observations of my own, and partly on things learned from other people—that the universe we live in has what one might call a Platonic character. More especially, my hypothesis (temporarily setting aside my previously expressed reluctance to engage in general classification) is that this world not only contains a vast number of concrete particulars or individuals—objects, events, states, facts, properties, and so forth—but objectively real generals or universals as well. Second, the universals that exist in our world can, and sometimes do, have definite, causal influences on some of the concrete objects, properties, and states of affairs that also are found there.

It might be more accurate to describe my position as more like that of Plato's student, Aristotle, than as similar to Plato's own view of things. I think of universals as existing within the natural world itself, and as influencing particular things from their standpoint within that world, rather than supposing that they somehow exist outside of nature, and manage to have a causal influence on natural entities from that removed, "intelligible realm." Nevertheless, it is still appropriate to describe my position as broadly a "Platonic" one, if only because of the obvious fact that Aristotle's view of these particular matters was deeply influenced by Plato's, and therefore also deserves to be called Platonist, in an extended sense of that term.

I once was attracted by the notion that there were at least some mathematical universals, in addition to universals of other sorts. But further reading and reflection finally convinced me that this last idea was neither a necessary nor even a defensible one. Accordingly, it now seems to me that we have no good justification for supposing that any so-called mathematical categories, processes, or objects—such as long division, squaring, the number 224, the number π, the square root of minus 1—count as literal existents. Instead, it is better to describe them as aspects or expressions of various intellectual techniques that people have devised to assist them in thinking about, and operating on, entities that actually do exist.

Thus, what are the main types of things that I believe have literal existence? The answer is that (for present purposes) I am willing to agree that all the things that exist—objects, properties, processes, facts, and so on—are physical in nature. Furthermore,

all those physical entities fall into one or other of two broad categories—namely, the ones that are particular, on one side, and
those that are general, on the other.

The most obvious alternative to the account just described is a
world-picture of a broadly nominalist or Ockhamist sort. To provide a sense of what the main characteristics of this alternative are,
let me now quote a short translated passage from the Latin writings of William of Ockham. Ockham was an English philosopher
who lived in the thirteenth and fourteenth centuries, and who now
is widely considered to be the originator of the view in question.

> [I]f a universal is that which is not numerically one—a meaning
> attributed by many to "universal"—then I say that nothing is a uni-
> versal . . . Hence we have to say that every universal is one singular
> thing. Therefore nothing is universal except by signification, by
> being a sign of several things. (Ockham 1962, p. 33)[7]

This second sort of metaphysical position still is very popular
at the present time. For example, many present-day philosophers
and scientists would express enthusiastic agreement with the following historical observation made by one of Ockham's editors
and translators, Philotheus Boehner:

> [When] Ockham refuses to admit that in the real world there is any-
> thing that corresponds to the universality of a concept . . . any uni-
> versal *in re*, common nature, etc.—anything which is not completely
> individual— . . . [he introduces] . . . a change of outlook almost as
> epoch-making as the Copernican revolution in astronomy." (*Ibid.*, p.
> xxvii.)[8]

Why, despite its current popularity (as reflected in Boehner's
glowing comment), have I decided to reject this doctrine? One

---

7. Although—as mentioned above—it is now common to associate Ockham's name
with this idea, he could not literally have been its inventor, since various other people
(such as Avicenna) thought of it before him. In fact, it was apparently the case that this
view formed part of the generally accepted intellectual background of Ockham's time, as
shown by the fact that he did not feel obligated to give explicit arguments in favor of it. In
other words, he merely assumed its truth, as if he believed it was something his readers
already would find clear and non-controversial, and therefore would be willing to affirm
(see Boehner's "Introduction" in Ockham 1962, p. xxiv).

8. Boehner intends to convey the impression here that this change of outlook was not
only important, but also justified and correct. In other words, he assumes that it describes
the world as it actually is.

reason for doing so is that any person who claims in the style of Ockham, that only single, individual items exist, must also be prepared to accept an additional hypothesis. That hypothesis (reminiscent of Tennyson's poem, "Flower in the Crannied Wall") is that the complete set of existing individual items always constitutes, provides, or contains, sufficient resources to account for absolutely everything that happens in our universe. But the trouble with this last idea is that recent empirical science evidently has uncovered certain facts that throw doubt on its truth. To be precise, those facts imply that, sometimes and under some circumstances, there simply are no concrete objects, properties, situations, and so on, that are available to accomplish the explanatory tasks, which Ockham and his followers assume that individual existents can and must do.

Consider a simple example. My *Concise Oxford Dictionary* (Seventh edition, 1982) defines the word "gold" in partly observational, partly theoretical terms, as a yellow, non-rusting, malleable, ductile metallic element of high density. It is clear to us from both ordinary experiences and more organized, scientific investigations that we are able to extrapolate in a predictive fashion from properties that belonged to instances of gold that we observed in the past, to future occurrences of those same properties in new, unknown, and yet-to-be-observed cases. On the other hand, experience also shows that we cannot make correct predictive extrapolations of the same sort in cases involving "non-natural kinds"—supposed types that have the status of being arbitrary, accidental, or merely verbal. For example, only a very foolish gambler would bet a great deal of money on the expectation that some fair coin, which came up heads the last 25 times it was flipped, also will show heads on the next trial as well. The reason (which ought to be clear to gamblers) is that this long string of heads was not a result of any form of necessity, but only of chance or luck. Similarly, suppose that today it is possible to find a copy of Euclid's *Elements*, and a small shark's jaw, on the shelves of the Lost and Found Department of the Toronto Transit Commission. That does not provide a basis for inferring that there will be another copy of that same book, and another shark's jaw, in that same place, one year, month, week, or day later. Again, at the present moment, some woman may be carrying a ticket to an opera in her purse. But that does not justify the belief that she falls under a natural category entitled, "opera-ticket-carrier," and therefore can be expected to have such a ticket in her purse at any given future date. Familiar points like these teach us a general lesson about what the world is like. That lesson is that words like "gold" refer to actually existing natural kinds or universals, which either are or express fairly definite, and perhaps even relatively permanent, sets of possibilities in our universe. But phrases like "this fair coin's disposition to turn up another head," "Toronto residents' tendency to lose copies of Euclid's *Elements* and shark jaws on the subway," and "Mrs. X's habit of always carrying an opera ticket in her purse," do *not* refer to real universals.

Now let us consider still another question: Precisely where, in our universe, is the location of the "projectable powers" that either constitute or express a given natural kind?[9] The reply Ockhamist or nominalist thinkers will be inclined to give this question is that those powers are identical with certain properties and dispositions that are possessed by concrete instances of the kind in question—for example currently existing atoms of gold. But that answer does not seem to me to be a good one, for the following reason. Even if we agree that the kind *gold* counts as a real and permanent part of our world, as that world exists here and at the present moment, there are, were, and will be many places, contexts, and times where there are no concrete instances of gold. For example, there is no gold—in fact, no atoms at all— in either black holes or neutron stars. Furthermore, there was no gold anywhere, at the past time when this universe first came into being (the so-called Big Bang that occurred approximately 13.7 billion years ago), as well as for quite a long period after that. Similarly, some cosmologists claim that, in a much later era, when our universe finally "winds-down," there again will be no gold at any point in space, because then only subatomic particles will be

---

9. Are some readers offended by the blatant "essentialism" that I am apparently expressing here? If so, those people should remember that I am only positing the existence of universals as part of the "metaphysical machinery" that seems to me to provide the best means of setting forth my general theory of mind. For my purposes, the most important consideration is the set of empirical facts that stands behind and (in my opinion) justifies this way of talking. However, if some readers prefer—and are able—to account for those same facts in an alternative way that does not presuppose the real existence of universals, then I have no objection to their interpreting what I said before in a way that fits this different manner of thinking. The essence, and truth, of my proposed account would not be affected by such a change.

able to form, but no atoms. Thus, to restate the above question, exactly what existential status is it appropriate to attribute to a natural kind like *gold*—including all its many and various powers—at those places where, and moments when, that kind has no instances?

Faced with this challenge, Ockhamists might adopt a second, "fall back" position, by saying that even when and where gold happens to be absent from our world, there always are plenty of other concrete things and properties—of other, non-gold kinds— that are capable of taking its place. In other words, all the potentialities of the kind *gold* (which, *ex hypothesi*, are not instantiated at the time and place in question) somehow are implicit, or contained in, and can be explained in terms of, properties of other concrete items. Again, however, I think this second proposal faces a serious and perhaps fatal challenge as well. That challenge is that present-day science tells us that it is possible for causal effects to occur (for example, matter can be created) even in cases where there are no previously existing, concrete individuals of any sort whatever. For example, quantum cosmologists like Stephen Hawking say that the Big Bang (and thus also, the entire universe that grew out of it) originated from nothing (or at any rate, nothing it would be appropriate to describe as an individual, concretely existing object). (See for example Morris 1993, pp. 135–36.) Furthermore, something similar also seems to be the case with respect to smaller, less unique, and more ordinary situations as well. Physicists now believe that pairs of material particles are constantly coming into existence from quantum fluctuations occurring in "empty" space—and that those newly-minted particles then last either a shorter or a longer time, depending on how much energy happens to be available in each instance (see *ibid.*, pp. 131–33).

An Ockhamist world-picture is one instance of the general view referred to before as "monistic naturalism." According to that picture, no matter where we look in our universe, or how deeply we delve into its inner nature, we are bound to find only one general type of items existing within it. Furthermore, all the items of that one special type are essentially similar to the concrete entities (pebbles, couches, elephants, stars, explosions, sounds, magnetic fields) with which we are familiar in our everyday experience. At one time, the results of modern scientific investigations might have seemed to support that particular way of looking at things. But I do not believe that still is true today. For example, consider the following statement by Richard Feynman, about how twentieth-century observations and theories forced physicists to change their earlier ways of thinking about very small natural objects and processes.

"Quantum mechanics" is the description of the behavior of matter in all its details and, in particular, of the happenings on an atomic scale. Things on a very small scale behave like nothing that you have any direct experience about. They do not behave like waves, they do not behave like particles, they do not behave like clouds, or billiard balls, or weights on springs, or like anything that you have ever seen.

[For instance,] Newton thought that light was made of particles, but then it was discovered, as we have seen here, that it behaves like a wave. Later, however (in the beginning of the twentieth century) it was found that light did indeed sometimes behave like a particle. Historically, the electron, for example, was thought to behave like a wave. So it really behaves like neither. Now we have given up. We say: "It is like *neither.*" (1995, p. 116)

Again, Albert Einstein (together with those experimenters who helped devise empirical tests to establish the validity of his ideas) reportedly proved—as summarized by the famous equation, "$E=mc^2$"—that every piece of matter was implicitly identical with, and under certain circumstances could be transformed into, a very large, equivalent amount of energy. But however one might be inclined to conceive of energy, or whatever speculative account one proposes of what energy *is*, it is not plausible to suppose that energy is a clear, unambiguous, non-misleading instance of what people have in mind whenever they talk about one, several, or many concretely existing entities. Instead of a "something," it is more natural to describe energy as "that which something (else) either does or is able to do."

Karl Popper claimed that twentieth-century physics had established the truth of the metaphysical system once proposed by the pre-Socratic, Greek philosopher, Heraclitus (see Popper 1965a, especially page 148). It is not entirely clear to me what Popper meant when he said this. But even so, it is reasonable to surmise that what he mainly had in mind was the Einstein-like thesis—typified by Heraclitus's comparison of the world to a river—that there were no stable, unchanging, individual objects in our universe, but instead only relatively permanent, relatively constant patterns of change.

If we are entitled to assume that the scientific doctrines mentioned in previous paragraphs are both coherent and true, then those doctrines apparently imply the falsity of the Ockhamist idea that everything that exists and happens in our world must be similar to the concrete objects and processes of familiar experience. Accordingly, I suggest it would be more insightful for us to follow the lead of Heraclitus and Einstein on this question, rather than to follow Ockham. In particular, reflection on various conclusions of present-day physics shows it is just as reasonable (at least in some cases) to account for the existence, properties, and behavior of singulars, in terms of roughly corresponding properties that belong to real and existing generals, as to proceed in the opposite explanatory direction—to explain universals in terms of singulars.

Let me try to make it still clearer how I propose to conceive of the Platonic universe in which we live, by making four additional comments. First, (a) it is not necessary for universals to have any "ultimate" ontological status, in order for scientific appeals to them to have legitimate explanatory power. For example, let us imagine that a researcher somehow succeeds in showing that it was possible to reduce a certain universal to various other, relatively simpler items—which, in their turn, might be either concrete or universal. This person's having demonstrated this point would not also prove that the universal in question was in some sense illusory or bogus, or that people now were under an obligation to expunge all references to that universal from the body of scientific knowledge.[10]

The second point I want to make is this: (b) There is nothing contradictory about the idea that universals exist as parts of the extra-mental world itself. (This—if true—implies in turn that there cannot be a necessary connection between universals on one side and human existence and thought on the other.) Consider the following. Humans are able to conceive of many more things,

---

10. Some philosophers are inclined to ignore the following two facts: (i) Scientists have never yet managed to find any basic level of reality, or in other words, any "theoretical bottom" of the world. And thus it follows that (ii), up to the present moment, absolutely all the effective explanations that scientists ever have proposed have been formulated in terms of one or another, "middle" ontological level.

properties, situations, and so forth, than just the ones that actually do exist and actually do occur. A simple instance: "If only that truck hadn't swerved to cut me off, I wouldn't now be lying in hospital with three broken ribs." How do people manage to do this? The answer is that they appeal to certain patterns in their ordinary, concrete, empirical experiences, as a means, a test, and a criterion, for the general distinction they make between real things and events, and merely possible ones. So in a similar manner, I claim that one also can appeal to experiences of that sort, in order to distinguish real from merely possible universals, and other "thought-objects." For example, a man's being able to conceive of a round square (in one or another vague, and perhaps also vacillating sense) is not enough to prove that the round square he so conceives, or any other round square, is real. Rather, the way we succeed in discovering that this cannot be anything more than a fanciful, imagined object is that concrete experience gradually makes it clear that there is no room in our world for objects of that particular description.[11] Similarly, I claim that, also in the case of universals, the only means we have of deciding what is and is not real is by paying attention to certain implications of our empirical observations.

(c) Unlike Aristotle and D.M. Armstrong (see Armstrong 1989), I do not believe that the existence of any given universal is somehow identical with the fact of its being concretely instantiated. Referring once more to a previous example, we have reason to think that the natural kind *gold* had to wait a very long time, after the beginning of our cosmos, before it finally became able to acquire particular instances. But it does not follow from that fact alone that *gold* was not something real and existent, during the whole course of the time just mentioned. To formulate this same point in a still more general fashion, a universal's having instantiations depends on certain background circumstances being in force at the appropriate times. But the existence of the universal itself,

---

11. Descartes once maintained that God was capable of creating a world in which 2 + 2 was equal to 5. Of course, he also said, although God would be able to understand that world, we could not. It seems to me that Descartes was right to make that claim, if only because it serves as a useful reminder of the following, obviously true principle: A mere process of thinking or conceiving of something—or of failing to conceive of something—even when that particular process either includes or presupposes the "basic" laws of contradiction, excluded middle, and identity, does not, and cannot, determine the nature of reality itself.

and of the various properties and powers it "contains," need not also depend on the operation or effectiveness of those same factors.

Finally, yet another implication of the preceding point is this: (d) Universals (such as natural kinds) are capable of existing in our world, even if they do not have—and perhaps never did, and never will have—any instances at all.

How do I propose to answer critics who pose searching questions about the status and existence of a natural kind (and of its projectable properties and powers) during those times, and in those places, where the kind in question is not instantiated? My reply is to point out that the criticism that is apparently implicit in such questions is based on a false assumption. That is, I claim that real and physical natural kinds are abstract entities, not particular ones. Thus it begs the question simply to assume that the subjects or "owners" of all such kinds, and their properties, always have to be concrete objects with definite locations in space and time. For example (analogous to a doctrine once espoused by Hegel and Bradley), one might suppose that the proper subject of all the properties associated with natural kinds is the universe as a whole. Furthermore, it is not necessary to picture the universe as a very large, existing object, with definite spatial and temporal parts and characteristics, just like all the objects that exist "inside" the universe. Instead—parallel to one of the points Wittgenstein makes in his *Tractatus*—we can conceive of it as a set of general and abstract factors that determines the spatial and temporal properties of all the possible entities that ever *might* exist.

If this line of reasoning is on the right track, then the statement previously quoted from Philotheus Boehner must be wrong. That is, he says the "nominalist and anti-Platonic metaphysical insight" developed by Ockham and other thinkers in the late Middle Ages was a step towards enabling humankind to acquire a more solid, realistic, and scientifically justified grasp of the world and its contents. But it seems to me that precisely the opposite is true. In other words, from the perspective of hindsight, it is possible to see that this conception of things was a regressive step that (at least in one important sense) had the effect of taking us further away from such knowledge. Furthermore, we only came to be in a position to correct that particular philosophical error at a later time, when discoveries made by twentieth-century scientists provided us with an opportunity to start conceiving of the world in different terms.

It now is time for us to shift attention to other, related matters, central to the themes of this book. I do not consider it an especially important matter whether or not readers agree with the cosmological intuitions and arguments set forth in the last few pages. The reason I say this is that it is not my primary goal to draw large-scale, philosophical conclusions about the universe as a whole, from premises derived from various findings of recent science. Rather, my focus is on a much smaller part of the world—namely, those aspects of living things in general, and of primates in particular, that are capable of throwing light on the nature, characteristics, and status of the human mind. Therefore (in so far as it proves possible), I propose to confine attention in the remainder of the book to points of a relatively non-speculative sort, which the great majority of present-day empirical scientists, and scientifically inspired philosophers, would be willing to accept. (However—as mentioned before—it is important to note that, in my way of thinking, historians also count as "empirical, scientific investigators.")

Arthur O. Lovejoy claimed in his book, 1961, that the central organizing notion of Western biology prior to Darwin was "The Great Chain of Being." What does that mean? Early biologists thought of the Great Chain as an all-encompassing scale of life on earth—or in some versions, both heaven and earth—in which every possible species of living creatures (they claimed that every possible species also was actual) occupied a place that was either "higher" or "lower" than all the other places. In fact, the picture in question was more like a steeply sharpened pyramid than like a staircase, ladder, or chain, because they thought of it as having a very wide bottom, comprised of the simplest, most microscopic organisms, and a very narrow pinnacle consisting of just humans—or God—at the top.

Later, during the eighteenth and nineteenth centuries, other biologists, prominently including Charles Darwin, began appealing to systematic observations of both living organisms and fossils, in order first to criticize, and then to improve upon, this previously accepted view of the organization of life. The main revision these people proposed for the Great Chain was to "temporalize" it. In other words, they no longer presupposed the existence of a single, static, unchangeable hierarchy among species.

Instead, they now maintained (a) that each separate species was an independent product of many past evolutionary factors and pressures. And they also said (b) that all those pressures were not necessary expressions of God's Plan, but instead were more or less accidental. For instance, they rejected the once fashionable idea that it always was possible to draw a clear, God- or nature-given line between different species (for example ducks, geese, swans), but that there was no correspondingly objective difference between the varieties included within any species (such as mallards, teals, and golden-eyes). Rather, many of these early modern biologists (including Darwin) said that, equally in the case of both species and varieties, all the categories that people usually recognized were nothing more than arbitrary, temporary, and subjective designations. In other words, the list of species that was commonly accepted at any particular point in time (similar to the list of varieties) did not comprise objective categories that reflected the general structure of the world itself. Instead, species were just categories that particular thinkers and observers had created, in a more or less arbitrary fashion, in order to serve their personal interests and convenience.

The upshot, as noted in Chapter 1, was that critics of the Great Chain no longer thought of biology as a neat, metaphysical system. Instead, they reconceived of it as a messy, genealogical science. According to them, to say the same thing another way, the new basic job that biologists had to perform was the historical one of reconstructing the contingent, accidental routes through which creatures had come into existence. And because of this change, it now was necessary to think about any given organism, species, or genus, in terms of its relations of descent within its own "family-tree," and not in terms of its relations to the larger, extra-organic environment.

It is an obvious fact of the history of science that the program just outlined—paying attention to organisms' descent, as opposed to their connections with the outside world—has played a pivotal role in the development of present-day biology. Nevertheless, at least in some respects, it seems to me that this shift in emphasis now has become a barrier to further progress in our long struggle to transform biology from the fanciful metaphysics it once was, into a substantively empirical field of investigation. For example— again, a case mentioned in Chapter 1—certain evolutionists are now embroiled in a controversy about "punctuated equilibria" (see for instance Dennett 1995, pp. 282–303). People on opposite sides of this debate give systematically different answers to questions like these: Was Darwin right to insist that evolutionary development always took the form of a series of very small changes? Or have discoveries in the fossil record now proved that Thomas Henry Huxley was right to rebuke Darwin for having ignored the possibility of large, relatively rapid "jumps" that transported species from one fairly static stage of development to another such stage?[12]

The only contribution I have to make to this discussion is to remind readers of an obvious but neglected point. This is the idea that we cannot understand the evolution of any species in a proper or realistic way, unless we also take account of its development in relation to the environment. After all, creatures are not able to change in any respect, at any speed, or in any direction, that their physical situation does not allow for and support. It seems clear, for example, that some physical surroundings encourage them to develop certain bodily forms, dispositions, and behaviors; and other surroundings would discourage the characteristics just mentioned, and encourage them to develop other properties instead. Accordingly, I do not think it should be a controversial or debatable point, but instead, should be something that one fully expects to be the case, that evolutionary development is not always, or even usually, smoothly progressive. To make the same point another way, we should not find it surprising that creatures often develop in a "jerky" way, by moving rapidly from one fairly stable position to another. And the reason this should not be surprising is that such a pattern is a natural consequence of an important fact about development. The fact I am talking about is that the principal means by which organisms manage to survive and reproduce is by adopting one or more adaptive tricks from the limited repertoire of such strategies that, at any moment, their environment makes available to them.

What do I mean by "adaptive tricks"? Again, I propose to make four points about them. The first of these, consistent with

---

12. The rapidity of such transitions is not measured in hours, years, or even centuries. Instead, the events in question are "quick," relative to a much more encompassing time-scale.

the Platonic view of the universe explained before,[13] is that organisms' basic survival strategies are responses they make to certain abstract and general, but nevertheless physically real and objectively existing situations in nature. Furthermore, those situations (another name for them is "niches") have causal effects on those creatures that employ or occupy them. The special sort of causality in question here—which niches exert on their occupants—is not the simple, "billiard-ball," or "push" variety that the philosopher, David Hume, famously discussed. To be more precise, it is not just a matter of two (types of) events standing in a relation of precedence, contiguity, constant conjunction, and necessary connection. Rather, it is more analogous to the "pull" causality, which Aristotle attributed to what he called final causes. For example, this last sort of causality is something like the efficacy Aristotle attributed to his Unmoved Mover. According to Aristotle, the Unmoved Mover did not act as the source of movement for all other things by means of direct, physical action. Instead, it was only through the "admiration" those things had for it (their desire and their striving to be like it) that the Unmoved Mover caused them to move. Analogously, for instance, I think the environmental reason that flying squirrels evolved, when and where they did, is as follows: The earth's gravity; the composition and density of its atmosphere; and certain competitive interactions among middle-sized prey and predators in a temperate, tree-dwelling environment; combined to create an ecological niche, where creatures of that particular type were able to survive. Furthermore, the niche just described "drew into itself" (if that is not an overly anthropomorphic way of speaking), both tree-living, placental mammal rodents living in North America—"flying squirrels" proper—and also tree-living, marsupial non-rodents—"sugar gliders"—who lived in Australia.[14]

Second, we know from observation (as contrasted with the static conception implicit in the Great Chain) that niches also are capable of evolving and changing, and of coming into existence

---

13. Roughly speaking, these points are applications—for a special purpose—of the four, more general observations about the relations between particulars and universals made earlier in this section.

14. Observers report that, despite the fact that they are not at all closely related, it is difficult to distinguish animals of those two types, just by noting the physical appearance and behavior of each in its natural environment.

and going out of existence. However, the nature, direction, and speed of those changes are not determined by the properties and evolutionary history of the particular organisms that happen to occupy the niches at any given time. Instead, the changes are determined by the niches themselves, or (to speak of the same thing in alternative terms) by the environments in which those creatures are located. Consider another simple illustration: Scientists say that after the North and South American continents became joined as a result of movements of their underlying tectonic plates, a new competitive environment was created for the creatures that previously had lived in mutual isolation on the two sides of the divide. In other words, at that time, both these sets of creatures now found it necessary to respond to a whole new set of conditions, challenges, and rivals. Paleontologists bestowed the informal name of "bear-dogs" on one species of large, marsupial mammal predators from the South American side. The reason this name seemed appropriate to them was that those animals were similar in various respects to (placental, North American) dogs, and similar in other respects to (placental, North American) bears. That species became extinct soon after the joining of the continents. And some scientists speculate that the main reason for this extinction was the following point: The majority of its members were too heavy to run as fast as the newly introduced placental dogs from the north (such as wolves, coyotes, and foxes); but on the other hand, they also were not sufficiently heavy to defend themselves against attacks from the newly introduced placental bears. More generally, then, we can describe what happened at that time and place, by saying that the niche these animals had occupied in their previous environment now had disappeared (at least temporarily). And because of this, the same characteristics that once had contributed to their adaptive success, made it a foregone conclusion that they would not be able to survive for very long in their new circumstances, because those animals now "fell between" two other, newly dominant niches.

Third, there can be niches in nature that—again, at least temporarily—have no instances. For example, it is plausible to suppose (see Newman 1997 and Turner 1997) that, although there are no such animals alive at the present moment, the kind, *saber-toothed cat*, counts as a fixed and permanent natural category in this particular era of the earth's development. The reason I say this is that creatures of that sort have shown a strong tendency to reappear in the history of life, despite a long series of apparent "extinctions." (In fact, some people speculate—again see Newman 1997—that, if humans were to disappear tomorrow, saber-toothed cats again would inhabit the earth, within the space of no more than seven million years.)[15] Geological and fossil records show that ecological niches apparently can exist for quite a long time, before any group of organisms happens to discover them and learn to exploit them. For millions of years, for example, there were no predators that were capable of harvesting the rich potential bounty of night-flying insects, until certain small mammals—bats of certain types—finally learned to do this, by means of sonar and echo-location. (I also have mentioned this same example in another place. See 1990.)

Fourth and finally, even though humans have a habit of thinking of themselves as separate from the rest of nature, it is necessary to admit that similar points apply to our own species as well. Consider a simple example from the history of economics. There was a flurry of excitement when certain merchants first introduced the innovation of warehouses designed to sell goods (furniture, hardware, drugs, and so forth) in large quantities at discounted prices to retail customers. The crucial point was that these customers had to be willing (i) to reach these shopping destinations by driving long distances in their own vehicles, and (ii) to transport their purchases home by the same means. Some commentators predicted at the time—a prediction which later turned out to be accurate—that retail outlets of that sort would be part of our lives for many years to come. Why did these commentators say this? What justification did they give for their prediction? They said that the entrepreneurs in question had "discovered a new niche in the market." This case, and others that might have been mentioned instead, do not seem to me to be merely analogous to

---

15. The plausibility of this idea depends on one's specifying the category in question in fairly wide terms. For instance, it is not plausible to claim that "uniformly brown, four-toed, heavier than 80 kilograms, saber toothed cat" is the name of any objectively existing natural kind, because details included in that last formula are properties of the sort that are typically determined by concrete, accidental conditions in which a species happens to develop. To simplify even further, the reason *saber toothed cat* is a projectable kind but *uniformly brown saber toothed cat* is not, is that biological facts give us a right to expect that further instances of saber toothed cats eventually will appear, but do not justify the expectation that those animals will have any particular color or bodily form.

the biological topics we were discussing before. Instead, I think they are more or less literal instances of some of those same biological properties, conditions, and facts.

One might wish to ask various "background questions" at this point. For example: (a) Precisely which, and how many, ecological niches are investigators entitled to recognize in any given situation? (b) Can there be different levels of abstraction and generality among such niches, so that (for instance) some are relatively more specialized, derivative, "versions" of others? (c) If the answer to the preceding question is Yes, then what precisely is it that shows that the two niches stand in this special sort of relationship—i.e. the relationship of "general *vs.* particular"? (d) Which niches count as currently dominant, effective, or "live" in any given context, and which others are either inactive or merely potential?

Unlike Plato (see for instance his dialogue, *The Sophist*), I do not think these are questions of the sort that I, as a philosopher, am qualified to answer. Instead, working scientists must decide how to interpret and answer them. Furthermore, scientists' answers ought to be based on what their observations have shown to be the case, and even more specifically, on the hypotheses they have been forced to make, in order to account for empirical facts in the best possible way. In particular, they should decide whether any proposed ecological niche does or does not count as an actual constituent of the world, according to the causal force they find that niche to have. In other words, they should understand the words "existence" and "causal force" as reflecting the concrete explanatory value they have found posited niches to have. For example, if empirical investigation shows the best means of accounting for observed facts is to refer to the operation of hypothetical abstract places in nature A, B, and C, then this is a good reason for supposing that the posited niches A, B, and C really exist. On the other hand, if appealing to *prima facie* niches D, E, and F does not have such explanatory value, then one is justified in concluding that those last niches are merely "thought objects" that in fact do not exist.[16]

---

16. In this sense, the positions of scientific realism and instrumentalism are not necessarily incompatible. In fact, in some respects, they can be combined. To state the same point more specifically: We are justified in assuming that (aside from certain obvious

4.3 (Wide) Mind As a Lately Discovered Ecological Niche

What precisely is belief? Some philosophers of mind (such as P.M. Churchland 1981) deny, and others (such as Lycan forthcoming) affirm, that this category of mental activity amounts to an objectively existing, natural kind that scientific investigators someday will be able to discover, describe, and clarify, by means of neurological studies of the brain. In my opinion, the question of whether there actually are such things as beliefs and desires—considered as physically existing, discoverable parts of the brain (or any other part of the natural world)—is neither sharply enough defined, nor sufficiently meaningful, to be informatively explored by means of scientific investigation. Nevertheless, if one focuses attention on mind in a relatively broad sense of the word, rather than on the narrow and proper sense that has been the main topic of discussion in this book so far, then it seems to me that there is one fairly clear respect in which anti-eliminativists like Lycan are right, and eliminativists like P.M. Churchland are wrong. What I mean by this is that the existence of both belief and mind (again, in broad senses of these words) follows from the simple, observable fact that certain organisms engage in certain types of behavior.

Let me explain this further. I propose to interpret mind (and derivatively also, belief), in a broad sense, as an objectively existing, abstract, adaptive niche. Furthermore, this niche was one that had no instances—and in that respect, remained merely potential—for a long time. In other words, no species succeeded in identifying and occupying it, until a comparatively late date in evolutionary history. Still more specifically, I think the event just mentioned happened roughly two million years ago, at the time when certain early members of the branch of the primate order known as *Homo* apparently became the first earthly organisms to begin exploiting that niche. Thus, at least in one sense, the situation I am talking about is roughly analogous to the previously mentioned case of echo-locating bats.

---

exceptions) the hypotheses that scientists find most practically useful are also likely to be those that accurately describe and explain the world itself—those which posit real existents. (Discussions with Pavel Davydov helped me clarify my ideas on this point.)

Present-day biologists usually follow the method of trying to account for the vast majority of the adaptive relations in which organisms stand to their environment, by appealing to both innate and acquired attributes of the organisms themselves. But I think there are some respects in which that method now has shown itself to be inefficient, shortsighted, and misleading. To take a simple example, such an explanatory program might lead us to be puzzled about the following historical fact. Why were certain hominid primates able to occupy that which I refer to as the (broad) mind-niche, while their close cousins, common chimpanzees in the genus *Pan,* were not, even though these two groups were similar in their physiology and (at least to begin with) in their behavior? I suggest that the key to finding a solution to that problem is to take note of the fact that primates of those types were attempting to exploit, or fit themselves into, different ecological niches. Furthermore, the two niches in question had dissimilar (pull- rather than push-) causal effects on the animals themselves, which finally resulted in their developing importantly different physiological properties. A second example: Theorists often say (or assume) that bodily attributes already belonging to early hominids like *Homo habilis* and *Homo erectus,* were the factor that started those creatures down a distinctive adaptive path that increasingly diverged from the conservative, "backward looking" course taken by the ancestors of present-day chimpanzees.[17] But that way of looking at things seems to me to put the explanatory cart before the horse. It is better to say that

---

17. Here is still a third example that reminds us of how misleading such reasoning can be. Some paleoanthropologists were troubled by recent discoveries made beneath the ruined medieval fortress of Dmanisi in the republic of Georgia (part of the old Soviet Union). In that place, Georgian scientists unearthed remains—including several skulls and mandibles (jaws and teeth)—of a group of apparently very ancient (1.75 million years old), and very primitive, hominids. Yet, the story previously accepted among the great majority of experts had been that a later species, *Homo erectus,* was the first group of hominids to leave Africa. Furthermore, according to the accepted tale, that which allowed members of *Homo erectus* to do what they did was the fact that they had relatively large brains, as well as lanky bodily proportions, including long legs. However, the Dmanisi hominids, who apparently pre-dated *Homo erectus,* had small brains that were not much larger than those of the "founding" hominid, *Homo habilis.* (The leg bones of the Dmanisi hominids have not yet been found.) (See the account of these discoveries, and some of their revolutionary implications, in Rick Gore's article, 2002. It is surprising that, when Richard Klein and Blake Edgar discuss the Dmanisi hominids in their book, 2002, pp. 119–122, they fail to mention the point that the brains of those animals were considerably smaller than those of *Homo erectus.*)

the new behavioral niche that early hominids discovered—the new adaptive survival trick they learned to perform—was what led, prompted, and determined them to develop a new set of physiological properties that were missing in their chimpanzee-like cousins. Of course, this is not to suppose that there were any necessary laws that forced hominids to evolve in the direction they did, as opposed to the many other directions that also happened to be open to them at the same time. Rather, the causal processes involved here were "attractive" ones, whereby selective pressures gradually brought it about that those hominid offspring that were most likely to survive, were the ones who were relatively more capable of doing those things that allowed them fit into the newly uncovered niche.[18]

The nature of competition seems to dictate that only one species at a time is able to exploit some single, narrowly defined niche or, in other words, a certain economic or social opportunity.[19] For instance, it is conceivable that chimpanzees someday might move into the same (broad-mind-) niche that we now occupy. But—as analogies with other cases show—that situation would not be likely to occur, unless and until we sapiens first vacated that niche.[20] On the other hand, it is perhaps easier to imagine dolphins eventually developing into fully minded, symbolically and technologically sophisticated creatures like ourselves. The reason this last hypothesis is more plausible is that we live on land and dolphins live in water; and this fact largely prevents them from coming into direct competitive contact with us. Still another apparent implication of the picture I now am sketching is this: Imagine a future where all the primates on earth were destroyed

---

18. As Steven Mithen remarks (somewhere in 1996), if we keep in mind their respective histories of development, we should not find it surprising that human beings and chimpanzees behave in radically different ways, in spite of their similar bodily characteristics. In particular, according to him, all the features of humans that make them distinctive appeared during a single, extremely short amount of evolutionary time—namely, the period since the *Homo* branch of the primate order first began to diverge from the common ancestor of both humans and chimpanzees.

19. *Pace* Tattersall who (in 2000) argues on the basis of several instances that it is possible—and (for example) 1.8 million years ago, it also was actual—for several different, culture-bearing species of hominids to co-exist. However, my reply to Tattersall is that all his examples apparently show that the co-existence in question was a temporary one, since competitive pressures in each of those case made it likely that one of the species eventually would "win" and all the others would "lose."

20. Anthropologist Richard Alexander made roughly this same point in another place. See the report and discussion in Wenke 1999, of Alexander's 1979.

(or—looking backward—a possible past where primates never evolved in the first place). In that future (or past), we also can imagine that some entirely different type of (land) animals—such as raccoons, pigs, or dolphins with (re-) evolved legs—might have come to occupy roughly the same ecological place that we now have learned to exploit. This reflection reminds us, then, that primates of our particular type do not have any "natural right" to be the only group of earthly creatures who live, think, and operate in terms of highly developed symbol systems, cultures, and explicit—for example, written—histories.

Incidentally, the same, "exclusivizing" characteristic of competition just mentioned also might throw light on the fact that only a single species of hominids—*Homo sapiens*—continues to survive at the present time. Why, as far as we know for sure, are we no longer accompanied on earth by any of the numerous species of *Australopithecus* that once existed, or by representatives of other presumed ancestor- or cousin-species like *Homo habilis*, *Homo erectus*, *Homo heidelbergensis* or even the very recent *Homo neanderthalensis*? I think the most plausible answer is this: Even though all these species' ways of adjusting themselves to the world were not exactly the same as our way, their styles of life at least were sufficiently similar to ours, for all of them eventually to be replaced by us. One can formulate this point in a "neo-Darwinian" style, as follows: We survived and they did not because, up to the present moment, members of our species have learned to perform the general adaptive trick characteristic of the whole *Homo* line, in a more thorough, efficient, and effective fashion than any of our relatives.[21]

What are the characteristics of the particular ecological niche that I propose to equate with mind in the wide sense? Consistent with the style of investigation repeatedly illustrated in this book, my answer involves looking back to a beginning point in history. According to some scientists, the crucial thing that led to the evolution of the hominid primates—and thus eventually to us—was a geological occurrence. Roughly eight million years ago, tectonic forces created a new, "rift" valley running from north to south across eastern Africa, as well as a new range of mountains along

---

21. To be fair to Ian Tattersall, this is something like the view he also adopts in his 1998, Chapter 5.

this valley's western edge. These developments had a deep effect on the environment that existed there previously. In particular, as a result of it, east central Africa became drier than it had been in the past, so that a savanna, or sparsely treed grassland, was created out of what once had been dense forest. Furthermore, those changes segregated into two isolated groups, the once homogeneous population of chimpanzee-like primates that lived in central Africa. Thus, after the separation, each of those groups began to follow a somewhat different evolutionary path. More particularly, the animals in the west, who were not under great pressure to change their previous style of life, evolved into modern-day chimpanzees (the *Panidae*). But the ones in the east were faced with a stark choice. Either they had to develop a new repertoire of bodily forms and behaviors to allow them to adjust to life in an open environment, or die and become extinct. In response to that pressure, the eastern animals evolved into a much more variegated group of sub-species (the *Hominidae)*, than their western counterparts (see Coppens 1994, especially p. 92).

Despite this variation, there seem to have been some traits that all the eastern hominids shared. For example, they adopted, apparently without exception, an upright, two-footed posture that allowed them to see further on flat ground than primates who retained the all-fours posture typical of present-day chimpanzees and gorillas. This stance also enabled hominids to walk over land (as opposed to climbing trees) more proficiently than their chimpanzee-like cousins could do. And finally, this posture also provided a certain amount of protection against overheating, when the animals were exposed to direct, overhead sunlight.

In other respects, however, the groups that developed among the eastern African, hominid primates were quite different from one another. In general, paleontologists say, the eastern animals evolved in two directions. On the one hand (see *ibid.*, p. 95), the large australopithecines—in the style of modern gorillas—developed strong physiques, combined with a narrowly specialized, vegetarian diet. And, as opposed to this, primates in the *Homo* or human branch of the same genus evolved a large brain, which they used to support a more broad-ranging, opportunistic style of living and feeding—one that included stalking and catching prey animals for meat. Yves Coppens says this second strategy ultimately proved more fruitful, for at least two reasons. First, humans' larger brain gave them "a higher degree of reflection" and "a new curiosity" that allowed them to gain knowledge of things beyond their original situation. And second, the increased mobility these animals needed to satisfy their relatively unusual dietary needs enabled, or at least encouraged, them to venture far beyond the place, climatic conditions, and other environmental features, where they had evolved. (In fact, as Coppens remarks, it has resulted in their having spread over the entire earth, and even having begun to explore other planets in the solar system.)

Certain recent discoveries have shown that, even if Coppens's theory—commonly known as the "East-Side Story"—is basically correct, it is also far too simple. The first news I received about one discovery relevant to this point came from front-page stories in two newspapers—*The Toronto Star*, and *The Globe and Mail*—delivered to my door the morning of July 11th, 2002 (Peter Calamai 2002 and Stephen Strauss 2002). Investigators found an extremely ancient hominid skull—between seven and six million years old—in the central African country of Chad, located approximately 2,500 kilometers west of previous finds in the Rift Valley of east Africa. (See also Michel Brunet *et al.*—including Yves Coppens—2002.) What fundamental lesson can we learn from this discovery? Paleoanthropologist Bernard Wood suggested the following answer in a commentary he wrote for *Nature* (Wood 2002). We have a strong temptation to simplify history—especially our own. But in spite of that tendency, empirical findings are forcing us to recognize respects in which the world that existed several millions of years ago was just as complicated, tentative, accidental, and multi-directional as the one we live in today. Thus, he says, the newly found skull mentioned before is "compelling evidence that our own origins are as complex and as difficult to trace as those of any other group of organisms." For example, "because of the independent acquisition of similar shared characteristics (homoplasy), key hominid adaptations such as bipedalism, manual dexterity and a large brain are likely to have evolved more than once. So the evidence of one, or even a few, of the presumed distinguishing features of hominids might not be enough to link a new species with later hominids, let alone to identify it as the direct ancestor of modern humans." Also consider the following, summarizing remark of Wood's quoted in Calamai's article, 2002 (p. A23): "We keep thinking that the farther we go back, the complexity is going to fall away and we're going to be left with just one creature that is the origin of the human species. This discovery shows matters were no less complex seven million years ago."

However, nothing I have said or will say in this book depends for its truth or relevance to our general topic, on the issue of whether Coppens's account of human prehistory is precisely and literally correct. In fact, my claims about the importance for evolution of the causal power of ecological niches have received further support from some things Bernard Wood and other paleoanthropologists have said about "homoplasy."

Let us now move on to another matter. What were the first visible signs of the eventually world-transforming adaptive regime adopted by the human members of the primate family? Suppose that, *per impossibile*, we could transport modern observers back in time to east central Africa between three and two million years ago. This was the period when *Homo habilis* lived side by side with several other, upright-walking hominids, like *Australopithecus afarensis*, *Australopithicus africanus*, *Australopithicus robustus*, and *Paranthropus*. Some paleontologists say that about the only characteristic those hypothetical observers could use as a means of distinguishing primitive adult humans from other hominids is the special way early humans employed tools. Many other primates—such as chimpanzees, bonobos, gorillas, orangutans, and rhesus monkeys—are also users, and occasionally even constructors, of tools. Chimpanzees sometimes break off sticks to attack and beat their rivals, or pull branches off trees to get materials for building nests. Sometimes also, chimpanzees carefully assemble a number of tin cans or other metal objects in order to make noise for expressing anger, or to frighten off danger. And they strip leaves from twigs, to use for extracting edible termites from their holes. But these present-day, non-human primates (and, it is reasonable to surmise, the past, now extinct non-human hominids mentioned before) only make use of tools on a more or less opportunistic basis. In other words, if the tools themselves, or raw materials for their construction, are conveniently at hand whenever those animals feel a need to employ them, then they appropriate the tools for as long a time as strikes them as appropriate. By contrast, however, excavators often find stone tools of many different sorts along with remains of early humans. The regular proximity of such tools with human bones might be a sign that humans carried them constantly—on a non-opportunistic basis—almost as if they were permanent parts of the creatures themselves. (This is parallel to an argument the English political philosopher, John Locke, once proposed. According to Locke, our fundamental *prima facie* justification for laws against depriving any person of his or her property, is contained in the following two points: (a) Everyone is obviously entitled to have, and to exercise control over, his own body; and (b) possessions, in effect, are extensions of one's body.)

Of course, the apparent fact that early humans employed tools in a different fashion than their relations is nothing more than a surface phenomenon. What mental abilities prepared and allowed our ancestors to think about tools in this special way? It seems obvious that all the abilities in question were closely associated with humans' relatively large and complex brains. But aside from that point, what further, substantive proposals can we make about the mechanisms through which those powers worked? Extending a theme of Chapter 2, I suggest that one way those new mental capacities might have expressed themselves was by prompting humans to draw a sharper line than usual between themselves and the rest of the natural world. And this, in turn, might have made it comparatively natural and easy for them to get the idea of exploiting things in that world for their own purposes, by (so to speak) "drawing them across the line that divides non-self from self." Still another formulation of the same point is to say that evolution provided humans with an ability (also mentioned in Chapter 2) to "think objectively." That particular power is what I consider to be the kernel, core, or foundation of that which I refer to as mind in the wide sense.

4.4 Reason As a Still More Recently Discovered Way of Filling the Mind-Niche

It is possible to think about the changes that resulted in humans' occupying their present ecological niche in two, roughly complementary ways. The first is to consider matters from the viewpoint usually taken by evolutionary biologists, of simply listing the main "speciation events" that led to the appearance of *Homo sapiens*. For example, one might begin by noting the first appearance of the primates, about sixty-five million years ago—the date widely associated with the extinction of the dinosaurs (see Tattersall *et al.* 1988, p. xxvi). Then one might mention the beginning of the hominoid primates—the super-family containing both apes and humans) that occurred about twenty million years before the present (see *ibid.*, p. xxvii). After that, one could note the splitting off of the so-called australopithecines (such as the species *Australopithecus afarensis*) from the evolutionary line of the apes, which happened between four and three million years ago (*ibid.*, p. xxviii). Next, one could call attention to the earliest representative of the *Homo* line (*Homo habilis*) at a little under two million years ago. Then one could mention the apparently longest-lived species our genus ever had—namely, *Homo erectus*, which began about 1.7 million years ago (*ibid.*). Next, the theorist could take account of the appearance of our probable ancestor species, *Homo heidelbergensis*, which developed about 600,000 years ago in Africa (Tattersall 2000, p. 60), and our closely related, "cousin" species, *Homo neanderthalensis*, which originated in Europe or Western Asia a little over 200,000 years before the present (see Tattersall 1998, p. 151). Finally, one could end the series by pointing to the origin of our own species, again in Africa, probably between 200,000 and 150,000 years ago (Tattersall 2000, p. 61).

Alternatively, someone could consider human history from the point of view of cultural developments. For example, a person who took this second approach might begin by noting the appearance of the first stone tools, which seems to have been associated with early members of the *Homo* line itself, or their immediate australopithecine ancestors, and which happened between 2.5 and 2 million years ago (see Tattersall *et al.* 1988, p. xxviii, and Tattersall 2000, p. 61). After that, one could mention the development of bifacial tools (so-called Acheulean hand axes), which were the first to conform to an explicit plan or "mental template." They were apparently developed by the species *Homo erectus*, about 1.7–1.5 million years ago (see Tattersall *et al.*, p. xxix, and Tattersall 2000, p. 61). Then the person in question could point out that even if *Homo erectus* was not the first of our line to leave Africa, this species might have been the first to use fire, and to live in caves in addition to open sites (cf. *ibid.*, p. xxx). And he could note that the Neanderthals were the first hominids to wear clothing (see Tattersall 1999, p. 145), and to bury their dead (Tattersall 1998, pp. 161–64). Next, as also mentioned in Chapter 1, one could point out the innovations of art; of complex, syntactical speech; of religious consciousness; of long-distance trade, including sea-going navigation, which apparently did not begin until after members of the species *Homo sapiens* had entered the Upper Paleolithic—an event that took place between 60,000 and 30,000 years ago. Following that, there occurred the transition into the Neolithic era, about twelve to ten thousand years before the present. And later still—as argued in Chapter 3—there came the beginning of what we now commonly call reason, which (in my view) took place in Greece between 1100 and 750 B.C.E.

The theorists whose views I am criticizing in this book (people like Pinker, Lakoff, Chomsky, and the Churchlands) consider the first of these approaches far more important than the second. And I admit that these people are at least partly right to take this attitude. In particular, it probably is true to say that the first few items on the preceding, "cultural" list were produced in an automatic, "biological" fashion by certain innately given structures and powers present in early hominid brains. Nevertheless, it is almost certainly a mistake to suppose that the same thing happened in the case of the last few items. For example, consider humans' entry into the Neolithic age, which took place about 10,000 years ago. Were the advantages of farming, domesticating animals, living in cities, organizing governments, raising armies, and so on, so clear, obvious, and naturally inviting to humans that it was inevitable that they would "fall into" that mode of existence, at about the time, and in the places, that they did? Even more explicitly, can we talk about this and similar cultural changes in approximately the same terms as we also apply to biological events like the separation of the *Homo* line from that of the other hominids? The answer is No. Contrary to what Pinker and similar people say, the mind cannot simply be "what the brain does" in any of these last cases, because here the crucial thing is not just the brain, but what people decided, planned, and strived to do with, or by means of, their brains. For example, historians remind us that the "river-bottom" agriculture practiced in the original sites of civilized city-life—southern Iraq and the Nile valley—was a complicated, sophisticated, and therefore very non-intuitive style of life. And in view of that fact, it would have been virtual impossible for it to have come into existence through actions of individuals who were careless, disorganized, unreflective, and uneducated. To mention just a few of the relevant factors, this way of earning a living involved the selection, gathering, and storing of seeds of various wild grains; it presupposed a division of labor between farmers, artisans, administrators, and others; it required a co-operative program of irrigation and flood control; and it depended on a system of communal harvesting. Furthermore, all the things just mentioned could only have been results of foresight, planning, and cooperation between, a large number of trained, thoughtful, and talented people (see Wenke 1999, Chapter 6; Mithen 1996, pp. 217–226; and Starr 1991, pp. 14–23.)

To summarize, then, a "Pinkerian" approach may be capable of picking out and characterizing mind in a wide sense of this word. But it cannot also account for mind in the narrow, more proper sense that we also have come to consider important. Alternatively stated, even though it is plausible to describe early items in the preceding list of cultural innovations as "natural products of evolution," the same is not true of later ones. Instead, all the last events were not changes in thinking that people could share in equally, and all at more or less the same time, just by virtue of the way their brains were organized. Rather, those cultural transitions originated from special, unusually insightful individuals, who counted as their inventors and discoverers.

Which of the sciences we traditionally recognize today are capable of illuminating the general topic of mind? To answer that question, it is necessary to draw a distinction. If mind in the wide sense is the topic under discussion, then ordinary, evolutionary biology provides the best means of studying it. To be more precise, I maintain that mind in that sense is identical with humans' adaptive trick of making use of their innately given potential for objective thinking. And that adaptive trick, in turn, presupposes, expresses, and fits into a certain abstract—but nevertheless physical, and objectively existing—ecological niche.[22,23]

_____

22. *Human mind* may not be the only natural kind that scientific investigators need to consider in a special way. And if, in fact, there are a large number of other kinds that also require distinctive treatment, then this will show that we are not entitled to think of modern science as dualistic, since it does not just involve "twoness," but a still greater number of relatively unanalyzable categories as well.

23. Again, it is not necessary to attribute any deep cosmic significance to the existence of this or any other niche, in order to explain things in terms of it. In fact, the only

On the other hand, humans' adaptive strategy also has another aspect, part, or dimension. And therefore, as contrasted with mind in the broad sense, which is something that is primarily biological in character, mind in the narrower and stricter sense is primarily cultural. To be still more concrete, I identify mind in the narrow sense with what people nowadays call "reason."

Many philosophers have devised elaborate and subtle theories of reason. Consider two representative cases. Plato interpreted this word (or its Greek equivalent, "λόγος") as the ability, possessed by every normal person, to know and be guided by unchanging, abstract Essences, Universals, or Forms, located in an unseen, "intelligible world." That ability stood in contrast with the ordinary, non-controversial ability to be aware of constantly changing, sensible objects in the world of everyday experience. Similarly, Descartes claimed that "reason" (in French, "*conaissence*") was the innately given, inner light that allowed normal, sane, adult people to distinguish right from wrong, good from bad (especially, good from bad arguments), and which also allowed such people to separate truth from falsity. I shall not propose another such technical theory of reason here. Rather, I am content to understand this word in the same informal, fairly vague way as the majority of people do today, whenever they talk about reason in non-technical and unspecialized contexts.

Present-day humans have learned to occupy their niche in a way that, in some respects, is more efficient and productive than their ancestors' way of occupying that same niche. The means by which recent people managed to do this was by leaving behind the former strategy of using natural, innately given intellectual resources to fit themselves into the niche, and appealing instead to consciously adopted, *cultural* resources.

Let me explain this further. Throughout most of its history, Western philosophy has been divided between the views of "empiricists" like Aristotle, Aquinas, Locke, Berkeley, and Hume, and "rationalists" like Plato, Augustine, Descartes, Spinoza, and Leibniz, about the ultimate source and justification of human

---

evidence we have for believing the (wide) mind-niche exists is simply that evolutionary biologists find it useful to appeal to it. Thus, for example, to describe the ecological niche associated with wide mind as physically real is the same as saying that it amounts to what Daniel Dennett has called a "robust pattern among natural entities" (see his 1991).

knowledge. Thinkers in the first group say that all our knowledge only can arise from sensuous experience. For example, one shibboleth by which they define their position is: "Nothing in the mind that was not first in the senses." On the other hand, the second group claims that all knowledge (or at least its most important parts) is inborn; and therefore sensory experience only can stimulate or trigger the expression of such knowledge—for example, help us "recall" it—but cannot create it in the first place.

This debate is no longer a live issue. Today most philosophers do not accept either one of these positions, because they consider a choice between empiricism and rationalism to be unrealistically simple. In particular, it has become clear from experimental investigations that we cannot understand the human mind in terms of either of these two a priori hypotheses, because virtually everything humans "know" is a mixture of elements that are both empirical (learned) and innate (unlearned).

I consider this last point a triumph of scientific observation over a priori speculation. Nevertheless, it seems to me that the theorists I am criticizing in this book have drifted back in the direction of such an old-fashioned, a priori method once again. When they say that brain is always of more explanatory value than mind, this carries the implication that philosophers like Plato are consistently right, and those like Locke consistently wrong, since the sources of knowledge are always "tilted" in a Platonic rather than Lockean direction. But it is at least questionable whether empirical facts justify any such claim.

Almost all the cultural features of human societies depend in a crucial fashion on our species' ability to think, not just directly—in terms of the perceived characteristics of things—but indirectly—by means of arbitrarily defined, learned symbols. Similarly, the thought-strategies we now call "reason" are an intellectual invention that depends on that same ability to think symbolically. To be more precise, reason is an objective method of solving problems where, rather than trying to puzzle out matters by paying attention to how things "strike" us, or by appealing to various different innately given dispositions, and long-standing learned habits and traditions, one tries to arrive at answers by considering each puzzling phenomenon afresh, and strictly in its own terms.

Thus, reason's main effect on us is to strengthen our ability to think about things objectively, by making thought of that sort more uniform, consistent, and powerful than it otherwise would have been, if this strategy never had been thought of. In doing this, reason enabled some people—the ones who founded Western Culture—to find and occupy the ecological niche common to all humans ("mind in the wide sense") in a more efficient, complete, and successful way than their competitors.

Consider an analogy: I think of reason as something like clothes or, still more narrowly, like shoes. A few years ago, posters appeared in the Toronto subway describing a certain brand of running shoes as "Feet You Wear." This claim was meant to be paradoxical, since if someone already had two feet, what could possibly motivate him or her to buy another, artificially constructed pair of "feet" to wear on, over, and under those he already possessed? But the solution is this. We humans are better able to perform certain activities characteristic of our species, like walking and running upright over hard surfaces or through rough country, when we wear shoes or boots, than when we are barefoot. In this same sense, in fact, we are always "more ourselves" when clothed and shod, than when we appear in our unencumbered, God- or evolution-given, supposedly "natural" state. Similarly, I suggest that reason is a culturally based, artificial invention that has allowed us to improve upon one of our evolutionary, and in this sense *non*-cultural, adaptations.

Of course, there are also disanalogies here. For example, we do not find it easy to forget that clothes, along with many other things employed in everyday life (such as houses, automobiles, airplanes, clocks, shovels, and pencils) are artificial, invented, and manufactured items, because of the fact that we were not born with them. By contrast, it is much easier to overlook the artificial and cultural nature of reason, because it is an intellectual rather than physical invention, and therefore is "invisible."

Some modern historians of the ancient world assume that reason is part of the innately given, non-pathological condition that rightfully belongs to all adult humans. Accordingly, they also suppose it could not possibly amount to a cultural innovation that one generation of thinkers had to develop, and then pass along to succeeding generations by means of teaching and learning. For example, H.W.F. Saggs directs his readers' attention (see Saggs 1989, pp. 255–265) to certain examples of anti-superstitious, anti-magical thinking that appeared in Mesopotamian cuneiform medical texts of the third, second, and first millennia B.C.E. In place of the old-fashioned method of prescribing incantations against the anger of the gods, the ancient authors in question seemed to have learned to diagnose medical problems (wounds, diseases) in terms of intrinsic and objectively perceivable features of the diseases themselves. But Saggs talks about these cases as if they represented a transition from a previous dark, unnatural condition, where people were only capable of appealing to certain mysterious, "numinous" powers, into the light of healthy common sense, where the medical thinkers finally began to see things rightly, as they always had been meant to see them.

But is this way of talking correct? Did these particular Mesopotamian writers succeed in achieving the intellectual sanity that was always their birthright as normal, healthy, adult humans? If the answer to this question is Yes, then how is it possible to explain the fact that these people were not able—as Saggs also reports—to influence and convince other, later writers to keep moving in this "natural" (correct) direction? Why, instead, did subsequent generations of doctors in Mesopotamia revert to all the same errors of superstition that had been present in the great majority of the generations of medical workers that had preceded them? The answer, as Saggs himself admits, is that any such fundamental and relatively permanent change in medical thinking and techniques was not able to take place, unless and until the ground for it had been prepared by an upheaval that completely "smashed the mold" of previously accepted ways of thinking (p. 255).

What form did that intellectual upheaval take? And when did it occur? Almost all modern historians of the ancient period propose similar answers these questions. They identify the required upheaval with the event I referred to in Chapter 3 as "the Greek revolution." Saggs himself also seems to agree with this view, as shown by the paragraph with which he ends his book. That paragraph reads (in part):

Those who had begun to think over the problems of life in this non-mythological way were of course only a tiny segment of the population.

. . . But the presence of such men in the community, and of those in the scribal schools who read and copied and re-copied such works, was a leaven, which gradually—not in a few years or decades but over centuries—began to erode the old mythological verities, and to prepare the Near Eastern world to receive the new ways of thought about the world and man's place in it, which were to come *from Greece*. (Saggs 1989, p. 301; italics added)

If we assume that the change described by Saggs and other historians was not an inexplicable miracle, then it now is necessary to return to a theme discussed in a preliminary fashion before. That is the question of what characteristics of the pre-Classical Greek world explain the fact that the event just mentioned happened there and then, rather than at some other place and time, or not at all? Another, related puzzle is this: In what respects, and to what extent, does reason count as "natural"? In particular, did humans obtain reason by just extending and generalizing certain characteristics they already had received from evolution? Or was it necessary for them first to suspend, and then also to transform, many of those naturally acquired tendencies, in order to acquire it? It seems to me that the second alternative is right. In other words, even though reason is the "capstone" of the mind-niche— the adaptive strategy that most clearly separates us from all other creatures—in some respects, it is antithetical to many of the natural characteristics involved in being an animal, a mammal, and a primate. Thus, rather than a "culmination" of innate biological tendencies, the best way to think of the invention of reason is as still another cultural revolution in the development of our species—i.e. something that made a difference of kind rather than degree.

Chapter 5

A Short, Speculative History of Reason

[T]he answer to such questions as "Why can humans reason?" lies as much and as deeply in the quirky pathways of contingent history as in the physiology of neurons.

—Stephen Jay Gould (1989, p. 281)

5.1 Barbarian Simplicity

There is an intimate relation between the question of exactly what reason (or what I also call "mind in the narrow sense") is, and the further question of how reason came into being. Accordingly, the main thing I want to do in this final chapter is to shed light on the first of these issues, by telling a more or less plausible tale about the second.

Since I am not a professional historian, the story I shall set forth will be a broad, speculative one based on conclusions of other people, rather than a report of original investigations of my own. I do not claim that this story can be shown to be true. I only say that something more or less similar to it is likely to have happened in the past times and places mentioned in the following pages. Finally, my overall concern in this book has been to set forth a hypothesis about the number and nature of the main stages of human intellectual development, in the light of recent advances in scientific knowledge. And my reason for choosing to elaborate this particular imaginative tale is to make one more contribution to that general plan.

Let me begin by saying a few words about the special sort of "scientific knowledge" in question here. I do not believe that scientific work has established the truth of the claim, made by thinkers like Plato, Aristotle, Aquinas, Ockham, Descartes, Kant, and Chomsky, that reason is an inborn, nature- or God-given source of special knowledge and insight. Nor does it seem to me that such investigations have proved that reason is identical with mind, and that mind in turn is identical with certain parts and aspects of the brain. Rather, reflection on results of empirical investigations (prominently including those of historians) has led me to draw a different conclusion—namely, that reason is a cultural phenomenon. To be more specific, I am going to argue at greater length here for the idea, already defended in previous chapters, that the best way to conceive of reason in the narrow and most proper sense of this word is as a style, method, or program of thinking and behaving that one or several now unknown individuals living in the pre-Classical Greek world thought of, and thereby invented.

Reason in this sense includes at least the following three properties, phases, or marks:[1]

(a) recognition of a potentially sharp, mutually exclusive, and exhaustive distinction between truth on the one hand, and falsehood on the other, and a determination to try to preserve that distinction in as systematic and consistent a way as possible;

(b) acceptance of the ideal of the objectivity of truth, according to which every true declarative statement corresponds to only one existing state of affairs, all of whose properties are what they are, independently of any personal factors;

(c) commitment to the investigative method of establishing truth exclusively on the basis of intrinsic, perceptible evidence about the matter in question itself, as contrasted with considerations about supposed indirect, purposeful, or magical influences emanating from external factors (such as demonic or spiritual forces).

Skeptical readers might object that this combination of ideals and procedures is something obvious, inevitable, and therefore also trivial, as proved by the fact that there is no coherent alternative to it. My response is to say that there in fact is such an alternative, and Western history shows what that alternative is. In particular, careful examination of the human past shows that the vast majority of our fellow species members who lived before the time of pre-Classical Greece did not think in terms of the points just listed. For example, these ancient people tended to conceive of the world as controlled by invisible, Animistic forces. To refer again to an example proposed by Saggs, which I discussed at the end of the previous chapter, most of them considered it fruitless to try to cure a disease by paying attention to properties of the disease itself. This was because they assumed that all such properties were nothing more than impotent and misleading surface

---

1. In previous chapters, I mostly talked about reason and the mind in a fairly informal way. But in this paragraph (mainly just to show it is possible to do so) I express my views more rigorously. Nevertheless, what I say now is still only a tentative hypothesis. And therefore, not a great deal hangs on the precise number or precise formulation of the above points.

phenomena; but the crucial thing was the intentions, plans, values, and desires of the hidden, intelligent, (usually evil) agents who had brought about the disease in the first place.

Why do I think pre-Classical Greeks invented reason, rather than members of some other, superficially similar cultural group that existed around the same time? Consider the following. In the course of a funeral oration for Greek soldiers killed in battle against the Persians at Marathon, the Athenian politician Pericles made the now famous prediction that "future generations will marvel at us." Later events showed that this was not an idle, arrogant boast, but was literally correct. Thus, what exactly about the ancient Greeks should later observers like us find marvelous? Of course, it is appropriate for us to be impressed with Pericles's period, city, and cultural environment, because that was when and where all the major arts and sciences now recognized throughout the world received their first clear expressions and definitions. We also should honor the fact that this was where the democratic form of government was invented, under which many inhabitants of the earth now either live or aspire to live. But something that should strike us as even more impressive is the earlier, hypothetical intellectual event that apparently started it all—which inaugurated the brief, brilliant period that later culminated in the achievements of Classical Greece. I claim that this "foundational" or "seed" event was nothing more nor less than the devising of a novel set of methods for thinking, inquiring, and assessing evidence. Those methods then provided the intellectual underpinning, not just for the era of Pericles, but for our own, world-wide society as well.

Theodor Gomperz was a philosopher and historian who lived in Austria in the late nineteenth and early twentieth centuries. I find him an interesting person, if only because of the fact that he also devoted a great deal of thought to the question of what made the early, pre-Classical Greeks distinctive (see 1901/1964, pp. 3–42). According to him, for example, one possible source of the special accomplishments of those people was the geography of the Greek mainland. At the time in question (the Greek Middle Ages), the population of the mainland was going through a phase of rapid expansion. But in spite of that, it was very poor in natural resources. Greece had a relatively small landmass. And its terrain was mountainous, with thin, rocky soil, so that its inhabitants could only farm a few narrow river valleys.[2] As a result, local agriculture and forestry were not able to support its inhabitants adequately. However, the country also possessed a long shoreline that included many sheltered bays and harbors. And therefore it was natural for Greeks of the period to look to the sea for alternative means of earning a living. In addition to the profession of fishing, this meant that many of them chose to become merchants who organized sea-going trading expeditions to the foreign lands and peoples along the shores of the Mediterranean and Black Seas. The way still other Greeks tried to support themselves was by emigrating from the mainland altogether, and establishing colonies among those same foreign groups. All these developments had an effect on the Greeks' usual habits of thinking. In particular, their exposure to other cultural groups quickly taught them that they would not be able to compete effectively as merchants and traders—nor could their colonies become important sources of wealth—unless they set about to learn as much as they could about those other cultures. Accordingly, this then led them to try to approximate (in their own way), or even to equal, the achievements of those other peoples.

What were the most important ancient civilizations to whom Greeks of that period were exposed? Some relatively recent philosophical commentators (as an example see Dewey 1920/1960) blandly assume that the Greeks must have been the dominant force in the eastern Mediterranean, almost from the beginning of their existence as a people. But Gomperz, who had a better grasp of the history of that time and place, did not agree. He considered it significant that the shorelines of Greece "pointed in the direction" of the then principal centers of Near Eastern civilization, located in Egypt and in Mesopotamia (present-day Iraq). More especially, it happened to be the case that the Greeks were close enough to, and had sufficiently intimate dealings with, the people living in those two centers to be informed and inspired by them. But they were also far enough removed, to resist being dominated and swallowed up by either of these older, more powerful, and more confident civilizations.

---

2. Furthermore, many of its forests and much of its farmland had been effectively ruined by previous mismanagement. See Editors of Time-Life Books 1991, pp. 44–48.

Another geographical factor Gomperz emphasized had to do with the mountainous landscape of mainland Greece. He argued that it was difficult for ancient inhabitants of open, broad river-plains like those of the Nile and Tigris-Euphrates (where communal irrigation made every person more or less dependent on every other) to escape the notice and intimate control of centralized political, military, and religious authorities. And this in turn, he said, might have made it hard for people of that sort to devise ideals of objective, person-independent evidence and truth, like those summarized at the beginning of this chapter. By contrast, the steep mountain valleys in Greece provided their inhabitants with a certain amount of isolation and personal safety. And this may have made it relatively natural for Greeks to think of, and then begin to employ in their own lives, those once novel techniques and standards of thought.[3]

In any case, however, no matter whether Gomperz's claims about possible geographical influences are true or false, I now want to point out a *cultural* factor that, it seems to me, even sophisticated and informed investigators like him have failed to emphasize adequately. It is that many inhabitants of the Mediterranean, Black Sea, and Persian Gulf regions of the period (especially the Egyptians and Mesopotamians) considered the Greeks to be uncouth barbarians. More specifically, those relatively more cultivated people expected Greeks to behave, speak, and think in ways that were unsubtle, uninformed, careless, and lazy. In their opinion, for example, the Greeks tended to be insensitive to many realities present in the world around them—especially, spiritual and divine realities. Thus, consider the rituals that regularly took place in a typical Egyptian temple. The main job of an Egyptian priest was to accomplish the daily bathing, care, and preparation of a god (*not* just the god's image; see Wilson 1946b, pp. 71ff). But before he did anything else, his first duty was always to recite the ordered list of the various names and titles that belonged to the god in question, as well as to mention that god's relationships to the other gods in the large Egyptian pan-

---

3. Gomperz also hypothesized (as an aside) that the clear reasoning, sharp distinctions, and so forth, we now associate with the thought of ancient Greeks may have been causally connected with the weather conditions—"brilliant air and bright sky" (1901/1964, p. 27)—typical of many parts of that country.

theon. At the end of that recitation—which took a considerable amount of time—the priest would declare proudly, "I have not equated your nature with that of any other god" (see Hornung 1990, p. 185). Priests who performed those rituals probably assumed (and probably were correct to do so) that most Greeks were unsuited to perform, and perhaps even to comprehend, anything of the same sort. After all, their everyday experience with Greek visitors had taught them that these foreigners characteristically lacked the patience, delicacy, and sense of reverence for tradition and spiritual matters that would be required for such comprehension.

One illustration of the value the Egyptians attached to "civilized" behavior and thought of the sort just mentioned was the attitude they took towards the Hyksos. This last name is the one historians now give the "Asiatic" people who first infiltrated, then finally also invaded the Delta region of Egypt, from a home base somewhere in Palestine, at the end of the Middle Kingdom, beginning about 1720 B.C.E. The Hyksos went on to rule large parts of Egypt for about a century—setting up their own, parallel dynasty of pharaohs—before finally being expelled by armies of the native Egyptian pharaoh, Ahmose, at the beginning of what we now refer to as the New Kingdom period (see Grimal 1994, Chapter 8).[4] After the Egyptians had succeeded in defeating and banishing all the Hyksos from the country, how did the restored pharaohs of the New Kingdom try to explain and justify, both to themselves and to their people, the humiliating series of defeats and disasters, and the great suffering, that had been associated with the Second Intermediate Period just mentioned? The answer was that they blamed almost all the bad things that had happened on the now expelled invaders. To be more specific, they claimed the basic cause of the recent troubles was the fact that the Hyksos usurpers were ignorant, non-Egyptian barbarians, whose "priests" had been unable or unwilling to recite the names and titles of the

---

4. Some commentators on the Bible's first book, *Genesis*, speculate that one factor that allowed Joseph—an impoverished, unknown, and unconnected immigrant—to gain the attention and eventually the trust of the Egyptian pharaoh, so as finally to be appointed as his Overseer or Vizier, was the fact that this particular pharaoh was one of the Hyksos invaders. Because of that, according to the commentators in question, the pharaoh thought of Joseph as a fellow Palestinian, whom he found it easy to understand, accept, and choose as his deputy. See Wright 1974, pp. 30–31.

gods in proper order. Thus, because of this and similar failings, it was obvious to the Egyptians that the gods had not been willing to listen to them (see Hornung 1990, p. 165 and D.M. Johnson 2000).

Notwithstanding the uniformly negative attitude the Egyptians and Mesopotamians took towards people like the Hyksos and the Greeks, it seems clear that there are some circumstances in which—and purposes for which—a careless, lazy, barbarian-like attitude can be advantageous. (It goes without saying that whether or not this is true depends on many details—for example, on precisely what corners are being cut, how one proposes to cut them, and so forth.) For example, representatives of great civilizations often have a proud, conservative attitude that prompts them to try to preserve every bit of their "cultural baggage." And this in turn might unnecessarily complicate and confuse things. Thus, a simpler, more barbarian-like way of thinking sometimes could be preferable to pedantic precision, because it might make it possible to understand a situation more clearly and accurately, and to deal with it more effectively.

Consider the following example. From a modern viewpoint, the Egyptian system of hieroglyphic writing looks like a needlessly arbitrary, complicated, and inefficient hodgepodge. Some of its signs ("uniliterals") stand for sounds that English speakers and writers would express by means of single consonants. (It has no means of representing vowels.) For instance, the picture of an owl stands for approximately the same sound as the English letter "m"; the picture of a quail chick is a sign for the sound "w"; the jagged line that Egyptians used as a schematic depiction of water represents our sound "n." Signs of another sort ("biliterals") stand for syllables that we would write with two consonants. The picture of a face represents the sound "hr"; the picture of a swallow represents the sound "wr." Other signs ("triliterals") stand for syllables we would write with (at least) three consonants. The picture of a sandal strap stands for the sound "ankh"; the picture of a beetle or scarab for the two-syllable sound "kheper." Still others do not stand for any sounds at all, but have something like the pictorial function that presumably belonged to all hieroglyphic signs originally—the function of representing the things of which they were pictures. The Egyptians often added such non-sounding signs to phonetic formulas, to act as determinatives—roughly analogous to present-day dollar signs, hearts, smiling faces, etc.—to provide disambiguating guides to the intended meaning. For example, it is possible to pronounce the combination of hieroglyphic signs, "hnw" (square-spiral, water, quail chick), in quite a few different ways (for instance, as either "hinew" or "ohanow"). And each of these ways expresses a word with a separate meaning. Because of that, whenever those signs or letters occur together, the writer also must add to them, one of several different determinatives. When the signs are followed by a picture of a beer pot, they have the meaning (and sound) of "liquid measure." When they are followed by a picture of a seated man with a raised hand, they mean (and sound as) "rejoicing." When followed by pictures of a seated man together with a seated woman, they mean (and stand for the sound appropriate to) "neighbors" (see Casson *et al.* 1965, pp. 149–157).[5]

Why, in spite of the time-consuming labor and inconvenience associated with the hieroglyphic writing system, and the various possible misunderstandings it invited, did this system survive in essentially unchanged form for thousands of years? The answer, almost certainly, is that, after a short introductory period, this system acquired the authority and power of tradition. The accidental fact that many of the country's historical records, literature, rituals, spells, and so forth, already had been set down in that form, meant that any later attempt to adopt some less cumbersome method of writing would have rendered large parts of their cultural tradition inaccessible to many Egyptians. (A parallel: Why do we not adopt a more logical and efficient arrangement of the keys on our typewriters and computer keyboards today? The simple answer is that it is too late.) Probably also, the priests, who (as the name implies) were the principal users of hieroglyphics, must have found it advantageous to preserve the complexities of that way of writing, in order to make their positions more important, mysterious, and secure (see Saggs 1989, p. 74). Nevertheless, in comparison with all those other factors, I think a still more important consideration was that the Egyptians had come to consider hieroglyphics a time-honored, authentic,

---

5. Readers interested in looking further into these matters can find a useful guide in Collier and Manley 1998.

beautiful, and gods-given expression of the distinctive properties and values of their society.[6]

After 1000 B.C.E., the alphabetic system of writing gradually started to displace Egyptian hieroglyphics. Where and how did this new sort of writing originate? The answer is that it was not invented by the leaders of civilized life in the Mediterranean region. Instead, tradition tells us it began with the Canaanite Phoenicians who, at the time, were low-status inhabitants of an obscure cultural backwater. An explanation for this paradox may lie in the fact that, unlike the Egyptians, Sumerians, and Babylonians, the Phoenicians did not have much to lose by experimenting with new conventions for writing. Some of their contemporaries might have said of them, "They did not know any better" (see Saggs, p. 83).

Later (about 850 B.C.E.) the Greeks—who, again, had a reputation of being just as barbaric as the Hyksos and Phoenicians—also adopted alphabetic writing. Because they used it to write their own, Indo-European language, as contrasted with languages like Phoenician and Egyptian, it was natural for them to extend the system by employing symbols for vowels as well as consonants. This made alphabetic writing more uniform and consistent than it had been before (*ibid.*, p. 88).

Still another desirable result that apparently arose from "barbarian simplicity" was the development of more efficient techniques of elementary mathematical calculation. Saggs says (*ibid.*, pp. 220ff) that although the Mesopotamians had made quite a few advances in this area (even developing algebraic processes), the extreme cultural conservatism of the Egyptians had led them to "freeze" their calculating methods at a permanently primitive level (also see Gillings 1972, pp. 11–15).

In general, the Egyptians only employed the single arithmetical procedure of addition, but manipulated it in such a way as to achieve multiplication and division as well. Thus, suppose a scribe wanted to multiply one number, by another that was greater than 2. To adopt an example proposed by Saggs, consider the case of

---

6. Egyptians may not have considered foreigners to be genuine people at all. One indication of this is the fact that they used the same word ("*ramesh*") to mean both "human being" and "Egyptian" (see John Wilson 1946a, 41 and D.M. Johnson 2000).

19 multiplied by 23. First the calculator would multiply 19 by 2, by adding 19 to itself, with the result of 38. Then he would multiply 19 by 4, by adding 38 to 38, providing the result of 76. Next he would multiply 19 by 8 by adding 76 to 76, giving 152. And finally he would multiply 19 by 16 by adding 152 to 152, giving 304.

The scribe would set out these results as follows:

1	19
2	38
4	76
8	152
16	304

He would look to see which of the multipliers added up to 23. In this case, the answer was 1, 2, 4, 16. He then would add up the numbers in the right-hand column that corresponded to those multipliers in the left-hand column—he would add 19 + 38 + 76 + 304. And this provided the correct answer, 437.

For division, they employed the reverse or inverse technique. To take the corresponding example, suppose the problem was to divide 437 by 19. In that case, the scribe would begin by setting out the same numbers, in the same form, as in the preceding table—making sure that the numbers in the right-hand column were sufficient to add up to more than 437. He would inspect the numbers on the right to see if there was a set of numbers that added up to exactly 437. In this case, 304 + 76 + 38 + 19 did so. Then, by adding up the opposite numbers on the left side, 16 + 4 + 2 + 1, he obtained the right answer—namely, 23.

If the answer in a division problem was not a whole number, then it was necessary to introduce fractions. (With the exception of 2/3, according to Saggs, the only fractions the Egyptians recognized were unitary ones of the form 1/n. If no single term was able to provide the fractional number they wanted, then they represented the required number by means of two or more terms, each having the form 1/n. For instance, 5/6 was represented as $^1/_2$ (+) 1/3.) Again employing Saggs's example, suppose the problem was to divide 25 by 8. The scribe would write down

The numbers in the right hand column marked with an asterisk are the ones required to make up 25. Therefore the correct answer is the sum of the corresponding numbers in the left-hand column—1 + 2 + 1/8 = 3 1/8.

How could the Egyptians have allowed themselves to become mired in such awkward and labor-intensive methods of calculating as these—especially when the Mesopotamians were using more elegant, powerful, and quicker techniques at the same time, which the Egyptians might have borrowed for their own use? Again, the probable answer is that they followed these traditional rules, because those rules had become "fossilized" in their society. After all, many Egyptians arrogantly supposed that—at least on average—members of their own cultural group were more stable, loyal, reverent, and patient than other people. And this attitude often made them willing to act in ways that would strike outsiders like us as ponderous, awkward, puzzling, and stupid, as long as those ways had the desirable effect of affirming their "Egyptianness."

How could a Greek thinker like Euclid have developed an inferential system of plain geometry, in a way that summed up, and abstracted from, the work of many other mathematicians, when the Egyptians' achievements in this field were so different? (The Egyptian's geometry at the same time was not much more than a set of practical methods for constructing buildings, for sailing ships, and for surveying fields.) Part of the answer may be that the Greeks' intellectual abilities in this area resulted from the fact that—at that time—they were not burdened with any complex, ancient, prestigious, culturally validated system of thought that they felt obliged to preserve. Instead, they were prepared—with barbarian-like directness, simplicity, and freedom—to ignore the many, sometimes slight differences that always distinguish one concrete case from another. This freedom then allowed them, for example, to formulate principles, and draw conclusions, about *all* parallel lines, *all* circles, and *all* tangents. And, as is clear from the previous examples, the leaders of Egyptian society would have considered any such manner of thinking strange, troubling, careless, foreign, and barbaric.

I claim, then, that one method the Greeks used to compete with the older and wiser civilizations of the Mediterranean-Persian Gulf area was not to try to beat more sophisticated and established thinkers at their own game. Instead, they invented a new game that turned an Egyptian vice into a Greek virtue. They rejected the previously dominant notion that thinking (in a style analogous to seeing) should reproduce parts of the concrete world itself, in all their complexity, diversity, and particularity. Instead they began to grasp the point that all ideas were essentially general, and therefore the natural task of a thinker was to uncover general characteristics shared by many, superficially different cases. With the passage of time, this second program became the new "default position" that thinkers all over the world accepted.

Thus, it was not just relatively specific intellectual inventions, like alphabetic writing and more efficient techniques of mathematical calculation, which first came into being on the outskirts of ancient, Near Eastern civilization. Something like the same thing also happened in the more inclusive case of reason itself. To make the same point in slightly different terms, historians tell us that modern science began (in the Renaissance and post-Renaissance periods) as a reactionary, anti-intellectual movement that was as much or more concerned to denounce old falsehoods, as to discover and proclaim new truths. My thesis in this first section of the chapter is similar. It is that—at least in part—the method of thinking we now identify as "reason" also originated as a revolutionary reaction, in the name of directness and simplicity, against previously accepted methods that, by that time, had increasingly come to be seen as arbitrary, inefficient, and needlessly complicated.

5.2 *Lingua Franca*: Reason's Connection with Commercialism and Cosmopolitanism

There were many semi-barbarous nations in the ancient Near East. And quite a few of them lived in approximately the same physical and cultural conditions as those mentioned by

Gomperz—mountainous terrain, a long coastline, clear weather, impoverished circumstances, fairly direct access to important cultural centers. Why and how did the Greeks, as opposed to, say, the Phoenicians, the Hyksos, the Libyans, or the Hittites, manage to invent reason? Understood strictly, this question has no answer. That is, in the final analysis, all one can say about the events of contingent human history is that they occurred when, where, and how they did, and leave matters at that. Nevertheless, it also seems clear that some factors predispose history to move in certain directions rather than others. And by virtue of that last point, it cannot be a waste of time to inquire whether the thinking of pre-Classical Greeks, compared with superficially similar styles of thought typical of other groups sharing roughly the same conditions at roughly the same time, had any distinctive properties, which might have "nudged" them toward the invention of reason.

Now consider a simple story. One day, for recreation, I happened to read a magazine article on another, unrelated topic (Conlon 1997). That article contained the following sentence:

> Simon Weil in a 1940 essay on "the Iliad" argues that the greatness of Homer's epic lies in its equal treatment of enemies—treatment that makes it easy for one to forget that its author was Greek rather than Trojan.

That led me to begin wondering about two things: (a) Was Weil's (and Conlon's) statement about Homer true? And (b) did Homer count as a typical representative, not just of Greek literature of his time, but of the whole awakening cultural environment around him? If the answer to both those questions was Yes, then a promising way of summarizing the distinctiveness of pre-Classical Greek thought might be to say that it introduced a previously unknown capacity to observe and describe things, people, and events in terms that were relatively selfless, dispassionate, and fair.

Let me mention one apparently contrasting case, from the field of written history. There is no mention of the Israelite exodus from Egypt, in any surviving historical document authored by the Egyptians themselves. Should historians conclude from this that the supposed exodus mentioned in the Bible did not really occur, but was completely mythical? It is possible and conceivable that the biblical exodus was nothing more than a myth. But even so, modern scholars say one should bear in mind that the mere fact that an event, known from other sources, fails to be described in Egyptian historical texts, is not in itself a sufficient reason for supposing it never took place. What they mean is that the writers of ancient Egypt's historical documents operated in a different fashion, with different standards of evidence and proof, and with the goal of accomplishing a different larger purpose, than historians (including the vast majority of those still living) who started to appear after the time of the pre-Classical Greeks. More especially, it was standard practice among Egyptian writers before that period not to record failures and defeats, but only successes and victories, in public, relatively permanent documents. K.A. Kitchen says, (1992, p. 706):

> It is sometimes remarked that we have no Egyptian record of an Exodus such as the Old Testament narrates (however interpreted). But several pertinent factors must be borne in mind. Military mishaps (like the loss of a large chariot squadron) are never the subject of triumphal temple inscriptions—Egyptian theology could only be sustained by successes, not failures. The flight of even a large body of slaves would only have been recorded in administrative daybooks and journals, like that excerpted in Sethos II's reign about the flight of two slaves, but over 99 percent of such records for the [Egyptian] delta have long since totally perished. A handful of wine-jar labels under Rameses II is all we possess, and they only give vintage dates!

On the other hand, Greek historians in the tradition of Herodotus and Thucydides operated another way. Their works show a capacity to recognize and recount—in comparatively sober, non-triumphal, even-handed terms—defeats as well as victories, failures along with successes, the bad in addition to the good. (One might argue that this same change in procedures and goals of thinking was the basis for the Greeks' invention of the literary genre of tragedy, which was also apparently unknown before that date.)

Even if the preceding suggestions are on the right track, they still do not answer the question of what actually brought about the change in question. I propose that one factor that might have helped inaugurate the revised attitudes and goals just mentioned was Greek commercial practice. As noted before, the Greeks of the Middle Age period were different from the

Mesopotamians and Egyptians (but similar to the Phoenicians), because a large percentage of them earned their living as "middle-men" for trade-goods moving between cities on the shores of the Mediterranean and Black Seas. Commercial activity is intensely competitive. And it also presumably is true that traders who are relatively better able to assess people and situations, in dispassionate, objective, unemotional terms have an advantage over others who are less skillful at doing that. For example, any merchant who consistently overprices his goods will not remain a merchant for long. Similarly, another who is so excessively concerned with his own cultural traditions, history, family background, or religious status that he finds it difficult to understand and accommodate himself to the needs, manners, and hopes of his customers also will not be as successful as competitors who are not like this.

As mentioned before, the colonial cities the Greeks founded were basically commercial ventures. This was reflected in both the colonies' composition and their systems of governance. For example, Miletus—the traditional "birthplace of philosophy"—was fundamentally a Greek city. But it gradually came to have a very mixed population, drawn (for practical, financial reasons) from all over the Mediterranean area. Did the non-Greek citizens of that city think of their Greek leaders as representing a prestigious and attractive cultural background that they wanted to take as a guide and model for their own lives and personal behavior? Probably not. Therefore, the rulers of Miletus could not conduct themselves in the manner of the Old Kingdom pharaohs in Egypt, where written laws apparently were unneeded, because all aspects of life were subject to dictates of the currently reigning monarch (see Saggs 1989, p. 170, and D.M. Johnson 2000). In Miletus, rather, the laws had to be explicitly written down so that all members of the public could read and comprehend them. Furthermore, it was necessary for those laws to be framed in a manner that applied to every citizen in the same way, irrespective of his or her mother tongue, religion, racial and cultural background, and so on.

Accordingly, the Milesians' commercial experience might have helped them cope with the cosmopolitan nature of their city, because it made them used to abstracting from culturally specific values, interpretations, questions of rank and privilege, etc., in order to focus on intrinsic and factual aspects of the matters at hand. More generally, it also might have disposed them to adopt the methods, ideals, and principles of reason. Still later, when those famously wise men we now call "philosophers" began to appear, first in Miletus and afterwards in other Greek cities as well, they were able to appropriate and expand the scope of the same kind of thinking that already formed part of their cultural heritage. In particular, the distinctive achievement of the philosophers was to apply thinking of this sort to various "theoretical" areas, in addition to immediately practical concerns. For example, the metaphysical question of what the world is "made of" is similar in form, and in the way one might set about trying to answer it, to many of the commercial questions the fathers, grandfathers, and great grandfathers of the Greek philosophers once asked themselves—such as "What trade goods are needed right now on the island of Cos?"[7]

Finally, let me bring this section to a close, by speculating about how and why reasonable, Greek-like thinking survived, grew, and flourished, rather than proving to be one of history's many dead-ends. One crucially important reason for the success of such a style of thought might have been the fact that the world itself, considered generally, evolved into a smaller, more crowded, and much less homogeneous place—a place, in fact, much like Miletus. For instance, classical Egyptian civilization might have continued for an indefinite time, in more or less unchanged form, if there had been sufficient space, resources, peace, and other favorable conditions, for members of that society to continue living in the Nile valley in undisturbed isolation. But—as any standard history of Egypt tells us—that was not the case. Instead, Egypt had to face many economic and military challenges from outside its borders. As a result of those challenges, its population became diluted with, and finally dominated, by foreigners. And

---

7. There is a rough analogy between this historically based account of reason or mind in the narrow sense that I now am exploring and some non-realist, evolutionary accounts of mathematics. Thus, Jean-Paul Changeux says: "Mathematics is taught in school as a coherent set of propositions, theorems, axioms. One forgets that these have appeared successively in the course of the history of mathematics and of human society—in short, that they are cultural objects subject to evolution. Putting mathematical objects back in historical perspective 'secularizes' them, shows them to be more contingent than they appear" (Changeux and Connes 1995, p. 18).

that finally led to that society's breakdown, and the end of its long historical tradition.

It seems fair to say that Greeks of the pre-Classical era were pioneering cases (and Greeks of the Classical era, paradigm cases) of individuals suited to thrive in the "post-Egyptian" historical situation that developed after 1000 B.C.E. The cosmopolitan world that took shape then—which the Greeks learned to mold and exploit for their purposes—is essentially the same one we live in today. If anything, the methods of thinking the Greeks invented have become even more important in our version of that world, than was true for their version of it. The reason for this is that those methods constitute a valuable *lingua franca*, in terms of which virtually all the people now alive can "understand" one another.

5.3   Reason's Connection with Indirect Practicality

Taking a cue from writers like Dewey and Russell, some readers might object that my account of the advent of reason is strange and unnecessarily complicated, and that it should be replaced with a simpler, leaner, and more intuitive view. They might hypothesize that early thinkers came to prefer a Greek-like way of organizing knowledge over an Egyptian-like procedure simply because they discovered that the first was able to make better sense of their experiences than the second. For example, ancient people gradually came to notice that supposed explanations of things in terms of values and activities of invisible beings were less successful and predictive than accounts formulated in terms of impersonal generalizations and laws. Accordingly, therefore, their deciding always to appeal to anti-superstitious, non-magical, reasonable explanations of phenomena was nothing more than a means of bringing their thinking into line with what their eyes and ears already had told them the world was like (see Dewey 1920/60, especially Chapter 1).

This objection is a familiar one today. Since 1912—the year Russell wrote *The Problems of Philosophy*—scientific research apparently has supplied further evidence in favor of the claim Russell made in that book, that the universe itself has a "reasonable structure." For instance, the sort of thinking that most mathematicians employ today can be understood as an application, to the special case of numbers and figures, of the same rules, standards, and intellectual methods that are characteristic of Greek-like reason. Furthermore, mathematical thinking, so understood, has proved remarkably (in fact, "unreasonably") successful at providing correct descriptions and explanations of reality. The mathematician, Alain Connes, says that the scientific career of Albert Einstein provides a good illustration of this point. According to Connes, when Einstein first began his project of reflecting on the general structure of the world, he assumed that modern mathematics was nothing more than a handy tool for organizing knowledge—a tool that (by fortunate accident) sometimes corresponded to the properties of actual existents. But later he came to believe that mathematics' applicability to the world was not something arbitrary or accidental, because of the fact that the world itself had a mathematical—or in other words, reasonable—inner nature. In Connes's words:

[Einstein] spent a very great part of his scientific life trying to devise a theory that would unify electromagnetism and gravity. The success of the mathematical model of general relativity was such that he came to think that the solution to his problem lay in mathematics. In 1921 he was still able to say, apropos of relativity: "I am anxious to draw attention to the fact that this theory is not speculative in origin; it owes its invention entirely to the desire to make physical theory fit observed fact as well as possible. . . . The general theory of relativity owes its existence . . . to the empirical fact of the numerical equality of the inertial and gravitational masses of bodies." But in 1933 we find him saying, to the contrary, "If, then, it is true that this axiomatic basis of theoretical physics cannot be extracted from experience, but must be freely invented, can we ever hope to find the right way? . . . I am convinced that we can discover by means of purely mathematical constructions the concepts and the laws connecting them with each other, which furnish the key to the understanding of natural phenomena. . . . The creative principle resides in mathematics." (Changeux and Connes 1995, pp. 51–52)

Does it really make sense—and is it correct—to describe our universe as intrinsically reasonable? If the answer is Yes, it follows that when the Greek founders of Western Civilization invented the intellectual and methodological techniques of reason (or mind in the narrow sense), they also discovered the key to a proper understanding of reality itself. I consider this an interesting idea that deserves further comment and study. But I am not able to engage in such a task right now, since doing so would take me too far from the main concerns of this book. Thus, for the time being, I shall content myself with reaffirming the claims, already expressed in Chapter 3, that the Egyptians, Babylonians, and other ancient cultures, on one side, and the pre-Classical Greeks on the other, developed two contrasting ways of relating themselves to their physical environments. And we are not entitled to assume that either of those ways is superior to, or "more correct" than the other.

Let us now return to the question of what led an increasing number of individuals to accept the ideals and procedures of reason, starting from the date of approximately 1000 B.C.E. One point I want to make about this is the following. It is easy for us to think of *ourselves* as responding to common-sense, directly evidential considerations of the sort proposed by Dewey, Russell, and perhaps also Einstein. In other words, we can conjure up a mental picture of earlier versions of the same people we are now, facing a choice—at around the date of 1000 B.C.E. That imagined choice is between deciding to employ reason as a general means of explaining the occurrence of diseases, wars, accidents, etc., and trying to explain those same things in terms of gods, demons, magical spells, and occult influences. Then we also can go on to picture ourselves as making an explicit decision to appeal to reason in every such case, because of the fact that we have learned from ordinary observations that reason always works better than mythological thinking. But this trick of imaginatively transporting ourselves backward in time neither implies nor proves that our ancient ancestors also must have engaged in thought processes that correspond to the ones just mentioned. Their world was not our world. And modern investigators interested in the ancient period are not justified in assuming, in the absence of independent evidence in favor of such an idea, that their own habits of thought provide a meaningful standard for describing, measuring, and assessing the correctness of thinking that occurred long ago.

What, more particularly, do I think is wrong with the Deweyan or Russellian story just mentioned? And if I am right to say that story is mistaken, what is the alternative to it? In other words, what do I believe actually happened to bring about our present historical situation—a situation where reason plays a central role in the thinking of virtually every living person? In order to clarify these questions, consider three related points.

(1) Humans do not always (or even frequently) choose to do what appears to them to be practical, advantageous, and adaptive. The widespread persistence of smoking at the present time is one clear testament to this fact. However (in agreement with Saggs— see his 1989, Chapter 12), I surmise that our ancient ancestors, who found it natural, honorable, pious, and time-honored to think in terms of magic and the workings of invisible spirits, were even less likely to be motivated by "common-sense" considerations, than we are now.

We noted, in the preceding chapter, the claim some people make that human cultures cannot be literal products of Darwinian natural selection, because there is no natural way of understanding cultural developments in terms of independent traits that might have been caused by separate genes. More especially, evolutionary processes are always automatic and "blind"; but cultural traditions and institutions come into existence largely through foresight, planning, and conscious choice. I now want to add a further point to this one, which justifies the idea that all the planning involved in creating a culture is very unlikely to be reasonable. It is that (cf. Munz 1989, 284ff.) many of the choices humans make in the course of establishing and elaborating their cultural practices are bound to be *im*practical and *non*-adaptive ones, because only such non-adaptive choices provide a means of distinguishing one culture from all others. Another, related aspect of the same point is that non-adaptive choices also create bonds of cohesiveness between members of a culture. That is, the more bizarre, unreasonable, and impractical the policies and traditions of any group of people are, the less likely it will be that any other group will have adopted those same traditions. Furthermore, the stranger they are, the more fanatically loyal members of the group will have to be, in order to defend those institutions against the opposition, ridicule, and sabotage of outsiders.

Accordingly, I surmise that the individuals who first invented, and then applied in their own behavior, the set of techniques for thinking that we now call "reason" were not likely to have done this because they considered those techniques useful. Nor, probably, did they even think of the practice of those rules as a harmless diversion or game. Instead, my guess is that ordering and assessing thoughts in terms of reason seemed to them to be something unnatural, daring, difficult, and dangerous. They were willing to undertake this program despite its costs, because they expected it to have the desirable result of making their own cultural group distinctive.[8] If I am right to speculate along these lines, then we are also justified in assuming that reason did not enjoy an immediate success—its adoption did not launch a mass, popular movement. Instead, it probably began as a secret, quasi-ritualized procedure, around which the members of an embattled, exclusive group (similar to the Pythagorean brotherhood) were able to unite.

(2) The second point I want to make is that reason only could have become practically useful, when the number of its advocates reached a "critical mass." How did that happen? Some philosophical commentators will say the personal and legal conflict between Socrates and Anytus in classical Athens, recorded in several of Plato's dialogues, provides a good example of the struggle to adopt reason as a central intellectual ideal, and to overcome previously dominant themes of authority, habit, and prejudice. But this case was both too late in time, and too superficial in character, to teach us anything about the change in question. For example (as Dewey also notes in 1920/60), Plato's account shows that Anytus and Socrates were not opposed in any fundamental respect, since they agreed about ends, and merely disagreed about means. Thus, their quarrel seems to have occurred at a time when reason already had attained an undisputed place in civilized Greek society, since it boiled down to a dispute about the best way of understanding and employing reason in the situation at hand. Accordingly, I think that their conflict was only a faint echo of a deeper and more serious intellectual clash that had occurred several generations earlier.

---

8. On my first trip to Greece in the summer of 1997, I was surprised to find quite a few taxi drivers in Thessaloniki and Athens who did not wear seatbelts, and who actively discouraged their passengers from wearing them. The justification they gave for this was just to say "That's the way we do it (or do not do it) here." In fact, one driver commented with what seemed to be obvious pride—whether truly or falsely I am not in a position to say—that Greek airline pilots also regularly refused to wear seatbelts.

Let us now consider the metaphysical views of the pre-Socratic philosophers, Parmenides and Zeno, (who were also discussed by Plato, in his dialogue entitled *Parmenides*). Do these people provide a better sense—and in particular, do they count as a more authentic remnant—of the original struggle mentioned before? I think the answer to this question might be Yes. After all, the most remarkable thing about those philosophers was their absolutely fanatical commitment to the ideals of reason, which led them to affirm everything reason apparently dictated, without regard to any considerations of the usefulness, plausibility, or even (paradoxically) the consistency of doing so. In fact, the way they characteristically expressed their conclusions was in the form of seeming contradictions or "paradoxes." Furthermore, it is a fact of history that those paradoxes had a confusing, even debilitating effect on the practical and theoretical work of the whole generation of Greek thinkers who immediately followed them (see Solmsen 1960, pp. 3ff). What motivated Parmenides and Zeno to formulate their ideas in this strange way? Part of the answer may be that they found this particular method of investigation attractive, because it was a means of recalling, and of partially recreating, the terrifying experience of those few, courageous, earlier individuals who first set out to put reason into practice in their lives.

(3) Napoleon Bonaparte once made the profound remark that, in war, the moral was to the material as 3 to 1. Analogously, the third and last point I want to make here is that people are not usually prepared to incur the discomfort and risk of introducing fundamental changes into their lives, just in order to bring about improvements in some of their physical circumstances—increased efficiency, wealth, safety, and the like. Instead, in typical cases, the motivation one has for making such changes is something that is either intimately personal or spiritual in nature. People are often willing to endure the stress of radical changes, because of religious or ideological commitments, or in order to bring about an advancement in prestige, rank, or class. But they rarely do it just to achieve more convenience, money, or food (assuming that those items are considered in and by themselves, as opposed to what they might symbolize and represent).

I want to return now to another problem discussed previously. If it really is true to say that reason received its initial impetus in

the Mediterranean area about the year 1000 B.C.E., what explains
the fact that it then succeeded in spreading from that source to all
other parts of the world as well? What happened to bring about
that diffusion? In the light of the above points, I now propose
that reason's eventual triumph might have received some crucial
help from the conquests of Alexander the Great.

Even as late as the close of the Greek classical era (around the
year Aristotle died), the vast majority of inhabitants of the
Mediterranean region (except for Greece and its colonies) continued to ignore the Aristotelian-like intellectual method of systematically applied rules and standards of reason. And that was so, in
spite of certain obvious advantages that were apparently connected with that invention—such as the fact that it allowed people
to develop a more complete and coherent system of mathematics
in general, and better calculating techniques in particular. One
consideration that might have encouraged this nearly universal
rejection of reason was the fact that the best-known sponsors and
employers of that technique were a small number of conspicuously pedantic, unworldly, and relatively ineffectual thinkers—
people like Thales, Parmenides, Zeno, Empedocles, Plato, and
Aristotle. However, all that changed with Alexander's appearance
on the world's stage. In association with his father, Phillip II of
Macedonia, he was obviously someone who had gone to a certain
amount of trouble to identify himself, in an explicit way, with the
Greek intellectual tradition of reason. (For example, he had been
a pupil of Aristotle.) Nevertheless, he was not just an academic,
theoretician, or teacher. Instead, he was the brilliant leader of the
victorious army that had swept through all the countries of the
Mediterranean, Persian Gulf, and Black Sea regions, that had top-
pled the Persian Empire; and that even had conquered large parts
of India. Accordingly, the admiration and respect he commanded
may have prompted ordinary people in Egypt, Mesopotamia,
Persia, or India to pose certain questions to themselves that they
had never asked before. They now may have begun to wonder
whether reasonable inquiry might have been one of the decisively
important tools that Alexander and the Macedonian army had
employed to transform the world.

It is clear that certain military advantages flow from a consistently applied policy of avoiding superstitious, mythological, and
merely authoritarian habits of thought. But in addition to back-

ground considerations of that sort, non-Greek observers might have wondered if even some of the specific battlefield techniques employed by Alexander's army could be usefully interpreted as expressions of Aristotelian-like, rational thinking. One key innovation that distinguished Greek and Macedonian armies of the day from their counterparts in other places was the central role of the phalanx. This was a close, rigorously organized formation of infantry soldiers which, at least when it was operating on level ground, was capable of generating an overwhelming forward thrust. The warriors in the first rank of the phalanx carried spears of normal length (approximately 6 feet), which pointed towards the front. Those in the second rank carried longer spears (approximately 8 feet), which they leveled and extended past the first rank, so as to point towards the front as well. Soldiers in the third rank carried still longer spears extending past the first two ranks; and so on back for several ranks, ending with soldiers in the last rank whose spears were enormously long (at least 15 feet). Now imagine a hypothetical soldier who served in the rear rank of a Macedonian phalanx. He only had one weapon to employ and rely on. And it was one that was so unwieldy and awkward as to be completely useless, except in so far as it functioned in connection with all the other members of the entire phalanx. In a sense, then, this soldier had been trained to make war in a way that was extremely indirect, counter-intuitive, and unnatural. Nevertheless, even if he and his fellow soldiers in the Macedonian army had renounced most of the ways of fighting and defending themselves that were dictated by their inborn, "primate" dispositions, it was clear to everyone that their new way of working together constituted the most effective means of fighting that existed on earth.

What happened once a critical mass of people had begun to appreciate the value of reason, and had started to put its rules and ideals into effect in their behavior? The preceding illustration provides part of the answer. One soldier in a phalanx was not an effective fighter, by himself. But when all the members of that formation operated together, they were far more effective than any group of fighters of approximately the same size, in any other army. To say the same thing another way, what made Alexander's soldiers the new terror of the earth was the fact that their education and training had prepared them to rely, not on natural instincts, but on "pedantic" chains of inferential thinking, whose

practical consequences were extremely indirect. This, then, is
another element in my proposed non-Russellian story of how and
why early Greeks, rather than other people, became the source of
the revolutionary technique of thinking that was destined to
reshape all nations everywhere.

5.4   The Goal of Science Is to Discover Truth, and "Chauvinism" Sometimes Is True

Now consider an objection to the whole project of this book.
Some commentators maintain that no genuinely scientific
method of investigation can allow the viewpoint of the investigator himself or herself to function in any crucial capacity.
Admittedly, those same people will say, our shared human nature
can lead us to fancy that our private and personal opinions are
somehow embodied in things outside us. But an important part
of what it means to engage in scientific theorizing is that we
should resist all such inborn tendencies to "remake the world in
our image."

What about the case of this book? I claimed that, from the
perspective of history, there were no minds at all—at least not in
the strict sense—until certain inhabitants of the pre-Classical
Greek world began thinking, inferring, and assessing evidence in a
previously unknown manner. Furthermore, when that happened,
those same individuals inaugurated the tradition we now call
Western Civilization. But, these critics will say, since I myself am
obviously a representative of that same cultural tradition, it follows that none of my statements deserves to be accorded legitimate scientific standing, since they are all infected with the disease
of prejudiced, self-congratulatory chauvinism. (Ned Block has
provided classic expressions of this general idea—see for example
Block 1978, section 3.0.)

To reinforce this point, commentators might pose rhetorical
questions like the following: (a) Is it not absurd to suppose that
intelligent, sensible, refined non-Westerners—Japanese, Chinese,
Africans, East Indians, and others—do not have minds, simply
because they were born and raised in some "wrong place"? Still
more basically, (b) how could anyone be sufficiently vain and
naive to propose, as a "scientific" hypothesis, that all and only

those humans possess minds who are (or, to the extent that they are) similar to himself?

My reply has two parts. The first is to blunt the force of questions like (a), by reminding readers—yet again—that, because of the influence of modern mass media, it seems to me that there are very few normal, adult, human beings left on earth today who are "unminded." This is why I had to spend so much time in preceding chapters discussing examples from ancient history. Thus, suppose it really is the case, as claimed before, that almost all present-day adults have learned (mostly from models like Mickey Mouse, Elvis Presley, Superman, and the like) to assess issues in a way that is based on objective, impersonal evidence. Furthermore, suppose they also have learned—from the same sources—constantly to presuppose that there is a single, sharp, and consistent line between truth and falsity. Assuming that is true, the best, clearest, (and perhaps only) means of finding clear and unambiguous examples of contrasting types of thinking is to look for them in the past.

The second part of my reply—in response to (b)—is more complicated. I said before that I approve of attempts made by recent philosophers to support their views by connecting them, in various ways, with the methods, ideals, and discoveries of modern science (a project sometimes called "naturalizing epistemology"). I think this is a positive and progressive development, because it has made the discipline of philosophy more focused, realistic, useful, and coherent than it otherwise would have been, and than it was in the past. On the other hand, however, many of the same individuals who claim to employ this method have not really succeeded in setting their philosophical claims on a scientific foundation, in my opinion, because they are either unable or unwilling to "let science be science." To see what this means, consider a roughly analogous theological example that I have constructed, in the general style of Spinoza and Kierkegaard. A man prays to God to grant him some foolish wish. But he fails to understand that God could not continue to be God—the wise and just Ruler of the Universe—if He were to grant that wish. To be more explicit, if (*per impossibile*) God did what the petitioner asked, He thereby would have shown Himself not to be divine, because that would mean that He shared in something like the same greed, selfishness, and shortsighted ignorance of consequences that are proper-

ties of the supplicant himself.[9] In similar style, certain philosophers say their opinions must amount to more than groundless,
empty, merely *a priori* speculations, because those opinions have
been constructed on the solid rock of empirical, scientific findings. But then these same people proceed to "interpret" the
results and procedures that are supposedly relevant to their concerns in strangely idiosyncratic, and empirically unjustified ways.
And because of that, it cannot really be the case, after all, that
their views have been shaped and supported by fair, dispassionate
observation and reporting. Instead, these views are merely "dis-
guised" products of ordinary prejudice, special pleading, and a
priori preconceptions.[10] The moral of the story is this: Anyone
who desires to buttress the claims he or she makes, by representing them as having arisen from—or at least as being consistent
with—certain things already established by scientific observation,
experiment, and theorizing, needs to cultivate an honest, objectively informed, and passively receptive attitude towards science.
In particular, this person should be able to distinguish clearly
between that which, for various reasons, he is inclined to think
certain scientific methods and discoveries "ought" to be, and
what observation and experiment shows that they really are.

One means of cultivating the sort of conservative and realistic
appreciation of scientific accomplishments just mentioned (including those discoveries relevant to the topic of mind) is to think
about science from the perspective of history. Consider, for example, Jacob Bronowski's claim that "The most remarkable discovery made by scientists is science itself" (1958, p. 58). Even
though I approve of the general approach apparently expressed by
this statement, it cannot be literally true, just as a matter of logic.
To describe someone as a "scientist" presupposes that science
already exists. And therefore no scientist could have done this.
Nevertheless, I agree that one or more people who were not yet
scientists might have thought of the new ways of acquiring, organizing, and justifying knowledge that now have come to consti-

---

9. The following passage from the beginning of Spinoza's work, *The Ethics*, gives the
"flavor" of the preceding argument: "those who confuse the two natures, divine and
human, readily attribute human passions to the deity, especially so long as they do not
know how passions originate in the mind" (1955, p. 49).

10. I argued in Chapter 1 that, at least in some respects, this is true of some doctrines
set forth by Pinker, Lakoff, Chomsky, and the Churchlands.

tute the discipline of science. Similarly, it also seems to me that no member(s) of Western Civilization could have been the literal discoverer(s) of science. This is because, as argued previously, I think that distinctive civilization began when certain individuals first got the idea of what it means to have objectively true beliefs; and the basic features of scientific thinking are already implicit in that single idea.

The preceding points are also capable of throwing light on eliminative materialism. As noted in Chapter 2, eliminativists like Paul and Patricia Churchland argue that brain research someday will expose, then finally displace, the vague, mythological notions of belief and desire that have been bequeathed to us by "folk psychology." Later still, according to those theorists, informed people finally will learn to reject many of the false statements, formulated in terms of "mind-talk," that they once accepted, and replace them with true statements, formulated in precise, substantiated, and scientifically fruitful language about the brain. For example, instead of saying I believe I now hear my daughter calling to me, I will say I just have acquired low-level electrical stimulation in the layered column of neurons underlying cingulate area 23 of my cerebral cortex. Or instead of declaring that I am having hunger pangs, I will say I now have a relatively large, oscillating pattern of neuron-firings on the ventral part of my thalamus. However, my own intuitions about such matters differ systematically from those of eliminativists like the Churchlands, since mine are largely based on, and directed toward, cultural and historical considerations rather than neurological ones. Thus, I think the eliminativists' program contains the following fatal flaw. If we really were able to ignore, suspend, and get rid of the common-sense notion of (true) belief, in the manner proposed by eliminativists, then *ipso facto*, all scientific thinking (including neurophysiological research) also would be rendered impossible. The reason for this is that there is a strong connection between the notion of belief, on one side, and that of objective truth, on the other. In fact, it seems to me that they amount to virtually the same thing. Furthermore, truth in that particular sense plays an absolutely central role in scientific thought. Still more precisely, science basically amounts to the project of "getting things right"—attempting to understand objects, facts, and so forth, as what and how they are, irrespective of all subjective, or humanly influenced, factors. And therefore, it is a topsy-turvy, self-defeating claim to say that folk psychology (which, in my view, began around 1000 B.C.E.) is antithetical to science, or to predict that science someday will displace and cancel this way of thinking, for the following reason. Folk psychology (including a commitment to the notion of objective truth) is not just essential to science, but is its foundation.

What bearing do the preceding remarks have on the "chauvinist" objection mentioned earlier? I take the warning of people like Block seriously, that part of what it means to be a scientific investigator is that one always should be on guard against allowing a smug sense of self-importance to lead one into making unsubstantiated claims about what "must" be the case. But it is also possible to make mistakes of the opposite sort—for example, errors of false modesty, or exaggerated and unwarranted self-effacement. Under what kind of circumstances could an investigator be enticed into making mistakes of that second sort? Imagine someone who followed the fanatical, ideologically inspired policy of not admitting the truth of any statement that had not been shown to be based on complete, "scientific" objectivity. In such a situation—paradoxically—the person in question might be led to assume, without evidence, that nothing in his own cultural background possibly could have helped determine the general shape of the present-day world. Nevertheless, despite the methodological fears of Block and others, evidence presented in preceding chapters shows that reason (the rules and standards for thinking, whose invention marked the beginning of Western tradition) has had exactly that type of world-transforming effect.[11]

Turning now to a related topic, I claimed before that it was a mistake simply to identify the mind with the brain (or any other set of natural objects, properties, or facts, for that matter). The reason I said this is that I consider mind, in the strict sense, to be something cultural. In particular, analogous to the office of Chancellor, the game of cribbage, the folk song about the fox and geese, the injunction against eating with one's knife, and so on, it

---

11. A parallel point: It is arguable that this same invention also played a role in the general development of our species itself. The reason for this is that it had the effect of strengthening, and giving concrete form to, an important set of human capacities that, before then, did not amount to much more than a bare potentiality.

is an aspect of the activity, commitments, and values of the members of a particular human cultural community. How do I understand that last claim? What do I think it implies? And what proof for it can I offer?

There are at least three undesirable consequences that flow from the claim that the mind is necessarily independent of all considerations about human history and culture. I want to say something about each of those points in turn. First, some theorists accept the idea that the mind must be physical *as opposed to* cultural, because they believe the whole of modern science is built on a rabidly anti-dualistic foundation. Thus, they say, any legitimately scientific account of mind must represent mind as "nature's genetic gift to humans." (For example, some of the theorists I am talking about assume that all normal humans automatically acquire fully developed and functioning minds, as soon as they reach "the age of reason.") But we assume that genetically given properties of a species should be present in, and expressed in a fairly uniform way by, all its normal and undamaged members, for as long as that species continues to exist. Yet historians tell us that human beings passed through at least one radical change in their general way of thinking, without ceasing (or beginning) to be human, as a result of that change. I refer to the fact that they did not begin to use systematically rational rules and standards for thinking, inferring, and assessing evidence until about 1000 B.C.E. And thus it follows that this change could not have been a "natural" one. For example, we have no justification for conceiving of reason as analogous to any such thing as innate common sense, or a shared moral faculty, or an evolved human nature.

To pursue this last point still further, some people apparently believe that the appearance of the rules and standards of human reason was a cosmic, genetic accident that resulted from blind evolutionary forces (see for example Kayzer *et al.* 1997). But experienced, working biologists would dismiss such an idea as unscientific and non-explanatory, on the grounds that it would make reason's advent "miraculous." To be more specific, it would be just as absurd to say reason was an evolutionarily developed "mental faculty" as it would be to make a similar claim about trigonometry, the game of Snakes and Ladders, the New York Stock Exchange, or the Vienna State Opera. It is obviously wrong to think of any of the items just mentioned as a development or extension of natural parts, properties, or inclinations with which we were born, because all of them originated from insights, intentions, designs, and plans of particular human individuals. And so analogously, I have argued that the same was true of the founding of reason. Furthermore, the particular intentions and plans involved in the invention of reason were part of a *reaction* against many properties already present in humans' innately given nature. Again, the main evidence I offer in support of this last claim is simply to note the empirical discovery made by historians and archeologists that, until relatively recently, it was not true that all adult humans employed reason, but only the members of one special group.[12]

By the way, if it is right to reject the above, "miraculous" view of mind (in the narrow sense), then it apparently follows as well that it is wrong to suppose that all of modern science must be anti-dualistic in character. Why? The answer is that if scientific thinking is not a product of our genes, but an invention of specific individuals living in an identifiable cultural context, then whatever scientists do, imagine, and conclude must presuppose a dualist-like distinction between culture on one side, and the non-human world of nature on the other.[13] In other words, it seems to be the case that science is based on the same distinction between nature and culture that people in our society implicitly but constantly recognize.

Still another implication of the view I am defending is that it is not appropriate to think of the mind as just another, more or less ordinary object of scientific investigation, on a par with all other such objects. This is true because—unlike all the other things scientists investigate—if there were no minds, then scientific thought itself would be impossible. More simply stated, mind (in the narrow sense) cannot be just another, ordinary concern of scientific thinking, since it is implicitly identical with thinking of that sort.

Nevertheless, despite the preceding points, it still seems to me that we possess effective, though indirect, means of studying the

---

12. Also, in view of that origin, it is correct for us to continue thinking of the rules of reason as characteristic expressions of the one special culture out of which they first arose.

13. The sense of the word "dualist" I am employing here does not presuppose anything magical or supernatural. And because of this, it ought not to be a word that scientists find objectionable.

mind scientifically. However, a key to the effectiveness of those means is that researchers should be willing to accept history—and more especially, the archaeological, anthropological, and textual reconstruction of the pre-Classical Greek world—as a legitimate source of data relevant to understanding the mind scientifically. In my view, investigators who assume that history must be tangential or even antithetical to science considered generally, and cognitive science more particularly, already have made the mistake of putting something peripheral in place of what is essential.[14]

The second of the three comments announced above is this: Whenever someone sets out to understand mind exclusively in terms of objective, non-human matters like evolution, neuroanatomy, neurophysiology, etc., he or she enters into a strange situation where it is only possible to inquire about how minds happen to have been created, or how they now are expressed, but where one cannot ask what the mind is.

Let me explain this by means of a brief digression. I am not a supporter—especially in light of recent events—of unregulated access to firearms. Nevertheless, whenever representatives of the gun lobby tell us that "guns do not kill people; people kill people," I think they are saying something true and important (although arguably misleading). A forensic scientist examining a pistol's inner condition (scratches, powder burns, and so forth) might be able to determine several possible ways that individuals employed that weapon in the past. But he cannot provide detailed, concrete information about exactly what those past users did with the gun, or what other users will do with it in the future. In partly similar style, I claim that investigative examination of skulls, brains, and other bodily parts can inform us in a general way about what human beings are like, and what in general they are likely to do. But that approach also leaves many questions open. Prominent among the unanswered questions are ones that arise out of occasional inventions, made by creative individuals, of previously unknown ways of employing "standard" bodily organs.

Thus, some remarkable individuals (such as choreographers or gymnastic instructors) have thought of new and interesting ways in which humans can use their torsos, arms, hands, legs, and feet.

---

14. See Erneling 1997.

Similarly, certain other inventors also discovered important new uses for the brains, and other parts of the nervous systems, with which humans were born.[15] Accordingly, it was not the brain that created the mind, but people courageous enough to experiment with previously unknown ways of using the brain. And because of this, historians, rather than physiologists, are more likely to give us informative scientific answers to questions about how and why the mind came into existence.

Another digression: There may be some readers who—having forgotten preceding arguments, or never having found those arguments persuasive in the first place—may continue to believe it was a serious mistake for me to claim that the mind was an invention handed down from ancient times, rather than part of innately given bodily resources. In a last-ditch effort to persuade people of that sort to think again, let me mention a couple of informal examples from common language. Suppose it really were correct to identify the mind with physical, non-cultural items like parts of the brain. In that case, Shakespearean phrases such as, "Make up your mind!" or "Change your mind!," or a familiar question like, "What did you have in mind when you did or said _____?," ought to strike us as nonsense. But—of course—we obviously do not find these forms of words nonsensical. In other words, they do not strike us as artificial or forced, but as sensible and natural. The reason for this, I suggest, is that we are implicitly aware that the basic meaning it is appropriate to attach to the word "mind" in today's world is: "Thinking conducted in a clear, justified, ordered, and consistent manner!" To say the same thing another way, we have become used to associating the general notion of having a mind with the more particular idea of thinking logically. Nevertheless—and both the present and earlier chapters were designed to show this—that same association, which now strikes us as intuitively acceptable, would have seemed strange, pointless, and perhaps meaningless to the physiologically normal humans who preceded us in earlier historical times.

Finally, my third comment is to remind readers of a claim already made in Chapter 4. That is the idea that even though mind as I conceive it is a product of history and culture, that does

---

15. This is my principal objection to the method Steven Mithen employs in his otherwise excellent and useful book, 1996.

not mean it is unreal, in the sense of being without significance, as far as things in the objectively existing world are concerned. It is not true that every cultural innovation counts as arbitrary and idiosyncratic, in the sense of having no meaning except in relation to the cultural group from which it arose. On the contrary, some culturally determined innovations reflect or "capture" various aspects of the objective, non-cultural environment itself. Consider a simple example, parallel to another considered before. Imagine an oddly shaped hat festooned with an outlandish pattern of bells, spangles, whistles, and tassels. That hat might be nothing more than one cultural group's whimsical expression of exuberance and sense of fun. Furthermore, it might express that group's desire to be different, in view of the fact that it is nearly inconceivable that any other cultural group would have happened to dream up that same item of clothing. On the other hand, one cannot say the same thing about the wider invention of hats and other protective head-gear in general. This last case is different from the first, because it corresponds to a real need that humans have to protect themselves from the wind, to avoid losing body heat in cold weather, and to shade their eyes and faces from the sun in hot weather. I claim that the Greek innovation of reason—the intellectual techniques of believing, desiring, and appealing to objective, impersonal truth, which (if my arguments are sound) it is appropriate to call "mind"—is like the invention of hats generally. It is not like the invention of a strangely shaped hat with bells and tassels. And therefore, we have good reason to think that, if the Greeks had not discovered reason, some other group (or species) eventually would have done so instead.

To what objective aspect of the inter-subjective world do I believe the invention of reason most closely corresponds? One answer to this question is to say that the notion of reason picks out, and is motivated by, an innately given, non-culturally-relative property (probably located in the central nervous system) that belongs to all normal human bodies. That property then expresses itself as a tendency for humans to think and behave in certain ways. To be specific, since early times, human beings have been disposed (occasionally and temporarily, but repeatedly) to set aside usual, survival-centered, primate-like reactions, in an attempt to achieve "higher" goals. For example, why are the great majority of the cave paintings of pre-historic, European, Cro-Magnon people located in extremely remote, inaccessible places? The plausible answer is that the artists who created those paintings probably thought of them as ritual objects. And therefore, the longer, more laborious, and more dangerous the approach was to the "cathedral" that contained them, the more impressively awe-inspiring, powerful, and effective the paintings would be. (I have referred to this example in another place. See D.M. Johnson 1997b.) Humans' tendency sometimes to choose dangerous and difficult circumstances and behaviors—and by this means, bring about states of reverential fear and awe—is not clearly associated, so far as I am aware, with any other primate species.

Could our pre-historic human ancestors have applied this apparently inborn tendency occasionally to engage in impractical and daring behavior, to the usually humdrum task of thinking about everyday objects and facts in the world around them? If the answer is Yes, that special application might have resulted in that which Thomas Nagel called "humans' capacity for objective thought." More generally: It is not absurd to say that, before the pre-Classical Greeks, every ancient culture with which we are familiar tried in various ways to submerge, discourage, disguise, and hide the upsettingly unnatural, fear-inspiring tendency to think in this way. But the Greeks found a means of mastering our fear of such thought, and eventually began to channel it in useful directions. In other words, instead of blunting, foiling, or obliterating humans' disposition to think and act unnaturally, they invented a revolutionary means of systematizing such behavior. And that invention is the basis of the same "intellectual tool kit" we continue to use today.

This then is a summary of why I think that, even if the mind is a product of history and culture rather than part of the objective, natural world, it amounts to more than a figment. In my opinion, monistic naturalists who suppose otherwise, thereby allow the tail to wag the dog instead of the other way around.

5.5   How Reason Made the World a Dangerous Place

I now want to bring the book to a close by considering the following question. Does my preceding story about reason and mind have a happy ending? To be more precise, is it really true, as many have supposed, that humans' ability to contemplate and assess matters dispassionately, objectively, and reasonably has been a wonderful, unmixed blessing? The answer is No. The program of thinking that I equate with mind (narrowly construed) has had a transforming effect on virtually everything present-day people do. But those effects have been disadvantageous as well as advantageous, bad as well as good. In particular, one sign that reason involves losses as well as gains is the fact that this thought strategy is associated with high levels of danger and risk.

The basic way in which ancient people like the Assyrians, Babylonians, Hittites, and Chinese were able to occupy the ecological niche that all humans share ("mind in the wide sense") was by adopting a "compromise with nature." As argued in Chapter 2, this involved their trying to reproduce, in an artificial, symbolic manner, styles of life that belonged to certain other, non-objectively thinking creatures—such as birds, lions, bears, wolves, or apes. What made the thinking and behaving of those creatures so attractive to our early ancestors? My guess is that early humans felt the style of life that once had been natural to them was in danger of being lost; and therefore, they proposed—as a means of calming their fears—to "re-enter nature" in an indirect, symbolic way.

More generally, non-human animals' means of relating themselves to their surroundings is by appealing to a "default survival strategy" dictated by hard-wired aspects of their nervous systems. And humans also share that same "basic design." Because of that fact, it is not surprising to find thinking of that sort constantly reappearing throughout the whole course of human history.

Evolution would not have settled on that particular kind of thought as part of animals' basic nature—in fact, as their "default position"—unless it had some clear advantages. Its main advantage, I suggest, is that it is a strategy that is conservative and safe. Although it dictates that creatures never or seldom should do anything new, daring, or (*a fortiori*) intelligent, it also dictates that they never should do anything stupid. In other words, it is a policy of low gain, combined with low risk—something like betting on the red or the black in a game of roulette. By contrast, when humans abandoned their policy of thinking in a (pseudo-) natural fashion and instead began to think in explicitly non-natural, Greek-influenced ways, a new and dangerous form of instability entered the world. The reason for this was that their new way of directing behavior was a risky one that carried a greatly increased potential for harm as well as good. It was like betting on just a single number in roulette. Although there was not much chance of its paying at all, if it did succeed, it would pay handsomely. Our own time provides us with many reminders of the increased dangers reason has brought in its wake—such as starvation and disease associated with overpopulation; the threat of nuclear, biological, or chemical warfare; world-wide pollution; the accumulation of space-junk; and so on.

Nevertheless, there is no realistic possibility of going backwards. That is, we have committed ourselves to a style of living that demands that we continually try to adjust ourselves to our environment—and it to us—by engaging in ever more indirect and subtle patterns of observation, surmise, and experiment. And because of that, the option of "returning to nature" no longer is open to us—even in the seemingly simple and benign sense of attempting to recapture what the ancient Egyptians once had and were. Instead, our only chance of solving the new series of problems we now face is by proceeding even further down the path we already chose long ago—the path that separates us more and more from undisturbed nature. For example, we have to reconcile ourselves to the fact that, long into the foreseeable future, our world will contain an ever smaller percentage of its original "wildness."

The main point for which I have argued in this book is that it is not possible to obtain a sensible and scientifically justifiable sense of who and what we are, unless we look for answers in details of our history. On the other hand, our best hope of continuing to move towards a better world—or even of surviving—is by looking forward. Thus, in place of the once effective strategy of trying to tame wilderness, it now has become imperative to create the sort of dynamically evolving, experimental, *artificial* world that can help us meet our future needs.

Bibliography

Alexander, Richard D. 1979. Evolution and Culture. In Chagnon and Irons 1979, pp. 59–78.

Anonymous. 1976. *The New English Bible: Oxford Study Edition*. New York: Oxford University Press.

Ardrey, Robert. 1961/1972. *African Genesis: A Personal Investigation into the Animal Origins and Nature of Man*, New York, Dell.

Aristotle. 1985. *The Complete Works of Aristotle: The Revised Oxford Translation*. Two volumes, edited by Jonathan Barnes. Princeton: Princeton University Press.

Armstrong, David M. 1981a. *The Nature of Mind and Other Essays*, Ithaca: Cornell University Press.

———. 1981b. The Causal Theory of the Mind. In Armstrong 1981a, pp. 16–31.

———. 1989. *Universals: An Opinionated Introduction*. Boulder: Westview.

Attenborough, David. 1979. *Life on Earth: A Natural History*. Boston: Little, Brown.

Austin, J.L. 1964. *Sense and Sensibility*. New York: Oxford University Press.

Beach, Frank A., Donald O. Hebb, Clifford T. Morgan, Henry W. Nissen, eds. 1960. *The Neurophysiology of Lashley: Selected Papers of K.S. Lashley*, New York: McGraw-Hill.

Bernal, Martin. 1987. *Black Athena: The Afroasiatic Roots of Classical Civilization, Vol 1: The Fabrication of Ancient Greece*. New Brunswick: Rutgers University Press.

Block, Ned. 1978. Troubles with Functionalism. In Savage 1978, pp. 261–325.

Boehner, Philotheus. 1962. Introduction. In Ockham 1962, pp. ix–li.

Brunet, Michel, Franck Guy, David Pilbeam, Hassane Taisso Mackaye, Andossa Likius, Djimdoumalbaye Ahounta, Alain Beauvilain, Cécile Blondel, Hervé Bocherens, Jean-Renaud Boisserie, Louis de Bonis, Yves Coppens, Jean Dejax, Christiane Denys, Philippe Duringer, Véra Eisenmann, Gongdibé Fanone, Pierre Fronty, Denis Geraads, Thomas Lehmann, Fabrice Lihoreau, Antoine Louchart, Adoum Mahamat, Gildas Merceron, Guy Mouchelin, Olga Otero, Pablo Pelaez Campomanes, Marcia Ponce de Lion, Jean-Claude Rage, Michel Sapanet, Mathieu Schuster, Jean Sudre, Pascal Tassy, Xavier Valentin, Patrick Vignaud, Laurent Viriot, Antoine Zazzo, and Christoph Zollikofer. 2002. A New Hominid from the Upper Miocene of Chad, Central Africa. *Nature* 418, pp. 145–151.

Brownowski, Jacob. 1958. The Creative Process. *Scientific American* (September), pp. 58–65.

Burkert, Walter. 1996. *Creation of the Sacred: Tracks of Biology in Early Religions.* Cambridge, MA, Harvard University Press.

Calami, Peter. 2002. Skull Deepens Evolution Riddle: It's Been Pushed Back Another Million Years by Chad Discovery. *The Toronto Star* (Thursday, July 11th), pp. A1 and A23.

Capitan, W.H. and D.D. Merrill, eds. 1967. *Art, Mind, and Religion.* Pittsburgh: University of Pittsburgh Press.

Casson, Lionel, 1965. *Ancient Egypt.* New York: Time-Life Books.

Chagnon, N. and W. Irons, eds. 1979. *Evolutionary Biology and Human Social Behavior: An Anthropological Perspective.* North Scituate: Duxbury Press.

Changeux, Jean-Pierre and Alain Connes. 1995. *Conversations on Mind, Matter, and Mathematics.* Translated from the French by M.B. DeBevoise. Princeton: Princeton University Press.

Chomsky, Noam. 1959. Review of *Verbal Behavior* by B.F. Skinner. *Language*, vol. 35 (January–March 1959), pp. 26–58.

———. 1987/1990. On the Nature, Use, and Acquisition of Language. Reprinted in Lycan 1990, pp. 627–646.

———. 1997. Language and Cognition. In Johnson and Erneling 1997, pp. 15–31.

Churchland, Patricia Smith. 1986. *Neurophilosophy: Toward a Unified Science of the Mind-Brain.* Cambridge, MA, MIT Press.

Churchland, Paul M. 1981. Eliminative Materialism and the Propositional Attitudes. *The Journal of Philosophy*, vol. 78, pp. 67–90.

Coles, Paul. 1968. *The Ottoman Impact on Europe.* London, Thames and Hudson.

Collier, Mark and Bill Manley. 1998. *How to Read Egyptian Hieroglyphs.* Berkeley: University of California Press.

Concise Oxford Dictionary. 1982. *Concise Oxford Dictionary.* Seventh edition. Oxford: Clarendon.

Conlogue, Ray. 2001. Adieu. Sayonara. M'bula. Goodbye to Language Diversity. *The Globe and Mail* (March 24, 2001), pp. D8–9.

Conlon, Edward. 1997. Men in Blue: Why Do Cops Go Berserk? *The New Yorker* (September 29th), pp. 10–11.

Coppens, Yves. 1994. East Side Story: The Origin of Humankind. *Scientific American* (May), pp. 88–95.

Damasio, Antonio R. 1994. *Descartes' Error: Emotion, Reason, and the Human Brain.* New York: Grosset/Putnam.

Darwin, Charles. 1859/2000. *On the Origin of Species*, edited by Ernst Mayr. Cambridge, MA: Harvard University Press.

David, A. Rosalie. 1982. *The Ancient Egyptians: Religious Beliefs and Practices.* London: Routledge.

Deacon, Terrence W. 1997. *The Symbolic Species: The Co-evolution of Language and the Brain.* New York: Norton.

Dennett, Daniel C. 1981/1990. True Believers: The Intentional Strategy and Why It Works. In Heath 1981. Reprinted in Lycan 1990, pp. 150–167.

———. 1991. Real Patterns. *Journal of Philosophy*, vol. 88, pp. 27–51.

———. 1995. *Darwin's Dangerous Idea: Evolution and the Meanings of Life*. New York: Simon and Schuster.

Descartes, René. 1985. *The Philosophical Writings of Descartes*. Three volumes, translated from the Latin and French by John Cottingham, Robert Stoothoff, and Dugald Murdoch, London: Cambridge University Press.

———. 1641/1985. *Meditations on First Philosophy*. In Descartes 1985, Volume 2, pp. 1–62.

Dewey, John. 1920/1960. *Reconstruction in Philosophy*. Boston: The Beacon Press.

Donald, Merlin. 1991. *Origins of the Modern Mind: Three Stages in the Evolution of Culture and Cognition*. Cambridge, MA: Harvard University Press.

———. 1997. The Mind Considered from a Historical Perspective: Human Cognitive Phylogenesis and the Possibility of Continuing Cognitive Evolution. In Johnson and Erneling 1997, pp. 355–365.

Easton, Stewart C. 1965. *A Brief History of the Western World*. New York: Barnes and Noble.

Edey, Maitland A., and the Editors of Time-Life Books. 1975. *Lost World of the Aegean*. New York: Time-Life Books.

Editors of Time-Life Books. 1991. *The Natural World*. Alexandria, VA: Time-Life Books.

Erneling, Christina E. 1997. Historical Approaches. In Johnson and Erneling 1997, pp. 353–54.

Erneling, Christina E., and David Martel Johnson, eds. Forthcoming. *Mind As a Scientific Object: Between Brain and Culture*. New York: Oxford University Press.

Faulkner, R.O. 1969. *The Ancient Egyptian Pyramid Texts Translated into English*, Oxford: Clarendon.

Feynman, Richard P. 1995. *Six Easy Pieces: Essentials of Physics Explained by Its Most Brilliant Teacher*. Reading, MA: Addison-Wesley.

Flanagan, Owen. 1992. *Consciousness Reconsidered*. Cambridge, MA: MIT Press.

Fodor, Jerry A. 1975. *The Language of Thought*. Cambridge, MA: Harvard University Press.

———. 1983. *Representations: Philosophical Essays on the Foundations of Cognitive Science*. Cambridge, MA: MIT Press.

———. 1987. *Psychosemantics: The Problem of Meaning in the Philosophy of Mind*. Cambridge, MA: MIT Press.

———. 1994. The Elm and the Expert: Mentalese and Its Semantics. Cambridge, MA: MIT Press.

———. 2000. *The Mind Doesn't Work that Way: The Scope and Limits of Computational Psychology*. Cambridge, MA: MIT Press.

Fodor, Jerry A., and Zenon Pylyshyn. 1981. How Direct Is Visual Perception? Some Reflections on Gibson's 'Ecological' Approach. *Cognition*, vol. 9, pp. 139–196.

Frankfort, Henri, Mrs. H.A. Frankfort, John A. Wilson, and Thorkild Jacobsen. 1946/1954. *Before Philosophy: The Intellectual Adventure of Ancient Man*. Harmondsworth: Penguin.

Frankfort, Henri, and Mrs. H.A. Frankfort. 1946. Myth and Reality. Chapter 1 of Frankfort *et al.* 1946/1954, pp. 11–36.

Gaffan, David. 1997. Review of *The Mind-Brain Continuum*. In Llinas and Churchland 1996, p. 194.

Gillings, Richard J. 1972. *Mathematics in the Time of the Pharaohs*. Cambridge, MA: MIT Press.

Gomperz, Theodor. 1901/1964. *Greek Thinkers: A History of Ancient Philosophy*. Translated from the German by Laurie Magnus. New York: Humanities Press.

Gore, Rick. 2002. The First Pioneer? A New Find Shakes the Human Family Tree. *National Geographic* (August), pp. xii–xxi.

Gould, Stephen Jay. 1989. *Wonderful Life: The Burgess Shale and the Nature of History*. New York: Norton.

———, ed. 2001. *The Book of Life*. New York: Norton.

Gould, Stephen Jay, and E. Vrba. 1982. Exaptation: A Missing Term in Evolutionary Theory. *Paleobiology* 8, pp. 4–15.

Grimal, Nicholas. 1994. *A History of Ancient Egypt*. Translated from the French by Ian Shaw. Oxford: Blackwell.

Halweg, Kai, and C.A. Hooker, eds. 1989. *Issues in Evolutionary Epistemology*. Albany: SUNY Press.

Heath, A.F., ed. 1981. *Scientific Explanation: Papers Based on Herbert Spencer Lectures Given in the University of Oxford*. Oxford: Oxford University Press.

Horgan, Terence, and James Woodward. 1985. Folk Psychology is Here to Stay. *The Philosophical Review* XCIV: No. 2, pp. 197–226. Reprinted in Lycan 1990, pp. 399–420.

Hornung, Erik. 1971/1990. *Conceptions of God in Ancient Egypt: The One and the Many*. Translated from the German by John Baines. Ithaca: Cornell University Press.

Hume, David. 1775/1978. *A Treatise of Human Nature*. Edited by L.A. Selby–Bigge and P.H. Nidditch. Oxford: Oxford University Press.

Huntington, Samuel P. 1996. *The New World Order, and the Clash of Civilizations*. New York: Simon and Schuster.

James, William. 1890/1950. *The Principles of Psychology*. Two volumes. New York: Dover.

Jaynes, Julian. 1976. *The Origin of Consciousness in the Breakdown of the Bicameral Mind*. Toronto: University of Toronto Press.

Johnson, David Martel. 1987. The Greek Origins of Belief. *American Philosophical Quarterly* 24: 4, pp. 319–327.

———. 1988. 'Brutes Believe Not'. *Philosophical Psychology*, Vol. 1: No.3, pp. 279–294.

———. 1990. Can Abstractions Be Causes? *Biology and Philosophy*, Vol. 5, pp. 63–77.

———. 1997. Taking the Past Seriously: How History Shows that Eliminativists' Account of Folk Psychology is Partly Right and Partly Wrong. In Johnson and Erneling 1997, pp. 366–375.

———. 2000. Aristotle's Curse of Non–Existence Against 'Barbarians'. In Sfendoni-Mentzou 2000, pp. 126–135.

———. Forthcoming. Mind, Brain, and the Upper Paleolithic. In Erneling and Johnson forthcoming.

Johnson, David Martel, and Christina E. Erneling, eds. 1997. *The Future of the Cognitive Revolution.* New York: Oxford University Press.

Kates, Robert W. 1994. Sustaining Life on the Earth. *Scientific American* (October), pp. 114–122.

Kayzer, Wim, Oliver Sacks, Stephen Jay Gould, Daniel Dennett, Freeman Dyson, Rupert Sheldrake, and Stephen Toulmin. 1997. *'A Glorious Accident': Understanding Our Place in the Cosmic Puzzle.* New York: Freeman.

Kim, Jaegwon. 1998. *Philosophy of Mind.* Boulder: Westview.

Kirk, G.S., J.E. Raven, and M. Schofield. 1957/1987. *The Presocratic Philosophers: A Critical History with a Selection of Texts.* Second edition. Cambridge: Cambridge University Press.

Kitchen, K.A. 1992. Exodus, The. In *The Anchor Bible Dictionary*, Vol. 2 (New York: Doubleday), p. 706.

Klein, Richard G., and Blake Edgar. 2002. *The Dawn of Human Culture.* New York: Wiley.

Knauth, Percy, and the Editors of Time-Life Books. 1974. *The Metalsmiths.* New York: Time-Life Books.

Lakoff, George, and Mark Johnson. 1999. *Philosophy in the Flesh: The Embodied Mind and Its Challenge to Western Thought.* New York: Basic Books.

Lamberg-Karlovsky, Martha, ed. 2000. *The Breakout: The Origins of Civilization.* Cambridge, MA: Peabody Museum of Archeology and Ethnology, Harvard University.

Larsen, Mogens Trolle. 1989. Orientalism and Near Eastern Archeology. In Miller, Rowlands, and Tilly 1989, pp. 229–239.

Lashley, Karl. 1960. In Search of the Engram. Reprinted in Beach *et al.* 1960, pp. 478–505.

Leach, Edmund. 1981. Biology and Social Science: Wedding or Rape? Review of Lumsden and Wilson 1981. *Nature*, Vol. 291, pp. 267–68.

Leahey, Thomas. Forthcoming. Mind As a Scientific Object: An Historical-Philosophical Exploration. In Erneling and Johnson forthcoming.

Lehner, Mark. 2000. Absolutism and Reciprocity in Ancient Egypt. In Lamberg-Karlovsky 2000, pp. 69–97.

Lemonick, Michael D. 1992. The World in 3300 B.C. *Time*, (October 26th), pp. 52–55.

Llinas, R. and P.S. Churchland, eds. 1996. *The Mind-Brain Continuum.* Cambridge, MA: MIT Press.

Lloyd, G.E.R. 1970. *Early Greek Science: Thales to Aristotle.* London, Chatto and Windus.

———. 1996. *Adversaries and Authorities: Investigations into Ancient Greek and Chinese Science.* Cambridge: Cambridge University Press.

Lloyd-Jones, H. 1971. *The Justice of Zeus.* Berkeley: University of California Press.

Lovejoy, Arthur O. 1961. *The Great Chain of Being: A Study of the History of an Idea.* The William James Lectures Delivered at Harvard University 1933. Cambridge, MA: Harvard University Press.

Lumsden, C. O. and E.O. Wilson. 1981. *Genes, Mind, and Culture*: The *Coevolutionary Process*. Cambridge, MA: Harvard University Press.

Lurker, Manfred. 1980. *The Gods and Symbols of Ancient Egypt: An Illustrated Dictionary*, London: Thames and Hudson.

Lycan, William, ed. 1990. *Mind and Cognition*. Oxford: Basil Blackwell.

———. Forthcoming. A Particularly Compelling Refutation of Eliminative Materialism. In Erneling and Johnson forthcoming.

Mayr, Ernst. 1997. *This Is Biology: The Science of the Living World*. Cambridge, MA: Harvard University Press.

McCarthy, John. 1983. The Little Thoughts of Thinking Machines. *Psychology Today* (December), pp. 46–49.

Mellars, Paul. 1998. Neanderthals, Modern Humans, and the Archaeological Evidence for Language. In Jablonski and Aiello 1998, pp. 89–115.

Miller, Daniel, Michael Rowlands, and Christopher Tilly, eds. 1989. *Domination and Resistance*. London, Unwin Hyman.

Mithen, Steven. 1996. *The Prehistory of the Mind: The Cognitive Origins of Art, Religion, and Science*. New York: Thames and Hudson.

Moore, A.W. 1991. *The Infinite*. London: Routledge.

Morenz, Siegfried. 1960/1973. *Egyptian Religion*. Translated from the German by Ann E. Keep. London: Methuen.

Morris, Richard. 1993. *Cosmic Questions: Galactic Halos, Cold Dark Matter, and the End of Time*. New York: Wiley.

Munz, Peter. 1989. Taking Darwin Even More Seriously. In Halweg and Hooker 1989, pp. 278–293.

Nagel, Thomas. 1986. *The View from Nowhere*. New York: Oxford University Press.

Newman, Cathy. 1997. Cats: Nature's Masterwork. *National Geographic*, Vol. 191: No. 6, (June), pp. 55–76.

Nietzsche, Friedrich. 1878/1986. *Human All Too Human*: A *Book for Free Spirits*. Translated from the German by R.J. Hollingdale. Cambridge: Cambridge University Press.

———. 1887/1969. *On the Genealogy of Morals*. Translated from the German by Walter Kaufmann and R.J. Hollingdale. New York: Vintage.

Ockham, William. 1962. *Ockham: Philosophical Writings*. Edited and translated from the Latin by Philotheus Boehner. New York: Nelson.

Onians, Richard Broxton. 1951/2000. *The Origins of European Thought about the Body, the Mind, the Soul, the World, Time, and Fate: New Interpretations of Greek, Roman, and Kindred Evidence, Also of Some Basic Jewish and Christian Beliefs*. Cambridge: Cambridge University Press.

Penfield, Wilder. 1975. *The Mystery of the Mind*: A *Critical Study of Consciousness and the Human Brain*. Princeton: Princeton University Press.

Pinker, Steven. 1994. *The Language Instinct*. New York: Harper.

———. 1997. *How the Mind Works*. New York: Norton.

Plato. *Parmenides* (many editions).

———. *Phaedo* (many editions).

———. *The Sophist* (many editions).

Popper, Karl R. 1965a. *Conjectures and Refutations*. New York: Harper Torchbooks.

———. 1965b. Back to the Presocratics. Reprinted in Popper 1965a, pp. 136–165.

Putnam, Hilary. 1967. Psychological Predicates. In Capitan and Merrill 1967, pp. 37–48.

———. 1975a. *Mind, Language, and Reality: Philosophical Papers, Volume 2*. London: Cambridge University Press.

———. 1975b. The Meaning of 'Meaning'. Reprinted in Putnam 1975a, pp. 215–271.

———. 1997. Functionalism: Cognitive Science or Science Fiction? In Johnson and Erneling 1997, pp. 32–44.

Quasten, Johannes. 1958. *Patrology, Vol. II: The Ante-Nicene Literature After Irenaeus*. Utrecht: The Newman Press, Westminster, Maryland and Spectrum.

Quine, Willard Van Orman. 1969a. *Ontological Relativity and Other Essays*, New York, Columbia University Press.

———. 1969b. Epistemology Naturalized. Reprinted in Quine 1969a, pp. 69–90.

Reed, Edward. 1997. The Cognitive Revolution from an Ecological Point of View. In Johnson and Erneling 1997, pp. 261–273.

Reynolds, P. 1981. *On the Evolution of Human Behavior: The Argument from Animals to Man*. Berkeley: University of California Press.

Russell, Bertrand. 1912/1964. *The Problems of Philosophy*. London: Oxford University Press.

Ryle, Gilbert. 1949. *The Concept of Mind*. London: Hutchinson.

Saggs, H.W.F. 1989. *Civilization Before Greece and Rome*. New Haven: Yale University Press.

Savage, C.W., ed. 1978. *Perception and Cognition: Issues in the Foundations of Psychology*. Minnesota Studies in the Philosophy of Science, Volume 9. Minneapolis: University of Minnesota Press.

Searle, John R. 1992. *The Rediscovery of the Mind*. Cambridge, MA: MIT Press.

———. 1995. *The Construction of Social Reality*. New York: The Free Press.

Sfendoni-Mentzou, Demetra, ed. 2000. *Aristotle and Contemporary Science, Volume 1*. New York: Peter Lang.

Snell, Bruno. 1953/1960. *The Discovery of the Mind: The Greek Origins of European Thought*. New York: Harper.

Solmsen, Friedrich. 1960. *Aristotle's System of the Physical World: A Comparison with His Predecessors*. Ithaca: Cornell University Press.

Sourvino-Inwood, Christiane. 1981. To Die and Enter the House of Hades: Homer, Before and After. In Whaley 1981, pp. 15–39.

Spinoza, Benedict. 1955. *The Chief Works of Benedict De Spinoza*. Translated from the Latin by R.H.M. Elwes. Volume 2. New York: Dover.

Starr, Chester G. 1991. *A History of the Ancient World*. Fourth edition. New York: Oxford University Press.

Stich, Steven. 1986. *From Folk Psychology to Cognitive Science: The Case Against Belief*. Cambridge, MA: MIT Press.

Strauss, Stephen. 2002. Fossil Hailed as Root of our 'Family Tree'. *The Globe and Mail* (July 11th, 2002), pp. A1 and A13.

Stringer, Christopher, and Robin McKie. 1996. *African Exodus: The Origins of Modern Humanity.* New York: Henry Holt.

Tattersall, Ian. 1993. *The Human Odyssey: Four Million Years of Human Evolution,* New York: Prentice Hall.

———. 1998. *Becoming Human: Evolution and Human Uniqueness.* New York: Harcourt Brace.

———. 1999. *The Last Neanderthal: The Rise, Success, and Mysterious Extinction of Our Closest Human Relative.* Revised edition. Boulder: Westview.

———. 2000. Once We Were Not Alone. *Scientific American* (January), pp. 56–62.

———. 2002. *The Monkey in the Mirror: Essays on the Science of What Makes Us Human.* New York: Harcourt.

Tattersall, Ian, Eric Delson, and John Van Couvering. 1988. *Encyclopedia of Human Evolution and Prehistory.* New York: Garland.

Taylor, John H. 2001. *Death and the Afterlife in Ancient Egypt.* London: The British Museum Press.

Tobin, Vincent Arieh. 1989. *Theological Principles of Egyptian Religion.* New York: Peter Lang.

Turner, Alan (with illustrations by Mauricio Anton). 1997. *The Big Cats and their Fossil Relatives: An Illustrated Guide to their Evolution and Natural History.* New York: Columbia University Press.

van Gelder, Timothy. Forthcoming. Beyond the Mind-Body Problem. In Erneling and Johnson forthcoming.

Vinci, Thomas C. 1998. *Cartesian Truth.* New York: Oxford University Press.

de Waal, Frans. 2001. *The Ape and the Sushi Master: Cultural Reflections of a Primatologist,* New York: Basic Books.

Walker, Roberta. 1992. The Wolf Man. *Canadian Geographic* (November–December), pp. 24–33.

Wenke, Robert J. 1999. *Patterns in Prehistory: Humankind's First Three Million Years.* Fourth edition. New York: Oxford University Press.

Wernick, Robert, and the Editors of Time-Life Books. 1973. *The Monument Builders.* New York: Time-Life Books.

Whaley, Joachim, ed. 1981. *Mirrors of Mortality: Studies in the Social History of Death.* London: Europa.

White, Randall. 1989. Visual Thinking in the Ice Age. *Scientific American* (July), pp. 92–99.

Whiten, Andrew, and Christopher Boesch. 2001. The Culture of Chimpanzees. *Scientific American* (January), pp. 61–67.

Wiley, R. Haven, Jr. 1978. The Lek Mating System of the Sage Grouse. *Scientific American* (May), pp. 114–125.

Wilson, Edward O. 1975/1980. *Sociobiology: The Abridged Edition.* Cambridge, MA: Harvard University Press.

———. 1992. *The Diversity of Life.* Cambridge, MA: Harvard University Press.

Wilson, John A. 1946a. Egypt: The Nature of the Universe. Chapter II in Frankfort et al. 1946/1954, pp. 39–70.

———. 1946b. Egypt: The Function of the State. Chapter III in Frankfort et al. 1946/1954, pp. 71–102.

Wittgenstein, Ludwig. 1953. *Philosophical Investigations.* Translated from the German by G.E.M. Anscombe. New York: Macmillan.

———. 1961. *Tractacus Logico-Philosophicus.* Translated by D.F. Pears and B.F. McGuinness. London: Rontledge.

Wright, G. Ernest *et al.* 1974. *Great People of the Bible and How They Lived.* Pleasantville: Reader's Digest Association.

Wood, Bernard. 2002. Paleoanthropology: Hominid Revelations from Chad. *Nature* 418, pp. 133–35.

Zadwidski, Tadeusz, and William Bechtel. Forthcoming. Gall's Legacy Revisited: Decomposition and Localization in Cognitive Neuroscience. In Erneling and Johnson forthcoming.

Zimmer, Carl. 2001. How Old Is It? Solving the Riddle of the Ages. *National Geographic* (September), pp. 78–101.

Index

adaptive tricks, 30, 151ff, 166
Akhenaton, 103–04
Alexander the Great, 105, 196–98
Alexander, Richard D., 158n20
animal beliefs, 22–23
Anytus, 194
Apopis, 82–83, 97, 124–26
Apopis bound, 83
Aquinas, Thomas, 174
Arabs, 90
archeology, understood as part of cognitive science, 12
Ardrey, Robert, 71–73
Aristotle, xi, 9, 39n13, 60n5, 76–78, 129, 140, 147, 152, 174, 196–97; his Unmoved Mover, 152
Armstrong, David M., 68, 147
Attenborough, David, 29
Augustine, St., 56–57, 67
Austin, J.L., ix, 4n3, 17n8, 66
Avicenna, 141n7

barbarians: Hyksos thought of as, 179–180; Greeks thought of as, 178–79; Phoenecians thought of as, 182
bats, 30, 154, 156
Beach, Frank A., 61
bear-dogs, 153
Bechtel, William, 61
behaviorism, 21–22
cross-cultural problems with, 22
belief, Section 3.3, *passim*, 127–28, 156; and desire as the two central

elements in mind, 63, 107; as a cultural artifact, 113; as connected with the notion of objectivity, 201; invention of, 114, 128; three main theories of, 107–08
Bernal, Martin, 100
biology, 79n17
Block, Ned, 68, 198
Boehner, Philotheus, 141, 148
Boesch, Christopher, 26
Bonaparte, Napoleon, 123, 195
Book of the Dead, Egyptian, 128
brain: as supposedly of more explanatory value than mind, 6–7; as pliable, 6–7
Bremmer, Jan, 47–48, 51–53, 57
Brownowski, Jacob, 200
Brunet, Michel, *et al.*, 161
Burkert, Walter, 137

Casson, Lionel, 116n17, 181
cats, 112; as conceived of by the Egyptians, 105; a relatively unchanging, conservative family of species, 28; saber-toothed, 153–54
causality, billiard ball variety of, 152; mind-brain, 16; pull rather than push, 158; Hume on, 31
Changeux, Jean-Pierre, 189n7, 191
chauvinism, Section 5.4, *passim*
childishness, Section 3.2, *passim*, 106, 128; Egyptian conception of, 97–98; Greek conception of, 97

chimpanzees, 157–58, 162
China, ancient, 99, 136, 209; Lloyd
    on its ancient scientific traditions,
    35–38
Chomsky, Noam, 6, 8–10, 21, 24–26,
    89, 110n12, 137, 174, 200n10
Churchland, Patricia Smith, 6, 8–9,
    11, 21, 26, 62, 89, 165,
    200–01n10, 201
Churchland, Paul M., 19, 21, 26,
    60n6, 89, 156, 165, 200n10, 201
Cro-Magnon people, 207–08
cognitive science, 11–12
cognitivism, 24; picturing the mind as
    internal, 24
Coles, Paul, 57
Collier, Mark, 181n5
commercialism, Section 5.2, *passim*,
    especially 187–89
common sense, 114, 193
Conlogue, Ray, 7
Conlon, Edward, 186
Connes, Alain, 189n7, 191
conservative species, 28
contradiction, law of, 76ff
Coppens, Yves, 160–62
cosmopolitanism, Section 5.2, *passim*,
    especially 188–89
culture, 11, 112–13, 159; history of
    human developments, 164–66

Damasio, Antonio R., 75
Dart, Raymond, 71–73
Darwin, Charles, 8, 10, 28–29,
    149–151, 151
Darwinian biology, 8, 138, 159,
    193
David, A. Rosalie, 45
Deacon, Terrence W., 8, 11nn5–6,
    16, 73n14
default survival strategy, 209
Delson, Eric, 35, 164
Dennett, Daniel C., 108, 114n16,
    151, 166–67n23, 203
Descartes, René, 67, 109n11, 115,
    147n11, 174

Dewey, John, 42, 44, 177, 190, 192,
    194
diffusion theory, 98ff, 130
Donald, Merlin, 7, 86n19
dualism, Section 2.1, *passim*; defined,
    42; as supposedly rejected by
    modern science, 42ff; as
    presupposed by modern science,
    204 and n13
Dyson, Freeman, 203

Easton, Stewart C., 91
ecological niches, 152ff, 166; as real
    entities in nature, 152; as evolving
    and changing, 152–53; as possibly
    real, even in cases where they have
    no instances, 153–54
"economy" or "polity" of nature 28
Edey, Maitland A., 98
Editors of Time-Life Books, 177n2
Edgar, Blake, 157n17
Egypt, 44, 54–55, 177–78, 189–190,
    196
Egyptians, ancient, 93n3, 136, 192,
    210; as not conceiving of the
    world in terms of dualism, 44, 94;
    as not possessing what we now
    think of as minds, 114; their
    conception of childishness, 97–98;
    their conception of existence, 83;
    their conception of law, 105; their
    conceptions of the soul, 45–46;
    their hieroglyphic system of
    writing, 180–82; their arithmetical
    procedures, 182–85
Einstein, Albert. 145–46, 191–91
eliminative materialism, Section 2.2,
    passim, especially 58–61, 201
Empedocles, 60n5, 196
equality, 137
Erneling, Christina E., 205n14
essentialism, 143n9
evolution, 209
existence: known by the possibility of
    empirical explanation, 147, 156;

Egyptian conception as having degrees, 83; Western conception as all or nothing, 82

extraterrestrial intelligent life, 135ff

Exodus, the, 186–87

explanation, 17; not the same thing as existence, 4; but provides a scientific criterion for what exists, 147, 156

Faulkner, R.O., 110–12

Feynman, Richard P., 145

Fink, Robert O., 97

Flanagan, Owen, 67

flying squirrels, 152

Fodor, Jerry A., 3, 11, 22, 65, 110n12

folk psychology, 114; as the foundation of modern science, 202

Frankfort, Henri, 76–81, 97n6, 115–17

Frankfort, Mrs. H.A., 76–81

freedom, 137

functionalism, 68

Gaffan, David, 62–63

Gillings, Richard J., 182

gold, 142ff

Gomperz, Theodor, 176ff

Gore, Rick, 157n17

Gould, Stephen Jay, 8, 28, 38, 173, 203

Great Chain of Being, 149ff

Great King of Persia, 77–78

Great Pyramid, 116–17

Great Rift Valley, 159–160

Greek Middle Ages, 34–36, 47, 102, 123, 187

Greek Revolution, 34–36, 39, 85, 89, 100, 118, 130, 165; as having created the modern mind, 86, 123–24, 129–130; as having created Western Civilization, 198;

as having led to modern science, 101–02

Greek-like thinking, 100ff, especially 106, 108; adopted by all major present-day cultural groups, 98; finally accepted by the Egyptians, 104; how it came to exist, 108–09, 176ff, 184–85

Greeks, ancient, 192; considered barbarians by the Egyptians, 178–79; not dominating the Mediterranean area until late in their history, 177ff; their place in the history of the world, 97–98

Greece, 176; its geography, 176ff

Grimal, Nicholas, 54–55, 81–82, 90, 93, 97, 101n8, 104–05, 179

Halweg, Kai, 138

Hawking, Stephen, 144

Hebb, Donald O., 61

Hebrews, Section 3.1, *passim*; their conception of divine-secular dualism, 93–94; their invention of the notion of paganism, 93

Heraclitus, 145–46

Herodotus, 187

hieroglyphic writing, 180–82

history, 10–12, 95; should be considered a legitimate part of cognitive science 12

historical method, x, 115; "tracing back to origins" the primary method employed in this book, 90

Hobbes, Thomas, 33

Homer, 34, 46–51

Homeric Greeks, 46–53

Homo habilis, 13, 157, 159, 162, 164

Homo ergaster, 12–13

Homo erectus, 3, 157, 159, 164

Homo neanderthalensis, 14, 159, 164

Homo sapiens, 14, 16, 29, 31, 163–65; as the last surviving species of hominid 159

Homoplasy, 161–62

Hook, Sidney, 42
Hooker, C.A., 138
Horgan, Terence, 65–67
Hornung, Erik, 82–83, 93n3, 97,
124–25, 179–180
horses, 28; as an example of a
wandering species, 28
Hume, David, 31, 152
Huntington, Samuel P., 91n1
Huxley, Thomas Henry, 151
Hyksos, 179, 186; expulsion of, 179;
considered barbaric by the
Egyptians, 179–180

Iliad, 46, 117n18, 121–22, 124,
128
indirect practicality, Section 5.3,
passim, especially 197–98
infinity, concept of, 124–28; proof or
justification for, 125–27; time
when the (correct) concept was
invented, 126

James, William, 57n3, 133n1
Jaynes, Julian, 117–124
Jeremiah, 121, 124
Joan of Arc, 121
Johnson, David Martel, 2n1, 78n16,
64n8, 78n16, 82n18, 96n5,
139n6, 154, 180, 182n6, 188,
208
Johnson, Mark, 4–5, 8–10, 26,
34–35, 42, 46, 75, 89, 137

Kant, Immanuel, 174
Kates, Robert W., 101
Kayzer, Wim, 203
Kierkegaard, Søren, 113, 199
Kim, Jaegwon, 10n4, 18–21
Kirk, G.S., 56n2, 102n9
Kitchen, K.A., 187
Klein, Richard G., 157n17
Knauth, Percy, 98

Lakoff, George, 4–5, 8–10, 26,
34–35, 42, 46, 75, 89, 137, 165,
200n10
language, 70n10
Larsen, Mogens Trolle, 99
Lashley, Karl S., 61–62
laws: Egyptian conception of, 105;
Milesian conception of, 188;
"laws of thought", 76, 81, 83
Leach, Edmund, 138
Leahey, Thomas, 63n7
Lehner, Mark, 44
Leibniz, Gottfried Wilhelm, 112
Lemonick, Michael D., 15, 101
Llinas, R., 62
Lloyd, G.E.R., 35–39
Lloyd-Jones, H., 48
Locke, John, 163, 168
Lockeanism, 168
Lovejoy, Arthur O., 149
Lumsden, C. J., 138
Lüning, Jens, 15
Lurker, Manfred, 45
Lycan, William, 67, 156

Ma'at, 109
Manley, Bill, 181n5
Mayr, Ernst, 43–44, 50, 75
McCarthy, John, 107
McKie, Robin, 16, 72
Mellars, Paul, 14–15
"Mentalese", 110n12
Mesopotamia, 169–171, 177–78,
196; original settlement of,
165–66
Mesopotamians, 184, 188
Milesians, 104
Miletus, 104; as birthplace of
philosophy, 102n9, 188–89; the
commercial success of, 104ff;
government of, 188–89; laws of,
188
mind, 85, 95, 204; as a container,
133; as a product of the Greek
Revolution, 68, 86, 133–34, 207;

as an *explanandum* rather than an *explanans*, 66; as being centered in belief and desire, 134; as capable of being studied scientifically, 6, 204–05; as having a "center" and "outskirts", 133; as having three categories, 133; as something cultural that does not count as part of nature 69–70, 88, 134; conceived as what the brain does, 2, 165; defined, 86; in wide sense, Section 4.1, *passim*, 166; —as an ecological niche, Section 4.3, *passim*; —objective thinking the core of mind in this sense, 163; in narrow sense, Section 4.1, *passim*, 166; —as belonging only to humans, and only to some humans, 134–35; —identical with reason, and with a more specific form of the wide mind ecological niche, Section 4.4, *passim*

Mithen, Steven, 14n7, 16, 72, 158n18, 166, 206n15
Moore, A.W., 126–27
Moore, G.E., 66–67
Morenz, Siegfried, 105, 111–12
Morgan, Clifford T., 61
Morris, Richard, 144
Moses, 58, 121–22
Muggeridge, Malcolm, 84
Munz, Peter, 193

Nagel, Thomas, 32, 208
natural kinds, 142ff, 166n22; as possibly being real, even when they have no instances, 148–49
naturalism: ancient version of, Section 2.1 *passim*, 89, 106; modern version of, 57ff; monistic, 138, 144
nature: understood as completely physical, 140–41; understood as including both particular and general entities, 140–41

Nebuchadnezzar, 122
Neolithic Revolution, 14, 85, 165
new dualism, 137–39
New Testament, 58
Newman, Cathy, 28, 105, 153–54
Nietzsche, Friedrich, 41–42, 56, 95, 88, 95
Nissen, Henry W., 61
nominalism, 141ff

objectivity, 168–67, 208; definition of, 109
Ockham, William, 120n20, 141ff, 174; as a supposedly revolutionary figure, 141
Old Testament, 117, 124, 128
Onians, Richard Broxton, 46–50

Paleoanthropology, understood as part of cognitive science, 12
Paleontology, 12
Parmenides, 109n11, 196
Parthenon, 116–17
Paul, St., 58, 94
Penfield, Wilder, 7
Pericles, 176
Persia, 176, 196
Phalanx, 197
pharaoh, 58, 77–78, 122–23; his decrees as defining truth, 105, 109; his role in Egypt, 81, 105, 188; his representations in art, 81–82
philosophy, Western: divided in its history between empiricism and rationalism, 167–68
Phoenicians, 182, 186, 188; considered barbaric, 182
Phrenologists, 60–61
Pinker, Steven, 2–3, 5, 8–11, 16, 26–28, 30, 110n12, 133n1, 137, 165–66, 200n10
Plato, xi, 56, 67, 109n11, 115, 140, 155, 168, 174, 194–96; as one of

the fathers of the Christian Church, 56
Platonism, 56, Section 4.2 *passim*, 168
pope, 123, 130
Pope Pius X, 129–30
Popper, Karl Raimund, 145–46
projectable powers, location of, 143ff
punctuated equilibria, 151
Putnam, Hilary, 68, 75, 108, 114n16
Pylyshyn, Zenon, 65
Pythagoras, 55
Pythagoreans, 55–56, 194

Quasten, Johannes, 92
Quine, Willard Van Orman, 43–44, 114

Raven, J.E., 56n2, 102n9
Reason, 4–5, Chapter 5, *passim*; as dangerous, 208–210; age of, 202; conceived as a cultural phenomenon, 167ff, 203–04; conceived as a product of the Greek Revolution, 34–36 , 195; conceived as a property of the world itself, 76; conceived as a recently invented way of filling the mind-niche, Section 4.4, *passim*; conceived as an innate property of humans, 169–170; connected with the notion of objectivity, 168–69; definition of, 168, 175; identical with mind in the narrow sense, 167; invention of, 168, 174, 176, 203; its place in history, Section 2.5 *passim*; traditional theories of, 167
Reed, Edward, 23n9
Reynolds, P., 137
Rosetta Stone, 111
Russell, Bertrand, 76–77, 190, 192, 198

Ryle, Gilbert, 21, 66
Sacks, Oliver, 203
sage grouse, 102–03; conditions that dictate a "lek" system of breeding, 103
Saggs, H.W.F., 169–171, 175, 181–84, 188, 193
Sapir, Edward, 110n12
Schofield, M., 56n2, 102n9
Searle, John R., 4n3, 19, 51n1
Sellars, Wilfrid, x
Sheldrake, Rupert, 203
Skinner, B.F., 21, 24–26, 59n4, 66
Snell, Bruno, 18, 48, 109
sociobiology, 138
Socrates, 194
Solmsen, Friedrich, 195
Sourvino-Inwood, Christiane, 47, 52
speciation events, 163–64
species, 8–9, 13–14 149ff; as fixed, 149; as coming into and going out of existence, 9, 149ff; as a common-sense concept, 75
Spinoza, Benedict, 199–200
Starr, Chester G., 56–57, 85, 165–66
Stich, Steven, 63, 107, 113
Stravinski, Igor, 132
Stringer, Christopher, 15, 72
sugar gliders, 152
syncretism, 81

Tassy, Pascal, 161
Tattersall, Ian, 7–9, 12–14, 16, 20, 29, 35, 72, 158n19, 159n21, 164–65
Taylor, John H., 46
Tennyson, Alfred, 142
Tertullian, 92, 94
Thales, 102n9, 196
Thorne, Alan, 14
Thucydides, 187
Tobin, Vincent Arieh, 79, 94, 97, 105–06
Tocqueville, Alexis de, 136–37
Toulmin, Stephen, 203

tracing back to origins, method of, 90

Truman, Harry S, 84

truth: Egyptian conception of, 105, 109; invention of objective or non–relative conception of, 86, 123–24, 129–130

Turing, Alan, 3

Turner, Alan, 153

universals, 140ff; can explain singulars, as well as vice versa, 146; mathematical, 140; understood as part of physical nature, 140–41

Upper Paleolithic Revolution, 14–16, 26, 33, 38, 44, 68, 84–85, 88–89, 100, 165; marks of, 15–16; significance of, 101–02n8; time of, 14n7; why it took so long to appear, 31–33

Van Couvering, John, 35, 164

van Gelder, Timothy, 134n2

Vinci, Thomas C., x

Vrba, E., 8

de Waal, Frans, 3n2

Walker, Roberta, 26

wandering species, 28

Watson, John, 21, 66

Wayne, John, 22

Weil, Simon, 186

Wenke, Robert J., 100, 158n20, 166

Wernick, Robert, 98–99

Western Civilization, 90ff, especially 94–95, 128, 169, 191–92, 201–02; as having world-wide scope at the present time, 86n20, 90–91; origins of, 89, 198

White, Randall, 102n8

Whiten, Andrew, 26

Whorf, Benjamin Lee, 110n12

Wiley, R. Haven Jr., 103

Wilson, Edward O., 30, and n10, 73–74, 138

Wilson, John A., 178, 182n6

Wittgenstein, Ludwig, 148

Whittier, John Greenleaf, 119

Wolpoff, Milford, 14

Wood, Bernard, 161–62

Woodward, James, 65–67

Wright, G. Ernest, 93, 179n4

Yolton, John, x

Zadwidski, Tadeusz, 61

Zeno, 67, 195–96

Zimmer, Carl, 99n7